Proclaiming the Good News

Proclaiming the Good News

Mennonite Women's Voices, 1972–2006

Edited by Lois Y. Barrett and Dorothy Nickel Friesen

INSTITUTE OF MENNONITE STUDIES

Copyright © 2023 by Institute of Mennonite Studies

Anabaptist Mennonite Biblical Seminary

3003 Benham Avenue, Elkhart, IN 46517

All rights reserved.

To order copies or request information, please call 1-574-296-6239, email ims@ambs.edu, or visit www.ambs.edu/ims.

Library of Congress Cataloging-in-Publication Data

Names: Barrett, Lois, editor, 1947- editor. | Nickel Friesen, Dorothy, 1947- editor.

Title: Proclaiming the good news : Mennonite women's voices, 1972-2006 / Lois Y. Barrett and Dorothy Nickel Friesen, editors.

Description: Elkhart, IN : AMBS, Institute of Mennonite Studies, 2023. | Summary: "Proclaiming the Good News recounts changes in the ways Mennonite women have been leaders in the church in North America from 1972 to 2006. The chapters in Proclaiming the Good News are shaped by voices of a women who exercised leadership in an Anabaptist denomination during this period. Some are scholars; others are pastors; still others are leaders in publication, education, and administration. Together, these voices tell the story of Mennonite women who invested their gifts and talents in Mennonite congregations and institutions. In addition to recounting personal experiences, the book engages survey data (from 1972, 1989, and 2006) to document changes in attitudes and practices over the decades"-- Provided by publisher.

Identifiers: LCCN 2023015475 | ISBN 9780936273594 (paperback)

Full LC record available at https://lccn.loc.gov/2023015475

International Standard Book Number: 978-0-936273-59-4

Book design by Mary E. Klassen.

Cover design by Nathan Shumaker.

The cover illustration by Teresa Pankratz originally appeared on the cover of the Report from the Peace Section Task Force on Women in Church and Society 133 (July-Aug 1997) and has been reprinted with permission of the artist. Do not reprint without written permission.

Unless otherwise noted, all Scripture references are from the NRSV.

Contents

Abbreviations	vii
Introduction: Women remember Dorothy Nickel Friesen and Lois Y. Barrett	1
1. First gatherings: Women organize Dorothy Nickel Friesen	11
2. If truth be told: Women dare to be activists Dorothy Yoder Nyce	37
3. Peace Section advocacy: Women write Gayle Gerber Koontz and Ted Koontz	57
4. Blinders and power: Women of color proclaim Iris de León-Hartshorn and Regina Shands Stoltzfus	72
5. The great hurdle: Women are ordained John A. Esau, Nancy Kauffmann, and Karen Martens Zimmerly	89
6. Surveys and conversations: Women pastors speak Dorothy Nickel Friesen and Diane Zaerr Brenneman	132
7. Conferences and publications: Women do theology Lois Y. Barrett	158
8. Moving into church structures: Women govern Lois Y. Barrett	183
9. Woman are "adjunct": Women serve and learn leadership Anita Hooley Yoder and Marlene Harder Bogard	205
Conclusion: Women said something! Lois Y. Barrett and Dorothy Nickel Friesen	224

Appendix: Ordained Women in Mennonite Church USA
    and Mennonite Church Canada (1972–2005)   234
    Compiled by Dorothy Nickel Friesen

Study Guide   258

Contributors   263

Abbreviations

AMBS	Associated (now Anabaptist) Mennonite Biblical Seminary/ies
APTS	Austin Presbyterian Theological Seminary
BIC	Brethren in Christ
CHM	Commission on Home Ministries
CWC	Committee on Women's Concerns
GCMC	General Conference Mennonite Church
EMC	Evangelical Mennonite Church
IMS	Institute of Mennonite Studies
MB	Mennonite Brethren
MBCM	Mennonite Board of Congregational Ministries
MBS	Mennonite Biblical Seminary
MC	(Old) Mennonite Church
MCC	Mennonite Central Committee
MC USA	Mennonite Church USA
MLA	Mennonite Library and Archives (North Newton, Kansas)
MMF	Manhattan (Kansas) Mennonite Fellowship
Report	*Report from the Peace Section Task Force on Women in Church and Society*
WMA	Women's Missionary Association
WMSC	Women's Missionary and Service Commission
MWC	Mennonite World Conference
TF	Task Force on Women in Church and Society
WDC	Western District Conference

Introduction
Women remember
Dorothy Nickel Friesen and Lois Y. Barrett

Telling our stories

I (Dorothy) confess that I loved my children, but I did not provide a suitable car seat for them when they were babies. After all, it was the 1970s, and there were no laws concerning approved car seats. The hospital nurse simply put my daughters into my arms, and I gladly held them tightly. I took my two babies home (one in Indiana, then later one in Kansas) in my arms—a perfectly loving act. However, I am horrified today at the risks we took, and now our two grandchildren, born in the twenty-first century, have securely traveled many miles in their legal car seats. Times have changed; laws have changed; I have changed.

A lot has changed since the 1970s. The year 1973 was the year of Watergate, the standoff at Wounded Knee, the withdrawal of US troops from Vietnam, the introduction of bar codes on products for sale, and the ruling in *Roe v. Wade*. The women's movement was growing. The magazine *Ms.* began regular publication in 1972. In the United States, Title IX had been enacted, requiring schools to provide equal opportunity in sports for women. The Equal Rights Amendment to the US Constitution had recently started winding its way through ratification by state legislatures. (As of 2023, it still is not ratified.) Helen Reddy won a Grammy for the song "I Am Woman." There was backlash as well; 1973 was also the publication date for *The Total Woman*, an evangelical Christian book touting total submission of wives to husbands in the bedroom and elsewhere. A woman in the United States could legally be fired for being pregnant, and sexual harassment in the workplace had not yet been recognized by the courts. In the US

Congress, women made up 3 percent of those elected to the House and Senate.[1] In Canada in 1972, there had been only one woman in the House of Commons; in 1974, nine were elected to Parliament, bringing the percentage of women to 3.4 percent.[2] Change was starting to happen in the 1970s—in the dominant culture and among Mennonites in North America, where Mennonite women were being ordained and proclaiming the good news in Mennonite congregations and church institutions.

The scope of this book was in my mind for years. Where are the stories of women who were ordained for Mennonite congregational leadership in the late twentieth century? Who remembers this era and its different contexts? What truth was conveyed to power? How did the Mennonite church (in its many branches) view women's roles in the congregation? Is there evidence of change in congregational attitudes toward women in ministry? What factors played a role in expanding women's voices? How did denominational leaders encourage or discourage women's participation? How do women describe their preaching? How did Mennonite women mimic or depart from social and cultural movements in the late twentieth century? What motivated women to become pastors? How did Mennonite women leaders experience discrimination, harassment, or hostility? What voices were silenced? Which women left the Mennonite church? What are the lessons or wisdoms that women from this era would pass on to the Mennonite church and to young women today? And more personally, how did my life take a vocational shift from secondary teaching to congregational pastoring and administrative roles in Mennonite institutions?

Finally, in retirement, I shared my dream of telling the story of Mennonite women's leadership with my longtime friend and colleague, Lois Barrett, over a lunch. She responded enthusiastically and supplied the links to the Institute of Mennonite Studies

---

[1] See Center for American Women and Politics, cawp.rutgers.edu/.

[2] See *Women in Parliaments, 1945-1995: Worldwide Statistical Survey* (Geneva: Inter-Parliamentary Union, 1995), http://archive.ipu.org/PDF/publications/women45-95_en.pdf.

(IMS) at the Anabaptist Mennonite Biblical Seminary (AMBS) in Elkhart, Indiana. IMS extended both affirmation for this project and editorial suggestions for the manuscript. We selected writers who could tell the story of the early years of women in leadership from personal experience, from denominational perspectives, and as congregational pastors.

I was aware that three professional surveys had been conducted by Mennonite sociologists—in 1972, 1989, and 2005—surveying five Anabaptist denominations' attitudes on many issues of faith and identity. The studies included three specific questions documenting attitudes toward the role of women in the church and society and attitudes toward women in ordained leadership. Perfect! We could use those benchmarks to order our own stories of ministry and ordination. Each chapter of this volume tells that story of emerging ordained female leadership in the Mennonite church in both Canada and the United States.

My own story of ordination was an exercise in pastoral complication. Because of both General Conference Mennonite Church (GCMC) and Mennonite Church (MC) policies and efforts at church planting in the 1970s and 1980s, I (as well as Lois) was moving into pastoral leadership in "dual-affiliated" congregations. That meant we were trying a new role, "female pastor," in young congregations that were "planted" with multiple denominational parents.

My earlier licensure (May 1984 and valid for one year) was at Rainbow Boulevard Mennonite Church in Kansas City, Kansas. It, too, was a product of efforts at urban church planting from the late 1950s. It was affiliated with both the GCMC Western District Conference and the MC South Central Conference. My husband, Richard, and I (and our two daughters) had lived in Kansas City since 1974 and were active in the Sharing Community of Rosedale, an ecumenical center-city effort of three congregations (Rosedale Christian Church, Rosedale United Methodist Church, and Rainbow Boulevard Mennonite Church). I was thoroughly enmeshed in various theological issues and church traditions while teaching public high school English full-time. The Sharing Community was a vigorous, healthy, and thriving religious community with active investment in social justice activities in a lower-income neighborhood. One such project was the establishment of a voluntary service unit (through the GCMC) in 1976. I not only chaired the Mennonite Voluntary Service Support Committee but also hosted new "VSers" at my kitchen table, since we lived next door to the unit house. The Rainbow congregation and a small group that met every two weeks for a meal and sharing encouraged me to finish my seminary education, begun at AMBS in 1973, and to move into formal pastoral ministry.

My license toward ordination service in 1984 was weeks before my graduation with a Master of Divinity degree from St. Paul School of Theology, Kansas City, Missouri—another ecumenical venture for me into a United Methodist seminary. Even though this initial credentialing was formalized by the Western District Conference (GCMC), it was assumed that South Central Conference (MC) would recognize this milestone. We assumed we would stay in Kansas City.

Things got complicated. Assumptions fell apart.

After graduation, I was called to be the (sole) pastor, and second full-time pastor, of Manhattan (Kansas) Mennonite Fellowship (MMF), founded in 1978 by *three* Mennonite denominations with colleges in Kansas: Western District Conference (GCMC, Bethel College), South Central Conference (MC, Hesston College), and the Southern District Conference (Mennonite Brethren [MB], Tabor College). It was a natural development since the charter members of MMF were previous members of all three denominations and wished to model collaborative ministry in a university setting. We moved to Manhattan in the summer of 1984, and I began a pastoral journey with a tri-affiliated congregation. We navigated multiple area conference delegate meetings, divided offerings into thirds, and shared news, guest preachers, publications, and mission opportunities from our parent denominations and Mennonite Central Committee (MCC)—also with a regional office in Kansas (North Newton).

The complication arose in spring 1985: How would I be ordained?

The Western District Conference interviewed me, and I was granted ordination, even though the Ministerial Committee was not unanimous in its decision. One man said at the meeting's outset, "I am going to vote *no* regardless of your answers. Women should not be lead pastors." The others voted yes, and I was ordained April 28, 1985. The recognition that MMF was tri-affiliated complicated the ordination ceremony, although the South Central Conference offered their support by participating in the worship service. The MB Southern District sent a representative who did not participate in the ordination ceremony but read scripture as part of the worship service. (A Catholic campus minister and Sister of St. Joseph of Concordia was part of the circle who laid hands on me with prayers of blessing.)

It turned out that the South Central Conference ministerial committee had a problem. In the past, they had routinely enjoyed the ritual of recognizing the credentials of pastors who had been ordained in other Mennonite area conferences. When my name and Lois Barrett's were on the agenda for acceptance, concern stopped their process. Instead, a formal study conference was designed to allow the thirty-five congregations to send delegates to a special consultation. The interim conference minister, Leland Harder, suggested a survey to test the status of "Women in Church Leadership," and the conference was planned for May 31 to June 1, 1985, in Oklahoma City. The 3,500 members responded to the survey with a 38 percent return.[3] During the two-day consultation, the diversity of opinion regarding biblical teaching was ever present. The program included keynote addresses by a seminary professor, "buzz" groups composed of the 120 people attending, and an original drama where the officiating pastor for a wedding was a woman. A final formal resolution, which stated that "these related issues be further discussed within the year, and in the interim give authority to each [of the four] districts' leader-

---

3 Leland Harder, "Congregational Questionnaire Survey Findings Summary," May 31, 1985, in personal collection.

ship commissions to recommend the licensing of a woman to the pastorate in specific situations," passed by a 78 percent vote.[4]

Now, decades later, and after multiple leadership positions in both congregations and Mennonite institutions, my ordination is nothing less than an early victory. It also was a time of testing, of decision, and of tenacity. I loved teaching in the public schools and shed tears when I finally gave up my teaching certificate in 1990. I truly was moving in a new vocational direction and had paid the price of examination, public testimony, and rounds of criticism and disapproval.

I (Lois) was also recognizing that the story of women's increasing inclusion in church leadership needed to be told. As a seminary professor, I occasionally encountered a student who had no idea how things had been for women a generation or two earlier—or who would claim that there was currently absolutely no discrimination against women in the church. Earlier, I had been a church journalist trying to raise awareness of women's issues in the broader church. I had worried whether I could actually be ordained. At my ordination interview, one member of the Western District Conference ministerial committee, a pastor, had left the meeting before the vote so he would not have to tell his deacons that he had voted to ordain me. I had weathered public criticism in a South Central Conference session over being a woman in ministry, only for the same man who had vilified me in the plenary session to tell me privately in the hallway that I shouldn't take any of it personally! I had been a pastor in a Mennonite congregation composed of house churches that for the first few years was not sure whether it wanted to call anyone "pastor." I had been a denominational executive where there were few female role models for how to do my job. Had my students known what it was like to be the only woman in a committee meeting? Had they known what it was like to be one of two or three women students in a seminary classroom? Could they understand the more subtle

---

[4] Susan Balzer, "Consultation Views Women's Roles," *Mennonite Weekly Review*, July 18, 1985, 5.

discrimination now? How could others understand the changes that had taken place since those early struggles?

The result of our questions and reflections became this book. Its chapters trace the story of women pioneers in Mennonite leadership. We have included firsthand experiences, memories, and data about the complexity of faith lived out in daily life from 1972 to 2006. This book is not about all issues concerning women's lives: politics, biblical interpretation, gender roles in parenting and marriage, sexuality, sexual harassment and abuse, social justice movements, and so on. Those important topics, no doubt, already appear on bookshelves and in library stacks—and, hopefully, in forthcoming manuscripts as well. Our primary effort is to document the role of women in Mennonite congregational and institutional leadership—some women successful, some sidelined, some refused, some forgotten.

Overview of chapters

Each chapter in this collection is shaped by the voices of women who have exercised leadership in Anabaptist denominations. Some are scholars; others are pastors; still others were leaders in publication, education, and administration. Two men also join their voices in this narrative. Together, these voices tell the story of Mennonite women who invested their gifts and talents in Mennonite congregations and institutions. The various chapters include not only personal experiences but also survey data, where available, to document changes in attitudes and practices over forty years.

In chapter 1, Dorothy Nickel Friesen explains how Mennonite women started organizing for change in the 1970s and involving church institutions in the change process, buoyed by the second wave of feminism in society. What started outside the structures became supported by at least some of the church structures. In the 1970s, a survey showed that the vast majority of Mennonites did not believe that women should be ordained or hold office in the church—and they believed that women were *not* being discriminated against in society. In that setting, feminist

Mennonite women's voices—in conversation—became the seedbed of change.

In chapter 2, Dorothy Yoder Nyce recounts her own journey in promoting change within Mennonite church institutions. In particular, she notes the mentors, classes, conferences, colleagues, and writings that influenced her over more than three decades.

One of the Mennonite institutions most influential in amplifying Mennonite women's voices was the Mennonite Central Committee (MCC) Peace Section. In chapter 3, Gayle Gerber Koontz and Ted Koontz, former MCC staff, examine the influence the MCC Peace Section and its Task Force on Women in Church and Society had on feminist change in Mennonite churches. Through packets of articles, a periodical (quoted frequently in this book), and a staff person at a Women's Concerns Desk, the Peace Section gave a platform to women who wanted a larger voice in the church.

A larger voice in the church was also a goal of Iris de León-Hartshorn and Regina Shands Stoltzfus, who, in chapter 4, look back on their experiences as Mennonite women of color during the time period covered by this book. For de León-Hartshorn, breaking into a largely white, male-dominated church required passion, commitment, education, and supportive people along the way. In this chapter her Latina voice is heard in an interview format. Shands Stoltzfus writes about how her nurture in a mixed-race, mixed-tradition Mennonite church influenced her later work as a pastor, administrator, and anti-racism advocate.

In chapter 5, John A. Esau, Nancy Kauffmann, and Karen Martens Zimmerly—all former denominational staff for ministerial leadership—tell the story of Mennonite women's ordination through interspersing official documents with women's ordination stories. They show how the roots of women's ordination among Anabaptists in the sixteenth century, in the deaconess movement, among overseas missionaries, and with the first official ordination of a Mennonite woman pastor in 1911 all supported the blossoming of women in ministry in the 1970s and 1980s.

In chapter 6, Dorothy Nickel Friesen and Diane Zaerr Brenneman look at surveys of Mennonite pastors in 1992 and 2005 that bring to light the experiences of women pastors in this era. Attitudes toward women in ministry had improved from the Sauder study in 1992 to the Zaerr Brenneman study in 2005, but women pastors were still only 16 percent of the total pastorates. Women's overall satisfaction with the choice to be a congregational pastor, despite doubts and barriers, was increasing, as was their spiritual leadership.

In chapter 7, Lois Y. Barrett tells the story of Women in Ministry and Women Doing Theology conferences and analyzes the various ways Mennonite women did theology from 1972 to 2006. The most popular of these theologies were those looking to the Bible and Anabaptist-Mennonite history for women models as well as those discussing the use of inclusive language for God. Other theological writings explored the impact of women's bodily experience on theology, connected women's struggles with liberation theology, made sense of suffering and forgiveness in women's contexts, and saw expanding roles for women as the continuation of a trajectory begun already in the Bible.

Chapter 8, also by Barrett, relates the changes in Mennonite institutions as women became congregational deacons and elders, sat on churchwide boards and committees, and increasingly took on administrative staff roles in church institutions. In addition, Barrett and others tell of their experiences of being the "first" in male-dominated structures and of women's ways of decision making.

In chapter 9, Anita Hooley Yoder and Marlene Harder Bogard discuss how the traditional church women's organizations, the "auxiliaries," functioned and adapted during this period of feminist ferment among Mennonites. They also discuss the future of these adjunct structures beside the official structures.

In the concluding chapter, we editors reflect on the changes in Mennonite women's participation in the church through our own stories and offer some ideas for the future.

The appendix has the most complete extant list of Mennonite women ordained in North America between 1972 and 2006. (Readers from Mennonite churches may even find their name or the name of someone they know!)

We have also included a study guide because we hope that people will not only read this book but reflect on it, discuss it with each other, and continue to promote the gifts of women in the church.

Finally, the original surveys referenced in this book are available online at the Mennonite Women in Ministry Survey Collection of the Internet Archives: https://archive.org/details/mennonite_women_in_ministry. Special thanks to AMBS's director of library services, Karl Stutzman, for making these files publicly available.

From an ad hoc women's caucus in 1972 to a survey evidencing changed attitudes in 2006, this book contains the stories, statistics, and spiritual beliefs of Mennonite women who found new and challenging ways to proclaim the good news of Jesus Christ.

1

First gatherings
Women organize
Dorothy Nickel Friesen

The 1960s were a tipping point for women's liberation movements in the United States. Having finally won the right to vote (1920) in the United States, (white) feminists now critiqued every aspect of the culture through the lens of discrimination. This "second wave of feminism" ushered in a flood of protests, publishing, and pursuits for the equality of women. Urban centers were filled not only with civil rights protests by Black leaders in the church, such as Dr. Martin Luther King Jr., but also with protests by "women's lib" leaders like Gloria Steinem and "radical" theology professors like Rosemary Radford Ruether and Mary Daly.

Women as helpers

In the Mennonite world, women were noticing the cultural shift. Higher education, "the pill," and television added to a tsunami of changing cultural norms, especially in North America. Through Mennonite women's organizations,[1] the General Conference Mennonite Church (GCMC) and Mennonite Church (MC) clung to the notion of complementary roles of women and men, thus perpetuating separate, but unequal, organizations within the formal structures of the denominations.

---

1 Ably documented in Anita Hooley Yoder, *Circles of Sisterhood: A History of Mission, Service, and Fellowship in Mennonite Women's Organizations* (Harrisonburg, VA: Herald, 2017).

To be sure, these women's organizations were critical places of Christian witness, service, nurture, and education. Women had been sent to other continents as missionaries—some even "ordained" for that purpose along with their husbands. My own mother-in-law was such an example. The GCMC Foreign Mission Board assigned newly married Arthur and Viola Friesen for "foreign mission" ministry among the Cheyenne and Arapaho in Oklahoma (so designated before 1950). A letter dated June 17, 1940, to Arthur's California parents, who were unable to attend the service, described the ordination service at Salem Zion Church in Freeman, South Dakota:

> When the answering was completed, both [Arthur and Viola] kneeled down, the elders present: Rev. Claassen, Schroeder, Linscheid, myself [Peter Penner], placed the hands upon the head of Arthur, whereupon Rev. Waltner ordained him as a missionary. Then the same procedure was followed for Viola. This we have never seen done. However, she was ordained as a helpmate to Arthur, fulfilling her obligations as is expected from a missionary's wife.[2]

Another instance of the word *ordination* used in connection with Mennonite women appears in the early twentieth century. Deaconess work among the Mennonites of North America represents the continuation of a practice among the Mennonites of Russia and had its origin within the GCMC in the United States with the work of David Goerz of Newton, Kansas. He seemingly hand-picked Frieda Kaufman, a vocal young woman yearning to be of service just like the nuns she had seen in her German birthplace. In her early twenties, she studied at Bethel College for two years and then went to the Deaconess Hospital, a Methodist institution in Cincinnati, Ohio, entering as their first candidate in a fledging institutional arrangement with Bethel. She promised to return to serve as a deaconess, and the GCMC promised to ordain

---

[2] Letter in personal file. Her name does not appear in the official records of "ordained women" in the archives of the Mennonite Church USA.

her as such. Sister Frieda Kaufman, Sister Catherine Voth, and Sister Ida Epp were ordained when the Bethel Deaconess Hospital in Newton, Kansas, was dedicated on June 11, 1908. They were the first three deaconesses of this motherhouse.[3] It seems that ordination was a commissioning for a specific church vocation, blessed by the institutional structures of both church and college. This was also a bold statement on behalf of single women, particularly, who dedicated their lives to Christian service as nurses and caregivers and, in at least one case, a worker in a congregational role.

In local congregations, women dominated Sunday school teaching (and still do), though the role of superintendent, denoting leadership, often fell to men. The roles that women could occupy in local congregations were as partners with their husbands with no first names recorded—just "Mrs. John Schmidt," for example.

In my Minnesota home congregation, the women's organization published cookbooks to raise money for missions. In 1966, when my mother's famous recipe for *Zwieback* (a double bun with Prussian origins) was published (famous because she used oil instead of lard), she was identified as a wife. Her name, "Mrs. John Nickel," appeared on the same page as "Mrs. Herb Friesen" and "Mrs. Alton Penner."[4] The next cookbook, published in 1980, has the exact Zwieback recipe, but she was now "Edna (Mrs. John) Nickel" and appeared on that same page with "Ann (Mrs. Harold) Klassen" and "Sara (Mrs. Londo) Regehr."[5] By 1993, my mother was simply "Edna Nickel" with a new bread recipe, "60-minute rolls."[6] It appears that the nomenclature, even in cookbooks, noted shifts in identity for faithful Mennonite women who not only cooked but also raised money for missions.

---

3 *Mennonite Encyclopedia*, vol. 2 (Scottdale, PA: Mennonite Publishing House, 1956), s.v. "Deaconess," 24.

4 *Our Favorite Recipes* (Mountain Lake, MN: Worship and Sew Society, Bethel Mennonite Church, 1966), 43.

5 *From Our Kitchens: Good Cooking* (Mountain Lake, MN: Worship and Sew Society, Bethel Mennonite Church, 1980), 12.

6 *Sharing Our Blessings* (Mountain Lake, MN: Worship and Sew Society, Bethel Mennonite Church, 1993), 141.

The church kitchen was the scene of congregational activity, fundraising, and fellowship. Most church building construction in the twentieth century was done by volunteers with technical assistance from licensed electricians and plumbers. Women, as noted in the centennial history for Bethel College Mennonite Church in North Newton, Kansas, argued and finally persuaded the congregation (in 1955) that a kitchen should be built on "faster action, so that they could begin their 'women's work' of cooking and serving meals to raise funds. . . . If you want us to continue our cleaning, painting, and fundraising, give us our kitchen!"[7]

The women were lauded for their volunteer efforts, while the ordination of women as pastors was hardly imagined. It was not until 1973 that the Illinois Mennonite Conference (MC) ordained Emma Sommers Richards—as co-pastor alongside her husband, Joe. The Western District Conference (GCMC) ordained Marilyn Miller in 1976 as a co-pastor with Peter Ediger at the Arvada (Colorado) Mennonite Church. Conflict, confusion, and complexity dominated the role of women in the church. Changing roles from "helpmeet" to "pastor" seemed an impossible leap for many Christians and nearly all Mennonites in the early 1970s.

Women's voices emerge

A significant, long-standing scholarly lecture series at Conrad Grebel College (Ontario) featured the first woman lecturer in 1970: Lois Gunden Clemens, PhD, then professor at Temple University and formerly on the Goshen College (Indiana) faculty, who had a long history of international service and leadership in the Women's Missionary and Service Auxiliary of the Mennonite Church. She highlighted biblical and theological reasons for women as leaders. "The important contribution of her book *Woman Liberated* is the tying of woman's identity and her relationship to the total life of the church," read the jacket of her

---

7 Keith Sprunger, *Campus, Congregation, and Community: The Bethel College Mennonite Church 1897–1997* (North Newton, KS: Bethel College Mennonite Church, 1997), 63.

book.[8] Change was coming to the Mennonites, and women were speaking with authority. Clemens's scholarly work broke the ice in Mennonite academic publishing and raised the stakes for women in Mennonite leadership.

In the evangelical Christian world, feminist scholars emerged.[9] The Evangelical Women's Caucus was formed, and *Daughters of Sarah*, a feminist journal, began in 1973. *All We're Meant to Be: A Biblical Approach to Women's Liberation*, by Letha Scanzoni and Nancy Hardesty,[10] became a core reference for Anabaptist women. In 1975, the Commission on Education of the GCMC published a study guide for this book and commissioned five additional sections by Mennonite scholars on "Women in the Bible and Early Anabaptism."[11] It was clear that biblical documentation and education, often called consciousness raising, were tools for the church and critical material for discussion and feminist perspectives.

Caucus in Chicago

A significant institutional development was the birth of the Mennonite Central Committee (MCC) Peace Section Task Force on Women in Church and Society (TF) in March 1973.[12] However, the catalyst for the MCC Peace Section was an informal, momentous gathering in the fall of 1972 of a women's caucus in Chicago.

In early September of that year, Gayle Gerber Koontz, a college friend of mine, sent a letter to me and two other women (one "somewhere in Boston" and the other the news service editor for the GCMC) stating, "I have been thinking for some time

---

8 Lois Gunden Clemens, *Women Liberated* (Scottdale, PA: Herald, 1971).

9 Here *feminist* refers to those who favor and advocate women's equality with men.

10 Letha Scanzoni and Nancy Hardesty, *All We're Meant to Be: A Biblical Approach to Women's Liberation* (Waco, TX: Word, 1974).

11 Herta Funk, ed., *Study Guide* (Newton, KS: Faith and Life, 1975).

12 For an in-depth look at the role of the Women's Task Force, see chapter 3 of the present volume.

that someone somewhere ought to initiate a gathering of women interested in the Mennonite church and women's liberation."[13] She outlined an informal gathering for women following the annual Peace Section Assembly coming in early November (1972) at the YMCA hotel in Chicago. She suggested several questions: What is your reaction to this idea? Would you be interested in helping to plan the event? Could you suggest women's names to invite? In addition, there was a draft of an invitation letter with a handwritten note asking, "Have you had your baby yet?" Indeed, our first child had been born September 8. This letter from a trusted friend was the spark that ignited in me.

That fall, I was beginning a second year as editor of *forum* magazine, a monthly newsletter jointly published by the MC and GCMC denominations for university students attending non-Mennonite colleges and universities. I suspect Gayle's hunch that my editing (and therefore interest in young adult and liberation agendas) and access to Mennonite issues might attract me to such a newsworthy event. She was right.

Dress rehearsal for change

I had graduated from Bethel College, Kansas, in 1969 with a degree in English and a teaching credential but failed to find a job in Denver, Colorado, where I accompanied spouse, Richard, who was fulfilling his alternative service requirement during the Vietnam War. We were part of a five-person group from Bethel who formed the nucleus of a new Mennonite Voluntary Service Unit (GCMC) sponsored by the Arvada Mennonite Church in the suburbs of Denver. Women were "supporting members," donating their salaries at secular jobs so the males could perform "service assignments." Instead of teaching (or even substitute teaching), I found employment through the Kelly Girls temporary employment service and drove Denver streets to businesses who hired short-term help. For no more than four to eight weeks per job, I careened from a typist for a credit card demand office to a legal assistant, a medical office receptionist, and an oil company

---

13 Gayle Gerber Koontz, letter, Sept. 11, 1972, in possession of the author.

receptionist. I was miserable. I experienced the world of disposable women—those who kept the office running but lacked any benefits, any permanent status, or decent wages and had no thought of future employment. Yet, the urban culture was exciting, challenging, and beyond my more parochial background. Women's liberation, civil rights, street marches for "La Raza," and gatherings with smart graduate students challenged and stimulated my thinking. All this societal change fit my own theology of Jesus as a liberator. Women, it seemed, were unaware of the Christian message of discipleship, and I determined that I would claim being a Mennonite feminist.

Meanwhile, Mennonite pastors in the Denver area were collaborating and scheming about a stronger urban witness and formed the Denver Urban Ministry, hired an urban minister (Don Schierling), and advertised for an office secretary. Eager to leave the "temp world," I immediately joined the staff of First Mennonite Church as Don's secretary and witnessed the vitality and creativity of pastors committed both to Mennonite nonviolent principles and to addressing current, hot-button social problems. I was hooked.

After six months in that role and still yearning to be a teacher, I was hired as an eighth-grade English teacher in the Aurora school system on the east side of Denver. I remember getting the phone call at work and jumping up and down with joy at finally getting to teach. At Aurora Junior High, my boss, the principal who was a retired Army officer, had hired me when another first-year teacher walked off the job in early December. I was the cheapest long-term substitute teacher he could find, and, true to stereotype, he was strict, stern, and suspicious of young "agitators." Nevertheless, I thrived for the next nearly two years as an eighth-grade English teacher.

As my teaching vocation was blossoming, my spouse was ready to go to seminary, since he had fulfilled his required two-year service assignment. We were off to Elkhart, Indiana, where he would be a student at Associated Mennonite Biblical Seminaries (AMBS),[14] and I, again, planned to teach. However, I could not find a teaching job.

Within weeks of our move to Elkhart in 1971, I was invited to be the editor of *forum* magazine after the prior editor, John Rempel, resigned to go to graduate school. That half-time job, supported by both the MC and GCMC offices of higher education, provided an entrée into the world of denomination ministry and denominational polity. It fit me like a glove.

In our second year at AMBS, I was also continuing to attend seminary classes as an auditor, since spouses of full-time students were afforded free tuition to any classes. I took notes and participated in the class discussions but was spared exams. I loved learning and saw the melding of English literature with biblical literature. Seminary education seemed a great route back to the classroom—not a switch to a church vocation. My growing insight into church and institutional sexism festered. Not only was I a new mother, but I was also ready for a more active role in church politics as an educator.

Women respond

I accepted Gayle's invitation. She, Lois Barrett Janzen, and I agreed to invite women to a half-day post–Peace Section Assembly in the modest Chicago YMCA. (The letter of invitation, dated October 6, 1972, noted that the YMCA lodging cost $4.50 per night.) We posed the following questions:

> What does it mean to be a "liberated woman"? Can a liberated woman participate freely in the life of Mennonite churches? Why or why not? What is being done to destroy discrimination against women in the church? How can Mennonite women tackle the problem most effectively? What needs do women in society have that our churches are not ministering to presently? What can we do about it?"[15]

---

14 Now Anabaptist Mennonite Biblical Seminary.
15 Letter in private collection.

In a final paragraph, we invited specific suggestions for planning the meeting set for November 18, 1:30–5:00 p.m. A request to be informed of the proceedings if unable to attend and suggestions for additional names of women who could be added to the mailing list were to be sent to Gayle. We wondered, Would anyone attend?

One woman from Baltimore wrote a two-page letter to me noting she could not attend the meeting in Chicago but then described her situation.

> As I read your letter, one thing that I thought of that a group like this might well work on is "women in MCC" or, maybe more generally, in overseas mission programs. In my own experience and that of quite a few women I've talked to, whose own qualifications do not dovetail neatly into their husband's job assignment (such as doctor-nurse, teacher-teacher), finding a satisfactory role can be a real problem. I ended up making my mark by having babies. I don't entirely blame MCC—it was partly my own lack of foresight that got me into that situation (the role conflict that is, not the babies—they, at least, were planned!). But I wonder if MCC now is doing any more on this when they make assignments or counseling women who are going into assignments with their husbands. . . . I think that my ideas and concerns about my role as a woman have not been very closely connected with the church as such because my energy in the last few years hasn't been put into the church, but in trying to work out a balance between being a person, a wife, a mother, and a social worker. I have seen (or see) myself as all these things before "woman in the church."[16]

Another letter arrived saying, "I most certainly will stay for the mtg. on Women's Liberation and the Church. . . . I am apply-

---

16 Janet Reedy, letter, Nov. 1, 1972, in possession of author.

ing for a nursing job now since the church likes me as a 'supporting wife' but this seems to require no additional salary."[17]

An undefined purpose: Just participate

Women's concerns gushed out when women were given an opportunity to speak out. After the caucus, a final summary report was sent to nearly one hundred names (nearly all women, but five men's names and one church were also listed). That list included those who had attended or wished to be informed of the gathering's agenda and findings. The report noted that the format for the afternoon began with an introduction by Lois: "The core of the gospel is peace and freedom; the church has been calling only men; women are not free to use all their gifts; [women are] not free to be responsible disciples."[18] Then seventy-five attendees were divided into small groups who brainstormed the following concerns:

- women discouraged from speaking in church
- Bible interpreted to keep women in certain roles
- God language is male-oriented
- women's projects seen as secondary
- women not given chance to develop talents
- token women on committees and boards
- single women often left out of church
- education gaps in history of women, Sunday school materials
- women identified by relation to husband, father, or children
- marriage and childcare

---

17 Norma Goertzen, letter, Nov. 4, 1972, in possession of author.

18 Gayle Gerber Koontz, "Report from Informal Meeting for Persons Interested in Women's Liberation and the Mennonite Church" (Nov. 1972), 1.

Six "Interest Group Discussions on Specific Concerns" developed goals, actions, and projects for each concern: Women and Theological Language; Combating Sexism through Education; Women in Church Leadership; Women, Child Care, and Marriage; Women in Seminary; and The Church and Single Women—Role of Women's Organizations. Specific ideas ranged from "stop using Mrs. in publications" to "sending liberation teams to churches" to "make information about Anabaptist women available" to "need women theologians." The voices were collecting energy with specificity in the context of women's roles in the church and society.

Finally, a large-group sharing session concluded the informal Chicago caucus. One specific suggestion was that the following year's Peace Section Assembly have input from women on the planning team. The only two women representatives on MCC Peace Section Board (Lora Oyer and Fern Umble) were noted as contacts for that future assembly.

In a closing announcement summarizing the Chicago caucus, Gayle noted that the GCMC Commission on Home Ministries was planning a fall meeting in Elkhart, Indiana, that would include "members and staff of several commissions, the Women's Missionary Association and a few seminary women." Women were urged to write to Harold Regier, staff, suggesting agenda relating to women in the church. The official GCMC news release, written by Lois Barrett Janzen, ended with this statement: "The group also suggested that women's role in the church be considered as the topic of the next Peace Section assembly." It was.

It had been a successful event. Our newborn infant attended her first churchwide meeting in a flimsy car bed, and I missed at least one session while I nursed her in the outside corridor. Exhausted from both leadership and motherhood, I had no doubt that women needed to be heard. And it seemed the institutional structures of MCC and maybe the GCMC the following year in Elkhart would provide opportunities for next steps. A network of women—young, mostly in the United States, MC and GCMC, mostly white, some in denominational women's groups, students, mothers—was merging into a fragile web of proclaimers.

Documenting attitudes

An ambitious research project began when J. Howard Kauffman, professor of sociology at Goshen College, and Leland D. Harder, professor of practical theology at Mennonite Biblical Seminary in Elkhart, Indiana, were secured to conduct a survey of church members in five denominations: Mennonite Church (MC), General Conference Mennonite Church (GCMC), Mennonite Brethren Church (MB), Brethren in Christ Church (BIC), and the Evangelical Mennonite Church (EMC). The study assessed that these five groups had a baptized membership in 1972 of 152,867 in the United States and 48,973 in Canada for a total of 201,840—or 70.5 percent of adult members of all recognized Anabaptist bodies in North America.[19] "The authors," wrote Kauffman and Harder in the preface to their book, "were asked to conduct a study that would yield information of use to church boards and committees, pastors, writers and editors, and others who carry responsibilities for the work of the church." The book's integrative theme, which formed the basis for organizing and interpreting the large quantity of data, was the concept of "Anabaptism, a vision of the Christian church that was hammered out in the fires of the Protestant Reformation. . . . Therefore, the central theme of this book is to learn how well the present members of these churches reflect that sixteenth-century vision."[20] A process of developing a questionnaire, securing funding, and consulting with church boards happened in 1971; the administration of the survey was conducted March through June, 1972.

I stumbled into this project when I was recruited and hired as a secretary for the "Anabaptist" study the summer of 1972. My role—along with Winifred Beechy and Betty Shenk—was to open the packets of returned questionnaires that flooded the mailboxes of the two research professors. We filled out numerous charts, completed reports, and checked the accuracy of each survey for

---

19 J. Howard Kauffman and Leland D. Harder, *Anabaptists Four Centuries Later* (Scottdale, PA: Herald, 1975), 21.

20 Kauffman and Harder, *Anabaptists Four Centuries Later*, 7.

established criteria. The role of support staff was ours. However, I was casually observing how sociologists did their work, as I saw the raw data from thousands of Mennonites across North America. I was privy to information that would either confirm or deny my own hunches about the state of the Mennonite church. After three months of secretarial duties, I returned to auditing seminary classes in the fall semester.

The two sociologists and collegial researchers processed the data over the next two years and finally published their findings in 1975. In the end, the questionnaires resulted in valid tabulating of 3,591 members from 174 congregations in the United States (2,878) and Canada (713), representing the five Anabaptist denominations.[21]

In part 3 of the report, The Work of the Church, the data was mined for questions surrounding leadership in the congregation. As the report states, "The responses of the samples of members of the five denominations to three questions probing the role of women indicate considerably more adherence to the traditional patriarchal view than to the radical Anabaptist view."[22] In an astonishing finding, the researchers wrote, "It is especially interesting to note that male respondents scored slightly higher on the Role-of-Women Scale than females. Thus, women struggling against tradition for the cause of equal participation in the work of the church should be aware that their own sex is the greater supporter of the traditional view on this issue."[23]

The first question asked, "In the future should larger numbers of qualified women be elected or appointed to church boards and committees at denomination, district, and congregational levels?" The *yes* response was an average of 32 percent for the five

---

21 Kauffman and Harder, *Anabaptists Four Centuries Later*. See the book's appendix, 364–85, for specific details on scope, method, and analysis of data.
22 Kauffman and Harder, *Anabaptists Four Centuries Later*, 195.
23 Kauffman and Harder, *Anabaptists Four Centuries Later*, 197.

denominations with a high of 40 percent for the GCMC, 36 for BIC, 29 for MC, 26 for MB, and a low of 22 percent for EMC.[24]

The second question was this: "Should the policy on ordinations in your denomination be changed to allow for the ordination of women to the Christian ministry?" Again, there was a high of 30 percent *yes* for GCMC, with 17 percent for BIC, 12 percent for MC, 12 percent for MB, and a low of 12 percent for EMC. Overall, a mere 17 percent agreed.[25]

The third question asked, "Do you believe that women in Canadian and American societies are being discriminated against and denied certain basic rights?" The *yes* responses were 20 percent for GCMC, 15 percent for MC, 14 percent for MB, 12 percent for BIC, and 10 percent for EMC—for a 16 percent average.[26]

It was not lost on me that my own hunches of limited options for women in the church and discrimination in society were critical issues for our time. However, most baptized members of five Anabaptist denominations were neither ready for nor open to qualified women serving in leadership roles in the church. The ordination of women pastors was not yet approved or possible.

I also witnessed the absence of full-time female professors at the Mennonite seminary in Elkhart and the near absence of women credit students in classes. Women who audited classes—as I did from 1971 to 1973—gave the impression of gender inclusion, but we auditors were add-ons. It was clearly a male environment meant for future male leaders of the Mennonite church.

Two institutional responses to "women's liberation in the church" in 1973

The dust from the Chicago caucus was not swept under institutional rugs; two institutional responses were made within a year. First, the GCMC planned a consultation for late October 1973. Organized by the Commission on Home Ministries (CHM) and

---

24 Kauffman and Harder, *Anabaptists Four Centuries Later*, 197.

25 Kauffman and Harder, *Anabaptists Four Centuries Later*, 196.

26 Kauffman and Harder, *Anabaptists Four Centuries Later*, 196.

staffed by Harold Regier, secretary for the Peace and Social Concerns division, the planning committee consisted of an Elkhart seminary student (me), two women representing the GCMC Women's Missionary Association (one from Canada, one from the United States), a GCMC news editor (Lois Barrett Janzen), plus Regier and Carol Epp, his administrative assistant. The invited list included key leaders of the GCMC structure charged to consider how this denomination could address the role of women in the broader church. There was pressure from others who wanted to attend, but the overwhelming nature of logistics, housing, and meeting space kept the invitation list to sixty people and a focus on GCMC.

The second major gathering that year was the MCC–sponsored Peace Section Assembly held at Camp Friedenswald in Cassopolis, Michigan, in late November 1973. Spurred by the Chicago Women's Caucus concerns, Peace Section staff Ted Koontz and Luann Habegger led the planning for the 1973 assembly.

Instead of the usual two main speakers, the 1973 assembly "offered a smorgasbord of speakers and interest groups on 'the interdependence of men and women.'" More than two hundred persons attended. "Probably a majority of those at the assembly were women, but no one thought of counting to make sure. It was evident, however, that most were under thirty."[27] There were short presentations from about seventeen participants, and more than forty others led interest groups on male and female roles in the church, society, and home. Many gave voice to the issue at hand: Would women and men be egalitarian or complementarian? Most said, in their evaluations in the last session, that they came because it was a Peace Assembly rather than because of the topic. The urgency and unrest because of the Vietnam War, no doubt, haunted this gathering. MCC Peace Section promised to continue to speak to churches on the issues of the assembly. The staff of the Peace Section projected a packet of literature on women's issues to be published the following year—and it was.

---

27 Lois Barrett Janzen, *The Mennonite*, Dec. 4, 1973, 705.

Dorothy Yoder Nyce was an early voice and prolific writer from College Mennonite Church in Goshen, Indiana. She was a speaker at the 1973 assembly on male-female interdependence in the Bible and dove into the ancient texts from Genesis to Paul. She quickly became a volunteer chairperson on the new "subcommittee for women in the church," as Ted Koontz assembled a working group to plan the 1974 assembly on behalf of women's voices. She brainstormed a book of essays featuring women's history—which did not materialize—and helped create a packet, "Persons Becoming," of over thirty articles, which she edited and for which she wrote several of the articles. She spoke at regional MC conferences and did research on male and female staff composition of MCC offices and of the Goshen College faculty and administration. Then, as a seminary student in Elkhart, she led workshops at regional MC annual meetings and used publications to write feature articles.[28] Two Dorothys—Nyce and myself—were now friends dedicated to the cause of women in the church.

The 1973 assembly also showed the small grip that women held in the church. Could we hang on? Shortly after the assembly, I wrote this observation:

> In doing some reflection, I noted that the Assembly, which has the reputation for activism, "fringe of the church" and the other "left" rhetoric, was mildly conservative and unenthusiastic as a group. There were few vocal feminists who pushed for hard thinking and soul searching—although the potential was (helpfully) there. . . . Clearly, there were some women saying they were interested in church-related work, jobs, service, but didn't feel they had a chance. It seemed the Assembly, for some, was the last stopping place before getting off the church's bandwagon altogether. . . . Some will go back, armed with new information, new friendships, ready to

---

28 See chapter 2 of the present volume for Nyce's reflections on this work. See also Dorothy Yoder Nyce, *Decades of Feminist Writing* (Self-published, 2020).

carry on. Others will be mildly disappointed, cynical and feel the church is five years behind on everything. Others will simply not care that much about anything. But at least they cared enough to spend several nights in a cold camp in southern Michigan listening and talking.[29]

In both Peace Section gatherings, the minutes and findings show integration of individual women's voices and institutional leaders who grappled with the issue of women's roles. Every angle was attempted: biblical lectures and input; the historical role of Anabaptist/Mennonite women; resources from Mennonite and other Christian publications; student research papers; challenges to individuals to write, preach, research, study, and inform churches about women's gifts. The implicit message was encouragement not to give up in the slow progress in freeing women to live out their Christian faith despite constant messages to the opposite.

AMBS offers first course on Women in Church and Society

Rumors that a new course would be offered at AMBS concerning the role of women in church and society were true. The course grew out of two ad hoc women's groups that formed and met during the 1972–73 school year at AMBS. One group was composed of women seminary credit students; the other group was wives of male AMBS students. Each group lobbied for formal education in the curriculum that would address the pressing agenda of the role of women.

Finally, in the spring of 1973, a course proposal for Women in Church and Society was submitted to the acting dean, John H. Yoder,[30] who carried this new course through the AMBS struc-

---

29 Dorothy Nickel Friesen, "The MCC Assembly: A Personal Response," *forum*, Dec. 1973, 14.

30 We editors are aware of the sexual abuse against women—including many Mennonite women—that John H. Yoder perpetrated during much of the time period covered in this book (until his death in 1997). We also want to acknowledge the ways in which Yoder both helped and hindered the cause of Mennonite feminism during that period. We believe that we can best evaluate his legacy in that regard by openly examining what happened.

ture—including the curriculum committee, the library, the business committee, and the registrar's office—on behalf of vocal women students. Miraculously, a student committee was appointed with all responsibility for the survey course—which required a minimum number of credit students in order to run.[31] In the end, fifteen (eleven women and four men) registered for three hours of credit and an additional thirty-four (twenty-seven women and

---

To that end, Yoder is mentioned several times in this book in the context of women's leadership in the church. We are in harmony with the AMBS faculty's "Statement on Teaching and Scholarship Related to John Howard Yoder," in which they agree that:

- The relationship between Yoder's influential work on theology, ethics, and peace and his violent behavior are open for examination by faculty and students.

- Faculty will address forthrightly questions or issues raised as students consider the possible connections between his thought and some of his actions, and will examine what these writings communicate to vulnerable women, men, and children.

- AMBS will use particular care to name the context of Yoder's abusive actions when utilizing his writing on singleness, marriage, and sexuality and how to interpret it.

- Yoder's work has been and will continue to be read and evaluated within a broader context of scholars and practitioners, especially those who are addressing similar issues related to theology, ethics, and peace.

- Yoder will be presented as the complex person that he was—intellectually brilliant, creative, shy, deeply caring, and generous to some; dismissive of persons who confronted him about his misuse of power; and manipulative while committing violence against women.

The entire statement is available on the AMBS website, https://www.ambs.edu/ambs-response-to-victims-of-john-howard-yoder-abuse/.

31 The committee included Rachel Hilty Friesen, Carole Hull, and Orlando Redekop in spring 1973 and then Daniel Schipani in fall 1973, and Dorothy Nickel Friesen, with Yoder as faculty advisor.

seven men) audited the evening course. Worries about participation in the survey course evaporated!

Patterned after some other topical courses, such as Church and Race, the women's course featured selected resource persons each evening session. Notre Dame biblical scholar Josephine Massyngbaerde Ford, for example, was a guest lecturer on the New Testament and the role of women. Peggy Way, a scholar from Chicago, spoke on "Christian feminists." All other sessions had local presenters—seminary students, college and seminary professors, community nonprofit leaders, a physician, and women leaders in Mennonite church–related organizations who were thanked but not paid. Credit students were required to read fifty pages each week from a selected bibliography, participate in class discussions, and write a major paper or make a major presentation. Auditors often dominated the class discussion—and warned in notes to the planning committee that some topics like "single women," "gay movement," "average woman in the church," and "ordination" were omitted from the course. A deeper concern was how to embed women's issues in all AMBS curriculum—or more immediately, whether the course would be offered again. In a memo to the new dean, professor and former dean Yoder wrote queries: (1) "This is the first course to be administered by a group of students. Is this a good idea?" (2) "This course had a disproportionately large attendance from off campus. Most of the off-campus people were not ministers. . . . Is this a good thing?" (3) "Should another course like this be offered?" (4) "The course made generous use of off-campus resources but also of other AMBS faculty. Does either the past or the future of this course provide a good sample to test team-teaching?"[32]

Ad hoc discussion groups among women on a seminary campus had been the catalyst for a bona fide credit course in the academic curriculum. This course was an example of women's voices proclaiming the good news, leading to the education of at least forty-nine future pastors and church leaders.

---

32 "Evaluation of Course: Women in Church and Society," memo from J. H. Yoder to C. J. Dyck, Jan. 21, 1974.

Women were increasingly entering AMBS in the early 1970s. Fewer than ten women were enrolled during the academic years 1966–70, but the increasing presence exploded in 1973–74 and then kept rising as a percentage of the student body to 44.1 percent in the 1988–89 year.[33]

Women in Ministry conferences begin

The Lombard Mennonite Church (Illinois) hosted the first Women in Ministry conference April 30 to May 2, 1976. About sixty-five people attended—mostly women—for a "weekend conference of mutual study, encouragement and sharing."[34] The featured speaker was Nancy Hardesty, co-author of *All We're Meant to Be*, a frequently cited book by Mennonites regarding the biblical view of male and female roles. Hardesty's evangelical voice calmed women and yet urged more assertive calls by Christians to accept women as leaders, even as ordained pastors. The ad hoc nature of this resourcing event was empowering, and registrants urged another meeting.

The loosely organized conferences quickly established a pattern of meeting at various geographical sites in the United States and Canada with volunteer local planning teams. The second conference, "Persons in Ministry—Women and Men," was held in Arvada, Colorado, June 16–18, 1977. The brochure noted six topics: pastoral and team ministry, making media as ministry, women and policymaking in the larger church, developing alternative ministries, teaching ministry, and theological and practical problems and possibilities.

The brochure for the third Women in Ministry conference (sometimes called Persons in Ministry) showed the frustration in language, whether all women were ministers or just women who were pastors. The conference was held at Akron Mennonite Church (Pennsylvania) October 27–29, 1978, with eighty-one

---

33 Information provided by registrars Weyburn Groff and Ruth Ann Gardner to author in 1978 and 1989.

34 Gloria Martin, "Conference Held for Women in Ministry," *Report* 11, Task Force on Women in Church and Society, July 1976, 4.

registrants. As in the first conferences, the speakers were household names in the Mennonite church. This time Ruth Brunk Stoltzfus, Emma Sommers Richards, and Willard Swartley were main presenters, with additional seminars. Participants urged a fourth conference with the explicit theme of "getting women into church leadership positions."

By the fourth Women in Ministry conference, held at AMBS November 2–4, 1979, attendance ballooned to 250 (230 women and 20 men). Provocative presentations by Diane MacDonald, then assistant professor of religion at Goshen College, stated this challenge: "We have to formulate a women's theology which will not necessarily be normative for me or all women."[35] An interesting strategic impact was that eleven women preached on that Sunday morning in eleven different Mennonite congregations across Elkhart and Goshen. The findings committee for the fourth conference became the planning committee for a projected fifth conference in the Kansas area.

And so the pattern for these ad hoc conferences continued: a fifth conference in 1981 at Bethel College (Kansas), "Whole Women Ministering to the Whole World"; a sixth in 1982 in Kitchener, Ontario, "Looking Beyond Ourselves"; and a seventh May 3–6, 1984, in Harrisonburg, Virginia, "In the Image of God." At the 1984 conference, Virginia Ramey Mollenkott was the keynote speaker, and films, fellowship, and twenty workshops were packed into a rich conference schedule. Attendance at these later Women in Ministry conferences generally was about two hundred, and many came with an amazing similarity in focus: women were recovering from a history of patriarchal teaching and near absence in leadership of the Mennonite church. Women as ministers—meaning pastors, chaplains, and ordained clergy—were still yearning for a chance to network and for encouragement. The opportunity to meet and form friendships meant that the loneliness endemic to most leadership roles would not be quite so chill-

---

35 Vic Reimer, "Where Are We Today? In, But Still Out," *The Mennonite*, Nov. 20, 1979, 694.

ing. With little institutional staff support, women carpooled, slept in local hosting beds, and paid their expenses just to be together.[36]

From individual voice to collective chorus

Just as Mennonite women were gathering to gain strength in the call to be a leader in the church, similar gatherings were taking place in mainline denominations. A large 1980 study research project of clergywomen in nine mainline denominations (about one thousand women) told the story of US change in both women's attendance in seminary and denominational ordination patterns.[37] The approximate dates when women were first ordained in mainline denominations is as follows: United Church of Christ in 1853, American Baptist Churches in 1882, Christian Church (Disciples of Christ) in 1888, United Presbyterian Church in 1956, United Methodist Church in 1956, Presbyterian Church US in 1964, Lutheran Church in America in 1970, American Lutheran Church in 1970, and Episcopal Church in 1977.[38]

The early 1970s were a sea change regarding Mennonite women in congregational and denominational leadership. The first three women had been ordained in the two largest Mennonite denominations in 1973 (Emma Sommers Richards, Illinois Mennonite Conference, MC) and 1976 (Marilyn Miller, Western District Conference, GCMC, and Anne Neufeld Rupp, Central District Conference, GCMC). Ruth Brunk Stoltzfus, speaker at the third Women in Ministry conference, who studied the 1978 Mennonite World Handbook for Statistics, reported, "The Mennonite Church has 2,009 ordained men and one ordained woman;

---

36 See chapter 7 of the present volume for discussion on extra-institutional gatherings.

37 Jackson W. Carroll, Barbara Hargrove, and Adair T. Lummis, *Women of the Cloth: A New Opportunity for the Churches* (San Francisco: Harper & Row, 1981). Although there have been greater numbers of women present in seminary in recent years, both women and men in this study were not likely to have attended seminary when even a third of the student body were women (92).

38 Carroll, Hargrove, and Lummis, *Women of the Cloth*, 102.

the General Conference Mennonite Church has 395 ordained men and five women ordained. I get enough affirmation to keep me encouraged, but not enough to boast about."[39]

Surely the next decades would provide opportunity for boasting as Mennonite women followed the call of Jesus and the desire to serve as leaders and ordained pastors. Progress in attitudes toward women in leadership was happening. The scope of this volume begins in 1972 with the first (informal) gatherings regarding women's roles in the church and ends with 2006. These years are marked with academic research (1972, 1989, 2006) using congregational surveys that measured attitudes toward women in leadership.[40]

In the 1980s, the researchers J. Howard Kauffman (retired sociology professor at Goshen College, Indiana) and Leo Driedger (professor of sociology at the University of Manitoba in Winnipeg) teamed to "take the religious temperature of church members at a particular time." They explained, "Valid comparisons between two surveys are possible when the samples are taken from similar populations and the same questions are asked. The two Mennonite surveys had 3,591 respondents in 1972 and 3,083 in 1989. In both cases respondents represented five related denominations: Brethren in Christ Church, Evangelical Mennonite Church, General Conference Mennonite Church, Mennonite Brethren Church, and Mennonite Church. Roughly two-thirds of the 1989 questionnaire repeated items from the 1972 instrument."[41] Fortunately, the three questions regarding the role of women from the earlier Kauffman-Harder study were repeated.

There was a significant change in attitudes among church members in a positive direction. The sociologists noted, howev-

---

39 Ruth Brunk Stoltzfus, "Women Call for Greater Involvement, Akron," *Gospel Herald*, Nov. 14, 1978, 906.

40 These surveys are available online at the Mennonite Women in Ministry Survey Collection of the Internet Archives: https://archive.org/details/mennonite_women_in_ministry.

41 J. Howard Kauffman and Leo Driedger, *The Mennonite Mosaic: Identity and Modernization* (Scottdale PA: Herald, 1991), 22.

er, that "male and female responses were similar on these items, except that the proportion of males that favored ordination (47 percent) was slightly higher than the female proportion (42 percent). Middle-aged respondents favored expanded roles for women in greater proportion than did the teenagers and the oldest respondents. Respondents with higher education and urban residence favored expanded roles more than those of lower education and rural residence."[42]

My involvement with this second major study was gratifying and serendipitous. As assistant dean at AMBS (1990–95), I was pleasantly surprised when Leo Driedger spent a semester in Elkhart on his sabbatical as visiting professor. I was equally thrilled when he invited me to reflect on the study that he and J. Howard Kauffman had conducted. Their resulting book had been part of many presentations that I had made about the role of the female pastor in the Mennonite world and encouraged women, especially, to heed the call to proclaim the good news. What changes did I see in women in leadership? What had Renee Sauder found in her research of Mennonite women pastors?[43] How did that compare to other Christian denominations? Finally, Driedger and I co-wrote our findings for *The Mennonite Quarterly Review*.[44]

A third churchwide survey, Church Member Profile 2006, was conducted by Conrad L. Kanagy, associate professor of sociology at Elizabethtown College (Pennsylvania). It examined only three denominations (Church of the Brethren, Brethren in Christ, and Mennonite Church USA). However, the findings were published with only data from the Mennonite Church USA (MC USA), a

---

42 Kauffman and Driedger, *Mennonite Mosaic*, 206.

43 See chapter 6 of the present volume for a discussion of Sauder's findings.

44 Leo Driedger and Dorothy Nickel Friesen, "Mennonite Women in Pastoral Leadership," *Mennonite Quarterly Review* 69, no. 4 (Oct. 1995): 487–504.

merger of the former GCMC and MC.[45] The survey also oversampled members and pastors from minority racial and ethnic groups.

The one question that repeated the earlier surveys (1972 and 1989) tested favor toward the ordination of women. Kanagy concluded:

> Although there is greater openness to the ordination of women today than in the past, members still prefer male leadership. Fifty-eight percent prefer a man as lead pastor of their congregation compared to 40% who have no preference and only 2% who prefer a woman. There is no significant difference between men and women in their gender preferences for pastoral leadership. While the ordination of women has freed women to use their gifts and callings in the church, the data suggest that it has not changed the deeper resistance of many members to having a women minister in their own congregation—few members prefer a woman over a man."[46]

I participated in the major presentation of Kanagy's 2006 findings when I attended his workshop at San Jose, California, during the MC USA convention in 2007. He and I had several discussions, which led to his survey's presentation to the Western District Conference (WDC) Reference Council (leaders of WDC) for discussion. My role as WDC Conference Minister from 2003 to 2010 brought the researcher, data, and application directly to area conference leaders—then 30 percent women in WDC pastorates.[47]

---

45 Conrad L. Kanagy, *Road Signs for the Journey: A Profile of Mennonite Church USA* (Scottdale, PA: Herald, 2007), 12.

46 Kanagy, *Road Signs*, 78.

47 Fall 2006 Directory, Western District Conference of Mennonite Church USA, where 70 congregations, including church plants, recorded 31 females and 72 males in "WDC Churches and Pastors," 17–28.

Conclusion

The stirrings of a feminist perspective in the late 1960s were met with informal gatherings and consciousness-raising groups and fledging, although momentous, educational and publishing efforts. For me, it meant a detour from a beloved profession as English teacher to editor for a Mennonite publication to seminary student and finally to pastoring and ordination. It is apparent that attitudes toward women in ministry made remarkable gains from 1972 to 2006 but were hardly resolved. With friendships, social justice movements, and determined—even feisty—attitudes, we can mark change in the Mennonite church. May there be more voices, more women proclaimers, and more witnesses of the power of a Jesus-inspired people.

2

If truth be told
Women dare to be activists
Dorothy Yoder Nyce

My mother, Bessie King Yoder, a graduate of Hesston College (Kansas), transferred her Kansas roots to Iowa in 1931. There she gave public speeches and for over five of ten decades was in demand as a Sunday school teacher with adult women. She shared beauty through flower beds, exuded hospitality, and canned vegetables from a huge garden. She "ministered" with my professionally trained father, meeting the public in contexts of grief. So, when I revised scripture misinterpreted by patriarchal leaders or advocated for women within Mennonite Central Committee (MCC), my mother, who feared that we would face flak, advised, "Just do it." Rather than cause conflict with church folk who conserved tradition, judged all feminists as "bra burners," or belittled Title IX—let alone history enriched with her-story—she encouraged, "Just do it."

Enabling women's self-growth, pursuing the half that had never yet been told, or engaging fields formerly dominated by men called for collective action. Mennonite women for decades served together via more than sewing circles. They encouraged each other and wrote books or articles in church journals to convey purpose or mission. They lived out truth as they understood it. Consider the following examples: (1) From the early 1860s, select women were "ordained" in Virginia to "visit the sick, relieve distress, or assist in (communion) foot washing procedures." (2) Inspired by deaconesses in the Netherlands and Germany, Mennonites in North America called women who served as nurses and teachers and with "rescue work" through Bethel Deaconess Home and Hospital in Newton, Kansas, and other deaconess ministries after 1903. (3) A Brethren in Christ (BIC) bishop ordained Anna Kraybill in 1921, and many who heard her messages recall her "fruitful ministry." Two decades earlier, sponsored by a faith missionary association, she worked seven years in India. In 1932 she married BIC bishop Millard Engle. (4) Olive Wyse, fifty-year home economics professor at Goshen College, requested of the Mennonite Board of Education more equitable salaries for women faculty in 1947.[1] Indeed, our grandmothers pioneered, prayed, made proposals to Mennonite officials, and produced children. This essay surveys this work across four decades.

The 1970s

The 1970s combined, for me, parenting two young daughters, studying at seminary, including women-themed research, and promoting diverse projects that proclaimed women's worth in church and society. Some women students at (then) Associated Mennonite Biblical Seminaries (AMBS) claimed the term feminist, commended women's value in scriptures, long semi-hidden, and discovered networking. (*Feminist* here means claiming equity for women and men: religious, social, economic.) The Genesis accounts affirm that humanity is created equally in God's image; women and men reflect divine care to all of creation. Students voiced concern, developed conviction, made choices.

While MCC Women's Task Force *Reports* will be analyzed in chapter 3, my first (1972) Task Force friends—Luann Habegger Martin, Lora Oyer, Ruth Stoltzfus Jost, Lois Keeney, and Ted Koontz, MCC staff person—shaped my volunteer engagement for

---

[1] Ruth Kady Lehman, "A Century of Deaconesses in the Virginia Conference," *Mennonite Historical Bulletin* 53:2 (Apr. 1992), 1–5. Ruth Kady Lehman, "The Deaconess and Her Ministry," *Mennonite Life* (Jan. 1948), 30–37. Miriam A. Bowers, "Anna Kraybill: A Woman Ordained," *Brethren in Christ History and Life* (June 1981), 38–47. Olive Wyse correspondence, Oct. 4, 1947 (writer's copy).

decades.[2] We determined to prove that justice for women merited the attention of the MCC Peace Section. We wished for Mennonite women to claim their strength. We studied the past to supply future integrity for Christian human relating.

For me, Luann Habegger Martin illustrated this vision. Her fine skills as organizer and analyzer enabled our team efforts while she managed the MCC Washington DC office and studied at American University's School of International Service. Her monograph, *Women and Development*, followed.[3] Her knowledge of the capital city enriched a seminar for Task Force friends on the family theme. We more rural participants met several women of Congress and the budding theologian Rosemary Radford Ruether. Luann elicited perspective, nudged Task Force members not to "worry about overexposure" through print for feminist causes, and complimented success. Before computers, she linked us through carbon-copied correspondence. She recommended forming an MCC advisory committee to review employment policies and practice. She reported after attending "The People's Meeting" at the United Nations' International Women's Year event in 1975 in Mexico City.

From its beginning, the Task Force linked personal with broader concerns. All members expected to learn about the women's movement local and global.[4] Luann addressed insight from Latina sisters about broad, male domination within power structures, anti-American feelings, and direct calls for governments to stop spending money on weapons of death. We, in turn, inquired into male control within Mennonite colleges and church patterns. All heads of Mennonite church boards were men at that time.

---

2 Comments here reflect what matters to me and other feminists. See articles about the Task Force in *Conrad Grebel Review* 23, no. 1 (Winter 2005).

3 Luann Habegger Martin, *Women and Development* (Akron, PA: Mennonite Central Committee, 1976).

4 For example, I read into the three-volume *Notable American Women* and Quaker Elise Boulding's *The Underside of History: A View of Women through Time* and received counsel from feminist Methodist and Roman Catholic women already organized.

Why were women not perceived as leaders? How might we foster change for such imbalance of duty? After Luann's death, her family donated to MCC a million dollars for maternal and child causes with which she had worked in African locations. What a fine feminist!

The Task Force vision was expanded by multiple writers. Research into church journals followed. Fellow enrollees at AMBS, like student Barry Schmell, noted 116 articles about women in *The Mennonite* between 1955 and 1981. Priscilla Stuckey-Kauffman noted over five hundred articles about women in *Christian Living, Mennonite Community, Mennonite Brethren Herald, Sword and Trumpet, Christian Monitor,* and *Mennonite Life* over several decades. I reported data from *Gospel Herald* at a Women in Ministry conference.[5] Three issues of the *Gospel Herald* in August 1973 printed my series "Women: In God's Plan and Man's World." That content followed research for the seminary course Hebrew Life and Culture, for which I charted 175 references to women in Deuteronomy through 2 Kings. For me, research matters, but tradition lingers. Editors misprinted the third article's title: "Freedom, Hope, *In*dependence" instead of "*Inter*dependence."

The *Mennonite Reporter*, February–March 1973, carried a series on "The Role of Women." (Note: women "play roles"; men

---

5 Five personal folders with *Gospel Herald* clippings written by or about women await analysis. Questions raised at the Women in Ministry workshop (one of 25): Types of *GH* material always read, percent of articles by women likely appearing on *GH* covers, five women writers within recent years, interest/import given to "Readers Say" (responses to prior articles). Data details include: "Why I Cover My Head" (Sept. 25, 1979) prompted 18 "Readers Say" letters. Of seven articles by women in 1981, "Sexist Language in Hymns" (Apr. 28, 1981) prompted 17 responses; "Women in the New Testament" (Dec. 29, 1981), at three pages, the longest, prompted 12; for both, more men responded. Whereas in 1979 ten cover articles were written by women, in 1983 seven of the 52 weeks focused on women writers. Only Mennonite Brethren Katie Funk Wiebe's writing appeared more often (50 times between 1979 and 1983). She pleased editors and many readers. I faced editors' attitudes through article rejections: "too long, general, or controversial." My "wisdom from the East" raised "thorny issues like different, valued approaches to God."

perform professions.) In print, women shared their experience, a key feature of feminism. What followed were short statements that prompted women readers to credit their own experience and urged male readers to affirm (or begrudge?) women's power. Writers like Ruth Klaassen carefully assessed women's liberation. She endorsed dialogue: open sharing, giving and receiving each person's gifts, encouraging Mennonite women to "keep up the prime standard set by Anabaptist sisters in the faith." Mary Regehr Dueck noted three items: being addressed as "Ms.," some church leaders' disapproval of change, and some church suppression. Patty Shelly boldly stated that prejudice against women reflects "the whole way we see reality: God and ourselves." She noted how language reflects beliefs and attitudes. Lois Barrett Janzen summarized activities and views related to seminary women at AMBS study groups, being pressured when addressing theology. Whether self-defined feminists or not, these women sought change for more just human relating.

Women's public voice often followed private, small group action. I sent seven pages of comments regarding a proposed document for the Mennonite Church (MC) General Assembly 1973 titled "Women in the Church." After the revised Assembly Workbook went to delegates (22 women, 255 men), I risked sending a three-page memo of personal conviction to all delegates whom I knew, about scriptures, resources, and questions. I felt driven to share my emerging vision. So also, when invited by General Secretary Paul Kraybill in spring 1975, Beulah Kauffman, Arlene Mark, Alice Roth, and I sent a memo to the MC General Board members and its Study Group on Biblical Interpretation. We urged welcoming genuine support for women in discussions expected at the July '75 Assembly.[6] We could not inhibit momentum.

Studying original biblical Hebrew and Greek had personal results. Through disciplined effort, I claimed texts for myself with new depth and gained tools for choosing among interpretations. No longer relying on traditional views, my lifelong task became

---

6 Beulah Kauffman, while chairing Women's Service and Auxiliary efforts, supported and connected with feminist leaders.

paying due attention to time and cultural distinctives of original speakers and hearers. All translation and interpretation reflected someone's bias combined with facts. Point of view—what matters or is valued—shaped decisions about content.

Research for the 1973 AMBS course Women in Church and Society led me to write a major paper on *The Woman's Bible*, compiled by Elizabeth Cady Stanton and her co-writers. What in their nineteenth-century context shaped the writers' views of a soul's existence, clerical influence, or concepts of God? While Stanton charged the Bible for degradation of women, my bias contended that translators, interpreters, and preachers (mostly men) often "propagate distorted teaching of biblical materials about women for reasons of self-defense or inadequate knowledge."[7]

The Woman's Bible conveyed how women's experience can enrich insight into that sacred text. Preacher Anna Howard Shaw (known as the "greatest woman speaker") spoke truth to me: "The great defect in the religious teaching to and accepted by women is the dogma that self-effacement and excessive humility were ideal feminine virtues."[8] During the 1840s, Julia Smith translated the Bible five times, twice each from Greek and Hebrew and once from Latin.[9] Lee Anna Starr's *Bible Status of Woman*, written thirty years after Stanton, added needed facts.[10]

Such women mentors called me to examine reasons for current attitudes about women as inferior. I bristled over biased translations or preaching that overlooked women's strengths. Therefore, I respectfully took issue—took feminist risk—with John Howard Yoder's "Revolutionary Subordination" chapter in

---

7 Dorothy Yoder Nyce, "The *Woman's Bible*: 75 Years Before and After," for AMBS Women in Church and Society course, Professor John Howard Yoder, Dec. 13, 1973, 1.

8 Aileen S. Kraditor, *The Ideas of the Woman Suffrage Movement 1890–1920* (New York: Columbia University Press, 1965), 92; Yoder Nyce, "*Woman's Bible*," 5.

9 Yoder Nyce, "*Woman's Bible*," 10.

10 Lee Anna Starr, *The Bible Status of Woman* (Zarephath, NJ: Pillar of Fire, 1955).

The Politics of Jesus.[11] Aware that Yoder would evaluate my paper, I faulted his categories of *sub* and *super* people. Those designations harm; they validate difference in worth. I asked, "When will the 'super' category (husbands) be 'revolutionary,' called to 'forsake and renounce all domineering use of status like a "super" mentality'?"

Further motivation for me followed the 1974 MCC Task Force's packet of articles titled "Persons Becoming." There, twenty-six Mennonite and three non-Mennonite scholars' views appeared. Themes reflected concerns: "Introduction: Feminism and Women's Liberation" (explained by Gayle Gerber Koontz and Dorothy Nickel Friesen), "The Bible and Women," "The Church and Women," "Changing Male-Female Relationships," and (briefly) "Minorities within a 'Minority.'" Young voices discussed history, language, and peace; several couples shared writing. More than 1,800 copies sold at $1.50 per copy. We were making a difference.

The 1973 consultation planned by the General Conference Mennonite Church (GCMC) Commission on Home Ministries, held at AMBS, resulted in Herta Funk being hired half-time to engage women's issues within the GCMC Commission on Education. (If only my MC group had such vision, I mused!) Her writing efforts included a brief history of women's public tasks with Mennonite World Conference (MWC), "Guidelines for Equal Treatment of the Sexes in the Foundation Series" (Sunday school curriculum), and "Study Guide on Women" with part 1 on Women in the Bible and Early Anabaptism, and part 2 consisting of lesson helps for *All We're Meant to Be*.[12] Funk's visits to GCMC women's groups linked with her newssheet "Accent on Women."

---

11 John Howard Yoder, *The Politics of Jesus* (Grand Rapids: Eerdmans, 1972). Yoder referred to pages 180–82 in his book. See chapter 1, note 30, for a discussion about referencing the work of John Howard Yoder in this volume.

12 Letha Scanzoni and Nancy Hardesty, *All We're Meant to Be: A Biblical Approach to Women's Liberation* (Waco, TX: Word, 1974). Funk's resource was intended for a 13-week Sunday school discussion.

A resource listing that she compiled reviewed twenty-two books and several films. Her speech to Church of the Brethren women—"Mennonite and Feminist: The Ongoing Struggle"—included responses that she gathered from twenty-seven of us regarding questions about gains, struggles, and frontiers. Funk attended, with six thousand women and men from eighty-one countries, the World Conference of the International Women's Year in Mexico City.

Whether for seminary courses or personal purpose, my typewriter flourished; research stimulated me. A 1974 AMBS New Testament course taught by Josephine Massyngbaerde Ford—a Catholic, University of Notre Dame woman professor—and the lengthy John 4 text about a Samaritan woman's theological encounter with Jesus drew my respect. That study, in turn, evolved into my writing a one-act play titled "Talking with a Woman . . . Can This Be the Christ?" Worshipers saw a memorized production of it during a College Mennonite Church (Goshen, Indiana) Sunday morning service.[13]

For some Mennonite women, the 1970s proved refreshing; others among us resisted change. We discovered networking, testing ideas with each other, and trusted common concern for defining peace with justice. In the process we explored a new vision of divine intent for personal worth with duty to confront the harm of patriarchy in the home, church, or society. We started believing

---

13 Gratitude for professors who valued my feminist research persists, like Orlando Schmidt's encouragement for this play-writing independent study at AMBS. When living in Cambridge, Massachusetts, in 1976–1977, I engaged in special course research at Episcopal Divinity and Andover-Newton Seminary, which proved exciting. I produced "Women in Pulpit Ministry: 19th-Century U.S.," with Suzanne Hiatt (early-ordained Episcopalian), "Exploring the Psychological History of Women, Focus: Exclusion," with Bessie Chambers, and "The Climate for Women in Early Anabaptism," with Eleanor McLaughlin. Being alone to explain Mennonite thought stretched me. I also treasured AMBS Hebrew professor Millard Lind's eleven pages of hand-written, energized notes to my forty-seven-page paper "Probing the Shape of Syncretism Known to Jeremiah."

in feminist thought, grateful for wise mentors. We claimed the usefulness of expressing our voice through print.

The 1980s and into the 1990s

The MCC Task Force on Women agenda led to publication in 1980 of the 150-page book *Which Way Women? (WWW?)*, which I edited.[14] I gratefully included forty-two Mennonite writers plus several journal reprints. Regrets from invited African American, Hispanic, and North American Indian writers reflected our ongoing effort to broaden the base of voices, plus we noted minority caution toward feminism. To expose Mennonites to broader influences, *WWW?* content was organized around International Women's Decade, 1976–1985, themes: equality, development, and peace.[15] Those themes accentuated a Mennonite, feminist, and global agenda. *WWW?* offered opportunity to communicate, cooperate, and even compensate, as my introduction stated.[16] Ever open to more women, my book vision stressed information, awareness of need for distinct, feminist leadership training, gratitude for our global heritage (people of 48 nations had attended the 1978 MWC in Kansas), and further commitment as capable women to God, neighbor, and family.

Numerous letters about *WWW?* reflected energizing power. "Thank you for the LOVE of it." "What a wonderful book!" "When I finished *WWW?* I felt very proud to be a Mennonite woman." "This is the best resource on women, women's issues

---

14 By 1978 members were Nancy S. Lapp, Mabel Paetkau, Gayle Gerber Koontz, Mary Dueck, Anna Mary Brubacher, Anita Buller, and Akron's Peace Section administrative assistant Linda Schmidt. (The original group's policy, to broaden opportunity, suggested that no one serve more than three years.)

15 The Decade evolved from the UN's special International Women's Year, 1975.

16 Articles by Susan Hill Lindsey, Marilyn Miller and Anne Neufeld Rupp, Dorothy Yoder Nyce, and Marthe Ropp received reference in the survey report *The Mennonite Mosaic: Identity and Modernization*, by J. Howard Kauffman and Leo Driedger (Scottdale, PA: Herald, 1991).

and responsibilities that I've ever seen." "I took time to read cover-to-cover the book. As a fifty-year-old member of the Franconia Conference (Pennsylvania), I join with you (in centers of Mennonite academia) in the movement toward justice for all children of God." Thirty college students who read *WWW?* for a course signed a note of thanks for it. Even my seventy-five-year-old father's only regret after reading the entire book was size of print. But a Lancaster Mennonite Conference bishop wrote of "concern, distress, and amazement after browsing *WWW?* The book betrays trust in MCC . . . is much in harmony with the political and ecclesiastical left. . . . A writer casts doubt on the veracity of Scripture." Aware that change triggers resistance, four of us wrote sensitive responses to that bishop. No one replied.

In 1981 the MC Assembly was held in Bowling Green, Ohio. Prior discussions during the 1970s assemblies prompted awareness of issues. A call for more direct action graced the 1981 Assembly. A dozen women from the Goshen-Elkhart area met to plan. Each introduced herself before voicing her response to the "Leadership and Authority in the Life of the Church" document scheduled for delegate, open mic discussion. Together we revealed women's experiences, clarified issues, shared silence, outlined tasks for Bowling Green, and nurtured desired outcomes. An ad hoc group of nine signed a two-page memo to MC delegates and General Board members. Assembly leaders received forty-two such unsolicited memos.

At the Assembly, pink sheets of paper alongside newsprint were posted inside restroom stall doors in all dorms where women lodged. In addition to providing space for women to write notes to each other, the paper invited women to a 7:00–8:00 a.m. meeting "For Women Only" on the first business morning. There women would discuss "Women in Church Leadership," a segment of the forty-five-page study document. Curious men who justified their "need to report the Assembly" were turned away. Newsprint from restrooms (48 sheets), later collected for archives, revealed women's views on being Mennonite, liberation, the Bible as authority, women preachers, humility, the helper role, and creativity.

Mary Schertz's four-page summary of women's activism at Bowling Green reflected the highlights. Fires of female friendship prompted commitment among ad hoc committee members. Two hundred women attended that morning meeting. (*Gospel Herald* reported 120.) After Anna Bowman and Diane McDonald invited all to address fears and joys, Alice Roth led the discussion. Twenty-five women voiced views, each adding her perspective to the richness of our being together. Change was a recurring theme. The ad hoc group had determined to create space and time from which women could emerge with such vision, an important feminist perspective. During the later delegate session, addressed by many men and articulate, bold women, the document passed with a provision to name a committee to "further study issues of women in church leadership."[17] The MC Church Personnel Committee chose none of the members of the ad hoc group for that task. Such a direct overlook prodded my further feminist concern for vision, justice, and trust in "qualified women." An implicit change for future assemblies later appeared: only *delegates* could address public sessions.

We continued our advocacy and exchange between general assemblies. Budding feminist women gathered informally in Kansas, Oregon, and Colorado, thinking toward Bethlehem '83. Thirteen women—a Mennonite Feminist Caucus—met in Goshen in 1982 to build trust, pool knowledge, and dream. Several issues emerged: assumptions about women due to long-practiced MC patriarchy, how creative women might change structures once admitted, where power resides and how women claim or share it. (A major MC board chair said, "I don't perceive of myself as having power.") Feminist-oriented goals and workshop ideas for Bethlehem '83 with names of people to lead them emerged. We accepted new tasks like writing news releases for church journals and preparing literature exhibits.[18] Meetings took place for mutu-

---

17 See also *Mennonite Reporter*, Aug. 24, 1981, and *Gospel Herald*, Sept. 8 and 15, 1981.

18 Articles sold at our booth during Assembly included: "A Model of Ministry for Women and Other Feminists" by Lois Barrett; "Women and

al clarity with male leaders or committees. Knowing what genuine effort for goodwill had transpired for a decade, calls for grace toward writers of a *Gospel Herald* article after Bethlehem '83 followed. Its title, "New Voices at Bethlehem '83; Young Women Speak Out," reflected the gist, chosen by an editor for bold type. "We are a pragmatic generation without the baggage of reactionary anger."[19] Understanding takes time!

Other Mennonite women studied denominational roots. Dorothy Nickel Friesen, Barbara Esch Shisler, Jan Lugibihl, Beth Brubacher, Mary Jean Kraybill, Lois Barrett, and Mary Beyler all brought Anabaptist women's stories to light for courses or church journals. Responding to historians who primarily report about men, women highlighted not being spiritually motherless.[20] Learning from each other about worthy women within our holy heritage led to claiming personal tasks for our day. An avid Anabaptist researcher for decades, Canadian Linda A. Huebert Hecht combined with C. Arnold Snyder in 1996 to edit *Profiles of Anabaptist Women: Sixteenth-Century Reforming Pioneers*.[21] Jenifer Hiett Umble's 1987 thesis, "Women and Choice: An Examination of the *Martyrs' Mirror*," delved into accounts of more than 275 women.[22] She commented on letters, personal testimonies, and

---

the Mennonite Patriarchy" by Anna Bowman; "Intersection: Feminist and Mennonite Theologies" by Mary Schertz; and "Bible, Bishops, and Bombs" by Dorothy Yoder Nyce.

19 Susan Huber, Rebecca Rittgers, Melanie Zuercher, and Julia Spicher, "New Voices at Bethlehem '83; Young Women Speak Out," *Gospel Herald*, Aug. 1983, 628.

20 See my "Are Anabaptists Motherless?" in *WWW?* 122–30. See also a chapter I co-wrote with my daughter Lynda Nyce, "Power and Authority in Mennonite Ecclesiology: A Feminist Perspective," in *Power, Authority and the Anabaptist Tradition*, ed. Benjamin and Calvin Redekop (Baltimore: Johns Hopkins University Press, 2001), 155–73.

21 Linda A. Huebert Hecht and C. Arnold Snyder, eds., *Profiles of Anabaptist Women: Sixteenth-Century Reforming Pioneers* (Waterloo, ON: Wilfred Laurier University Press, 1996).

22 Jenifer Hiett Umble, "Women and Choice: An Examination of the *Martyrs' Mirror*," MA thesis, Southern Methodist University, 1987.

eyewitness accounts of arrest or execution. She noted women's spiritual activities: being strong examples for children, claiming scriptural depth, creating hymns, fleeing persecution, and opening homes to refugees or for worship.

Feminist students raised theological questions. In "For the Healing of the Nations" (1981), Mary Schertz examined myth, the female divine in the biblical symbol of "the tree of life," the warrior-God, threat due to centuries-long Israelite worship of the goddess Asherah, and more.[23] My DMin study of Asherah built on work done for a seminary course in Jeremiah. Interfaith study has enriched my understanding of the female divine figure with links to Spirit and Sophia-Wisdom from our Jewish heritage as Christians. My Hebrew scripture mentor, scholar, and friend Phyllis Trible wrote *Texts of Terror*.[24] I gained new views of Christology by reading Jacquelyn Grant's *White Women's Christ and Black Women's Jesus* and pastor-professor Carter Heyward's *Saving Jesus from Those Who Are Right*.[25]

Diverse themes for disciplined papers shaped my lifelong views. Because Mennonite church history often examined Anabaptist accounts after noting the early church, it typically bypassed the church fathers or medieval centuries or Eastern Orthodoxy. I learned much from John Oyer's seminary teaching, yet I was left with much unexplored when I wrote "Medieval Women Religious: Some Sketches." Other AMBS student colleagues researched and wrote stimulating papers.

---

23 Sensitive to people loyal to religions with more balanced fe/male divine symbols, I gladly provided readers my related feminist thought: Dorothy Yoder Nyce, "The Female Divine Figure within Several World Religions," *Journal of Interreligious Dialogue* 9 (May 19, 2010), 31–37, http://irdialogue.org/journal/issue#9.

24 Phyllis Trible, *Texts of Terror* (Philadelphia: Fortress, 1984).

25 Jacquelyn Grant, *White Women's Christ and Black Women's Jesus: Feminist Christology and Womanist Response,* American Academy of Religion Academy Series 64 (Atlanta: Scholars Press, 1989); Carter Heyward, *Saving Jesus from Those Who Are Right* (Minneapolis: Augsburg Fortress, 1999).

Janette K. Zercher from Bethel College, Kansas, researched "The Organizational Role of Women in the Churches of Three Mennonite Conferences," aided by original questionnaires with resulting tables.[26] Zercher's purpose was "to study the role of women present and in positions on elected and appointed committees in local Mennonite churches in a five-state area"—in GCMC, MC, and Mennonite Brethren (MB) conferences. Zercher's hypothesis was confirmed: men served more important committees at the top of a church's structural hierarchy, while women served smaller, often male-chaired, committees at the bottom of that hierarchal scheme. Women's leadership had not greatly increased in Mennonite churches since Eva Harshbarger's 1945 study, "The Status of Mennonite Women in Kansas in Their Church and Home Relations."[27]

Rare among MB women during the decades here reviewed, feminist Sandy Wiens envisioned an organization called WOMEN-SAGE. Marginally linked with Fatima, a Roman Catholic retreat center in South Bend, Indiana, Wiens prompted me and others to explore plans for writing projects and retreats beyond Mennonite structures. Friends signed up for a short-lived newsletter to address issues of theology. Women gathered there to hear Carole Hull's retreat talks on spirituality and to shape a Mennonite version. Publications emerged. Christine Kaufmann and Priscilla Stuckey-Kauffman volunteered many hours to create the historic "Mennonite Women's Calendar 1984–86." For the calendar, many of us identified women's unique data from among GCMC, MB, and MC affiliations, compiled documentation, offered photos, and supported the project's goal: "to make worthy women known." For most days of each month, the name of a Mennonite woman along with a year and brief detail of her significance crowd the space.

---

26 Copy in personal files. Summarized in "Women's Role in Church Committees Examined," *The Mennonite* (Aug. 19, 1975), 464–65.

27 Eva Harshbarger, "The Status of Mennonite Women in Kansas in Their Church and Home Relations," MS thesis, Kansas State College of Agriculture and Applied Science, 1945.

To convey that women indeed were preaching by 1983, I edited *Weaving Wisdom: Sermons by Mennonite Women*.[28] Thanks to WOMENSAGE's vision, Suelyn Lee's graphics, and Mary Louise Bower's printing service, thirty-five women's voices spoke truth. Whereas Mennonite Dutch sisters had preached since 1911, and Ann Jemima Allebach was ordained in the United States on January 15, 1911, but not assigned to preach with Mennonites, *Weaving Wisdom* proclaimed a "cloud of witnesses." Styles varied. One writer called herself "a total rookie"; an African American woman reported her extemporaneous pattern. Another admitted the ever-revising feature of sermons.[29] Mentor for many Mennonite women preachers, Emma Sommers Richards from Lombard, Illinois, excelled with purpose, content, and delivery. She enabled others. She invited me to her pulpit when I was a seminary student, and my work with Psalm 8 remains a gift to her for her encouragement. Later in life she highlighted having initiated Women in Ministry conferences.[30]

Due to a notable part of the 1981–82 year at AMBS addressing sexual issues, three seniors requested an alternative, "women's only" MDiv seminar led by a woman. I was asked to be their teacher. Explaining their lack of space in which to be emotionally present, honest, and "free to spin out theological images without stopping to explain them" (among possibly judgmental men) in a context that expected self-disclosure, women risked petitioning administration. Presumed unfairly to have nudged the women, I was faulted by a president for not obstructing their wish. Having been a student with the original 1973 women's course on campus, I observed now, in 1981 as a faculty member, a distinct determination by better informed feminists truly to affect needed change

---

28 Dorothy Yoder Nyce, ed., *Weaving Wisdom: Sermons by Mennonite Women* (South Bend, IN: Womensage, 1983).

29 Helen Dueck's positive review of *Weaving Wisdom* appears in *Conrad Grebel Review* 2, no. 2 (Spring 1984): 168–69.

30 James E. Horsch, John D. Rempel, and Eldon D. Nafziger, eds., *According to the Grace Given to Her: The Ministry of Emma Sommers Richards* (Elkhart, IN: Institute of Mennonite Studies, 2013), 127.

within AMBS. My privilege to engage and learn with five women for that seminar shines in their signed message of friendship dated May 1982.

Another highlight of that semester was the celebration of Women's History Week. Sixty women shaped plans, including a women's art display, inviting a woman to teach each course once during that week, selecting women speakers for forum and chapel, hosting an international dinner, and posting quotes by men about women along the full length of AMBS's longest hallway.[31]

I both resonate with and recommend student Jan Lugibihl's significant MA Peace Studies thesis, "Feminism and Community at AMBS (1981–1984)." It honestly discusses feminist questions, the patriarchal model, and how threatened men resisted women's bonding. Among the comments made by many students and faculty interviewed by Lugibihl, history professor C. J. Dyck said, "Our Anabaptist theology is very well suited to a liberation motif of women. . . . We should have done better than we did. Maybe the fact that we continued to operate and basically cared for each other showed that community was there, but it was hurting."[32]

Mennonite college personnel both resisted and nurtured feminist thought. For example, the alert Goshen College librarian Kathy Kauffman ordered fine feminist resources for students and community.[33] I charted data about Goshen College faculty women in 1974 and noted the dilemma for students who might face only male teachers during their four years. *The Record* (Goshen College student newspaper) highlighted justice for women almost

---

31 Personal storage. Rolled up for posterity, and available for archival research, is the newsprint with quotes that include scriptures and influential statements from prominent Christian theologians, historians, writers, and a few Mennonites.

32 Personal conversation with Jan Lugibihl.

33 In 1995 to validate women's experience, Kauffman prepared and archived audiotapes with transcripts for an oral history project with retired women faculty. Women interviewed include Mary Bender, Viola Good, Mary Katherine Nafziger, Mary Oyer, Mary Royer, Edna Shantz, Lois Winey, and Olive Wyse.

yearly during the 1970s to 2000s. While professor emerita Olive Wyse urged student wisdom for choosing priorities, peace advocate Ruth Krall highlighted both frustration and hope, and social work professor Anna Bowman led key workshops and chaired the Women's Studies minor.

I taught "Bible and Sexuality" at Goshen College between 1981 and 1996. In addition to biblical texts, with reading keyed to themes of female/male relating, required reading praised Leonard Swidler's *Biblical Affirmations of Woman* and James Nelson and Sandra Longfellow's *Sexuality and the Sacred*.[34] Class enrollment grew from nine students to thirty-four, more women enrolled, and most men desired to credit women fully, in scripture and life. One semester a Michigan congregational board sent a church member to audit the class at Goshen College and report back. After the course ended, the church board asked me to meet with them to "explain" why I did or did not present certain things. But most students were appreciative. Another semester, five alert daughters of Mennonite pastors kept asking, "Why haven't we heard these perspectives before?" Discussion included sexual affirmation, orientation, and violation. One guest lecturer per semester conveyed gay and lesbian insight. I was ever stimulated by students' disciplined research on God-language, incest, Jesus's radical friendship with women, and more.

In 1987, a group of women then living in Goshen joined me to create a twenty-four-minute slide set. It combines the ancient, acrostic poem of the woman praised in Proverbs 31 with our slides from countries where each had lived.[35] Creating the set, "Women of Strength, Ancient and Modern," enriched our friendship and served church women's groups that rented it.

---

34 Leonard Swidler, *Biblical Affirmations of Woman* (Philadelphia: Westminster, 1979); James Nelson and Sandra Longfellow, *Sexuality and the Sacred* (Louisville: Westminster/John Knox, 1994).

35 Planners with country include Deb Byler (Guatemala), Frieda Shellenberg Erb (Bolivia and Argentina), Peggy Froehlich (Zaire), Dawn Yoder Harms (Zaire), Mary Yoder Holsopple (Uganda), Cynthia Yoder (Egypt), and Dorothy Yoder Nyce (India, script writer).

As is clear, during the 1980s and into the 1990s, Mennonite women increasingly practiced networking. More of us both shaped and trusted feminist truth through theology and scripture. How I longed for publication of academic women's voices! More congregations were trusting women as pastors, but qualified women were also leaving Mennonite circles. Without a woman to edit MC journals other than *Voice* (Women's Missionary and Service Commission) and the predominance of men published in *The Mennonite Quarterly Review*, how could educated women's research and writing be read? Computers made writing and communicating more accessible; competent voices published with non-Mennonite links. Had a vision for or convincing patterns of distinct women's leadership not evolved?

Feminism and more

My focus later shifted from collective to more personal growth and changed to include interdenominational and interfaith work. I have lived in India multiple times since 1962. I increasingly depended on ecumenical and interfaith truth. With diverse Christians on staff at Woodstock School in India, I combined my budding feminism, healthy ambiguity rather than rigidity, and love for religious difference along with loyalty. In 1988 I participated with a group of university women in a summer Fulbright study tour titled "Women, Family, and Social Change in India." That opportunity helped me compare how India's women experience worth, organize themselves, or alter ancient practice to fit today's realities. It prompted a lectureship and the writing of the 1989 self-published book *Strength, Struggle, and Solidarity: India's Women*. More book editing brought thirty-five voices of mostly Mennonite women with experience in diverse global settings into print in the self-published books *To See Each Other's Good* (1996) and *Rooted and Branching: Women Worldwide* (1998). In addition, the 1990 volume 5 of *The Mennonite Encyclopedia* included articles I wrote about nine missionaries and three topics: abortion, gender roles, and head covering.

From 1994 to 1997, I completed a Doctor of Ministry degree along with six men at Western Theological Seminary and linked my Mennonite heritage with the Reformed Church of America. Courses and thesis work engaged reading, workshop leading, congregation events, and the themes of interfaith arts; water; and goddess, women, and Wisdom, along with video creation.[36]

Mennonite-only worship or theology causes restlessness for me. My ecumenical connections have been useful: a year with Methodists in Detroit, a year with Disciples of Christ in Elkhart through grief ministry in Clinical Pastoral Education,[37] and a year in Cambridge, Massachusetts, that combined Peter Gomes's solid morning sermons at Harvard Memorial Church with Mennonites meeting in homes for evening worship. On receipt of a 2001 Worship Renewal Grant from Calvin Institute of Christian Worship in Grand Rapids, Michigan, funded by the Lilly Endowment Inc., I interacted with diverse denominations in Goshen. I created materials focused on Jewish holidays as well as original poems, prayers, and notes on ecumenical conferences from 1910 to 1990. I also wrote a script for a camping youth exchange and an adult Sunday school class.

Conclusion

My hope here has been to make feminist women's collective and personal concerns and actions during several decades better known. Regarding Mennonite surveys in 1972, 1989, and 2006, I am truly disappointed that no women designed or assessed questions and that no items expected engagement with people loyal to

---

36 Dorothy Yoder Nyce, "Dialogues to Foster Interreligious Understanding" (DMin thesis, Western Theological Seminary, 1997).

37 See Dorothy Yoder Nyce, "Grieving People," *The Journal of Pastoral Care* 36, no. 1 (March 1982): 36–45. To study at Episcopal Divinity (three courses), Andover-Newton Theological (one course), Western Theological (Reformed Church in America, three-year Doctor of Ministry degree), and the University of Notre Dame (Roman Catholic, interfaith, and biblical courses) enhanced my Christian feminist valuing of difference and my sharing and receiving of a particular perspective within universal potential.

diverse living faiths. Such reality reflects being unprepared to live in North American cities or to converse wisely with global missioning.[38] In the future, when capable women sociologists, theologians, and her-storians co-plan, conduct, and analyze surveys with women's interfaith insight, what might be the results?[39] What echoes of 1972 feminist advocacy might there be?

---

38 Occasional references in the surveys noted other Mennonite or Christian denominations but failed to address interreligious openness.

39 My international feminist women mentors include Aruna Gnanadason, Kwok Pui-lan, Chung Hyun Kyung, Riffat Hussan, Monica Melancthon, Amina Wadud, Ursula King, Helene Egnell, Karen Armstrong, Muriel Orevillo-Montenegro, and Mercy Amba Oduyoye.

3

Peace Section advocacy
Women write
Gayle Gerber Koontz and Ted Koontz

Ferment in Boston, tradition in Akron

In the summer of 1972 we arrived at Mennonite Central Committee (MCC), Akron, Pennsylvania, fresh from Boston. Our part of Boston had been a hotbed of protests—against the war in Vietnam, especially, and against segregation and racism. When we drove into Harvard Square in the summer of 1969, we wondered why the windows in many businesses were boarded up. "Peace demonstrations," we were told. The following spring the university canceled final papers and exams. Students and some faculty members and staff were too occupied protesting the invasion of Cambodia and the shootings at Kent State.

Boston had also been a place of ferment about women's roles in church and society. It was there that we first encountered the "second wave" women's liberation movement in a powerful, first-hand way.[1] Gayle joined Ted as a student at Harvard Divinity School for the 1971–72 school year. She took a class or two with Mary Daly, a pioneering Catholic feminist theologian from Boston College, and became friends with a number of feminist wom-

---

1 The first wave was the women's liberation movement in the late nineteenth and early twentieth century that receded after white women received the right to vote in August 1920.

en students.[2] It was there—partly in contrast to Daly's growing radical feminism that included significant separation from men but also her own growing appreciation for a theology of church quite different from Roman Catholicism—that Gayle consciously claimed an identity as a Mennonite Christian feminist.

The most memorable event symbolizing the atmosphere at that time happened on November 14, 1971. We attended Harvard Memorial Church that morning when Mary Daly preached the first sermon by a woman in Harvard's 336-year history, which she titled "After the Death of God the Father." As one observer described, at the end of her sermon she invited "'sisters and other esteemed members of the congregation' to join her in what she called 'an exodus from centuries of darkness.' More than half the women and some men in the congregation joined her in walking out of the church before the Sunday morning service was finished."[3]

The tranquil setting in Lancaster County, Pennsylvania, provided a striking contrast to our tumultuous setting in Boston. Mennonite Central Committee had invited Ted to serve as associate executive secretary at MCC Peace Section and Gayle to work part-time as assistant editor for MCC Information Services while she continued her education at Lancaster Theological Seminary. At the office we quickly noticed that there were no women seated at the desks along the windows in the large open space where the directors for various programs around the world were seated. Men at these desks used Dictaphones to record letters and reports that were then typed by the secretaries (only one of whom was a man) who sat at desks in the center of the room.

---

2 Two of them instigated a practice in Harvey Cox's class of blowing party noisemakers whenever lecturers used male language for God. This incident was recalled in Olivia G. Oldham, "When 'He' Isn't God Anymore," *The Harvard Crimson*, Oct. 18, 2018, thecrimson.com.

3 Barbara Flanagan, "Mary Daly Leads Exodus after Historic Sermon," *The Heights*, Nov. 1971, https://newspapers.bc.edu?a=d&d=bcheights19711122.2.4.

This seating arrangement (and the occupants of the seats) represented Mennonite gender role reality at the time. In 1972 there were no women heads of any Mennonite agencies or colleges, the MCC board had just elected the first woman (Betty Schmidt Epp) two years prior, the Peace Section board consisted of all men except for two women who represented the General Conference Mennonite Church (GCMC) and the (Old) Mennonite Church (MC) women's organizations, and there were no ordained female pastors serving MCC-related congregations. In addition, as Dorothy Nickel Friesen has noted in chapter 1 of the present volume, the Kauffman and Harder study from the early 1970s indicated that only 32 percent of respondents thought more women should be appointed to church boards and committees at any level, 17 percent thought women should be ordained to the ministry, and a mere 16 percent believed that women in Canada and the United States were being discriminated against. But in spite of this attitudinal picture, pockets of people calling for change in the roles of women were emerging across the church. One of these was within the MCC Peace Section.

How did the MCC Peace Section help to free women's voices?

Catalyzing organizational changes

Dorothy Nickel Friesen has described the energetic, spontaneously planned gathering of women in Chicago following the November 1972 MCC Peace Assembly (chapter 1). At the spring Peace Section meeting following the gathering, according to a report from the time, "a group of women presented their concerns regarding the role of women in church and society. It was proposed that Peace Section include women's interests in justice and peace as part of its continuing agenda to examine attitudes, actions, and institutional structures which deny individuals their human rights, depress human potential, and spawn a domination mentality."[4] The Peace Section agreed to add "women's concerns"

---

4 *Report from the Peace Section Task Force on Women in Church and Society* (hereafter, *Report*) 1, Aug.1973, 1.

to its peace (and justice, though we talked little about this at the time) agenda.

The Peace Section further appointed a subcommittee named the Task Force on Women in Church and Society (TF). The group included Lora Oyer and Dorothy Yoder Nyce, the two Peace Section members who represented GCMC and MC women's organizations; two Peace Section staff members, Luann Habegger [Martin] and Ted Koontz; and two younger women, Lois Keeney (GCMC) from Bluffton, Ohio, and Ruth Stoltzfus [Jost] (MC) from Harrisonburg, Virginia.

By August of that year Luann Habegger, on behalf of the TF, had compiled and mailed (primarily to the Peace Section and to those who had attended or wanted to attend the 1972 Chicago gathering) the first *Report from the Task Force on Women in Church and Society*. This six-page typewritten *Report* reiterated the importance of the Task Force and its purpose by citing Rosemary Radford Ruether:

> It has been said that the domination of women is the most fundamental form of domination in society, and all other forms of domination whether of race, class, or ethnic group draw upon the fantasies of sexual domination. This also suggests that the liberation of women is the most profound of all liberation movements, the most far-reaching revolution, because it gets to the roots of the impulse of domination.[5]

The Report noted that "the Exodus, the Crucifixion-Resurrection, and Pentecost are powerful reminders that liberation is a concept central to the Christian faith" and underlined the TF view that "liberation does not mean freedom without restraint or self-indulgence at the expense of others."[6]

---

5 Rosemary Radford Ruether, "Women's Liberation in Historical and Theological Perspective," *Soundings: An Interdisciplinary Journal* 53, no. 4 (winter 1970): 363–64.

6 *Report* 1, Aug. 1973, 4–5.

From this enthusiastic beginning, the TF slowly became institutionalized, developed, and changed. One of the first significant developments was the expansion of the TF to encompass members from MCC (US) and MCC (Canada). The new "transnational Task Force on Women in Church and Society" met for the first time in April 1975.[7] The structural inclusion of MCC (Canada) was evident in the increase of Canadian voices in TF newsletters after that point. This close cooperation continued until 1991 when "the decision emerged for Canada and the United States to have separate committees,"[8] although the *Report* planning continued to be jointly approved.

The name of the TF was changed to the Committee on Women's Concerns (CWC) in 1982. This accompanied a significant structural change at MCC. MCC (US) executive committee created a Women's Desk and appointed Linda Schmidt as a half-time staff person for women's concerns. Funding continued to be through the MCC (US) Peace Section, but Linda was "given access of accountability to both MCC (US) and MCC [international] in this expanded role." Committee members also encouraged Linda "to take leadership in developing long-range proposals for the direction of the women's committee and the staffing of women's concerns and that this should be done in collaboration with other MCC staff and denominational groups."[9]

The Women's Concerns Desk continued to oversee MCC work in this area until 2011, when major restructuring occurred, several staff positions were terminated or reconfigured, anti-sex-

---

[7] *Report* 8, Jan.–May 1975, 1. Members included Erna Klassen, Dorothy Yoder Nyce, Margaret Loewen Reimer, Sue Clemmer Steiner, Katie Funk Wiebe, Luann Habegger, and Ted Koontz (the latter two Peace Section staff). See *Report* 109, July–Aug. 1993, 16, for a list of the first twenty years of members and their conference groups. Brethren in Christ members were not added until after 1982. See *Report* 46, Nov.–Dec. 1982, 8, where the Committee on Women's Concerns decided to recommend to the Peace Section that a Brethren in Christ member be named to the committee.

[8] *Report* 109, July–Aug. 1993, 1.

[9] *Report* 45, Sept.–Oct. 1982, 12.

ism and anti-racism concerns were combined, and a restorative justice position included attention to sexual abuse. MCC (Canada) appointed its first half-time staff person for Women's Concerns in 1984 and ended its national women's concern program in 2004.[10]

Women in leadership

One of the first and central concerns that TF members raised with the Peace Section board was that there were few, if any, women in major leadership roles in Mennonite, Mennonite Brethren, and Brethren in Christ circles. Although the TF addressed this situation almost from the outset, it was stated as an explicit goal of the committee in a 1980 Report: "To urge church organizations to involve women in all dimensions of church life and establish guidelines to ensure full participation."[11]

Following a study by Ruth Stoltzfus and Luann Habegger on women, work, and the church,[12] the Peace Section passed a resolution in November 1974 stimulated by the TF, "urging MCC to study the effects of its employment practices and policies on women."[13] In response, MCC appointed a special advisory committee on the recruitment, assignment, and services of women in MCC programs. In March 1977 a review of MCC actions indicated "movement toward more women in field program administration, increasing use of hired help to ease heavy hosting responsibilities left to women in addition to their regular full-time assignments, steps to provide better pastoral care services, publication of a monograph on women in development, and plans for leadership training seminars for both men and women."[14] To some degree TF concerns were integrated early into other MCC structures.

---

10 Linda Gehman Peachy, compiler, "Milestones, Materials, Meetings: Partial Overview of MCC's Work Related to Women," unpublished paper in Peachy personal files, 2011, 2.

11 *Report* 31, May–June 1980, 7.

12 See their work in *Report* 6, summer 1974.

13 *Report* 8, Jan.–May 1975, 1.

14 *Report* 14, May 1977, 9.

In addition to encouraging changes in employment practices and policies in MCC, the TF set an ambitious research goal in relation to MCC-related colleges. Katie Funk Wiebe was to contact colleges to "discover what they are doing to help students achieve a better understanding of the Christian approach to the role of men and women in church and society." She was to request information on courses dealing with the role of women in church and society; human sexuality, family, and related law; copies of research papers in these areas; a list of library and audio-visual holdings on these topics; and a list of effective lecturers with expertise in these subjects. She was also to ask each school to appoint a contact person.[15] The intent was for the information she gathered to be shared with colleges as it became available. Subsequent issues of the *Report* did not mention this project again, but Women's Desk staff Linda Gehman Peachy found record of a letter sent in 1974 to Mennonite college deans and heads of sociology and religion departments encouraging them to promote studies on the involvement of women in church and society.[16] Over the years, events and resources available at various educational institutions appeared regularly in the *Report*.

The TF also took initiative in 1978 to compile a "Resource Listing of Mennonite Women" available to serve on boards and committees and to serve as seminar leaders and as speakers on various women's concerns.[17] The list was updated in 1980, 1982, 1985, and 1988. At the request of Mennonite deans, the TF also used the *Report* in 1979 to help compile "A Directory of Mennonite Women with Graduate Degrees." Resource lists were "made available to MCC offices, church conference boards and offices, colleges, seminaries, and other church-related institutions" at no cost.[18]

---

15 *Report* 9, Oct.–Dec. 1975, 4.

16 Peachy, "Milestones, Materials, Meetings," 1.

17 *Report* 18, Feb. 1978, 7–8.

18 *Report* 46, Nov. –Dec. 1982, 6. *Report* 84, May–June 1989, noted that the resource list was available free to organizations and to individuals for $2.00.

Because of the dearth of women from the Two-Thirds World representing their churches at Mennonite World Conference (MWC) assemblies, MWC invited women's organizations in the United States to raise travels funds for women from the global South to attend the conference in Wichita, Kansas, in 1978. The TF agreed to coordinate raising ten thousand dollars to be matched by MWC. The *Report* also had an appeal for funds for thirty women from the Two-Thirds World to travel to the 1981 MWC expanded General Council meeting in Nairobi and an additional request for funds for women's travel to the 1984 Assembly.[19]

Communication and consciousness raising in MCC-related constituencies

Along with leadership concerns, the TF immediately gave priority to networking and education. A comprehensive retrospective statement of this goal appeared among others in a 1980 *Report*:

1. To foster an awareness of problems and issues related to the status of women in church and society by a) disseminating information; b) promoting research of policies, practices and attitudes that may discriminate against women in areas of employment, education, representation on boards and committees and leadership positions; c) engaging in educational programs

2. To provide a forum for the sharing of concerns, ideas and resource materials relating to women's issues[20]

The Peace Section supported these goals that were implemented through regular issues of the TF/CWC *Report*, organizing or contributing to educational events for constituents,[21] carrying out or

---

19 *Report* 15, July 1977, 7; *Report* 35, Jan.–Feb. 1981, 11; *Report* 54, Jan.–Feb. 1984, 12.

20 These two points are quoted directly from *Report* 31, May–June 1980, 7.

21 For example, the TF—along with the Peace Section Washington Office—planned a two-day seminar for May 7–8, 1974, on the pressures facing families (*Report* 4, Feb. 1974, 1). Also see *Report* 7, Sept.–Dec. 1974,

reporting on research related to women's concerns,[22] preparing educational packets and booklets,[23] and initiating several books, including two books of creative works by Mennonite women writers and artists.[24]

The most long-lived TF undertaking was the *Report*, first distributed as a short newsletter in 1973, that ceased publication in 2004 as *The Women's Concerns Report*, an attractive twenty-page periodical with black-and-white illustrations. The issues of

---

with information on a male-female interdependence conference at Goshen College that involved a presentation by a Peace Section staff member. Concerns there moved beyond simply getting more women into church leadership. One of the remaining questions was, How do women avoid getting caught up in power struggles, typical in male hierarchies, yet push ahead for involvement in these structures? (p. 5).

22 In addition to the research by Katie Funk Wiebe noted above, another early example was the *Report* item summarizing a Bethel College (North Newton, Kansas) senior student's research on women's organizational roles in twenty-seven Mennonite churches in three conferences in the area (Janette Zercher, *Report* 8, Jan.–May 1975, 3).

23 The first packet of resource materials for individuals, congregations, and schools, *Persons Becoming*, was available already in 1974. MCC had distributed one thousand copies by late fall that year and was preparing a third printing (*Report* 7, Sept.–Dec. 1974, 1). More than eight hundred copies of *Which Way Women?*—a second packet that addressed themes of international women's year (equality, development, and peace)—had been sold 12 weeks after publication (*Report* 31, May–June 1980, 7–8). MCC later produced numerous other materials on sexual violence, domestic violence, abortion, and pornography—all significant "women's concerns"—that had begun to be seen as peacemaking issues.

24 In October 1981, the TF decided to publish a collection of "artists' approach to women's concerns" (*Report* 40, Nov.–Dec. 1981, 13). They raised some funds to make it available at an affordable price (*Report* 77, Mar.–Apr. 1988, insert). See Mary Schertz and Phyllis Martens, eds., *Born Giving Birth: Creative Expressions of Mennonite Women* (Newton, KS: Faith and Life, 1991). MCC (Canada) Women's Concerns supported *Braiding Hearts and Minds: A Poetry and Dramatic Arts Anthology* (MCC Canada, no place, n.d.). The CWC (US) and CWC (Canada) together sponsored the book *Women & Men: Gender in the Church*, edited by Carol Penner (Waterloo, ON, and Scottdale, PA: Herald, 1998).

the *Report*, mailed to a list that varied from four hundred to two thousand individuals and organizations over the years, are a rich resource documenting changes in the role of women over a thirty-year period in MCC–related groups.[25]

From our perspective today, mailed periodicals seem a slow and ineffective method of communication for people concerned about transformational change. Yet, it was only in the early 1980s, ten years after the beginning of the TF, that personal computers were beginning to become more available; they were also expensive and limited in what they could do. We bought our first computer and printer in 1980 as we began work on dissertations. They cost over six thousand dollars, but the computer amazingly allowed us to edit and move text around without endless retyping. Both internet research and e-mail were not widely available in the United States until the mid-1990s. Church communication channels before that (and often later) were primarily church papers, phone calls, letters, and personal face-to-face relationships. From the 1970s through the 1990s, the *Report* was a significant informative and networking instrument for women and men across Mennonite and Brethren in Christ denominational boundaries who were often feeling isolated in their convictions about changes in the roles of men and women in church and society.

The first issue of the *Report* clarified that the anticipated periodic reports were "*not* intended to negate the contributions of women in church and society, alienate women from men, or replace male power structures with female power structures." Instead, the TF hoped the mailings would:

1. provide a forum for sharing concerns, ideas, and resource materials. . . .

---

25 This extraordinary research resource is available online at a public site: https://archive.org/details/WomensConcernsReport. By November 1974 MCC was mailing four hundred copies of the *Report*, which illustrates the initial interest in it. Margaret Loewen Reimer noted in *Report* 50, July–Aug. 1983, 9, that MCC was mailing more than two thousand copies.

2. make visible and affirm efforts being made by women to create a more whole, inclusive church and society,

3. and alert readers to available leadership positions.[26]

To do this the TF invited readers to share what was happening in their geographic areas, write book reviews, and provide information about openings on church-related boards. As the first issue of the *Report* states, "By uniting together and sharing information, we can better coordinate efforts to bring about the emergence of a new consciousness in our churches."[27] From the outset until its closure, the *Reports* included information about these items, sometimes in brief articles, often in a section titled "News," later revised to "News and Verbs" that would occasionally cover several pages.[28]

Beginning with the first issue and continuing throughout its existence, the *Report* included lists of written and audiovisual resources related to women's concerns. By issues 4 and 5, the *Report* focused on a selected theme and related resources, an approach that became standard. Issues covered a wide range of topics—from ministers' wives to sexuality and disabilities, from native women to shopping cart power, from step- and single-parent families to how the Bible is vital for feminist women of faith. Of particular significance were courageous TF/CWC steps to address topics that were highly controversial or were not being addressed adequately in larger and more public forums in the Mennonite and Brethren in Christ worlds. These included experiential accounts and reflections on concerns such as women and divorce, sexual abuse, incest, abortion, rape, pornography, women and depression, lesbian women, mentoring for and by women, women and cancer, addictions and co-dependency, Mennonite

---

26 *Report* 1, Aug.1973, 1.

27 *Report* 1, Aug.1973, 1.

28 The term "verbs" highlighted the active or movement dimension of what was happening.

women leaders around the world, female images of God, and two-career marriages.[29]

A decision along the way that each issue would be compiled by different women on the TF or by others they knew who could address a theme had a far-reaching effect on the character of the publication. The result was an unusually wide network of contacts and the opportunity for many voices to speak and be heard. From August 1973, when the first *Report* was written, through 1986, representing the first thirteen years of its existence, more than 535 different writers or interviewees made contributions, not including more than fifteen women who submitted experiential material anonymously.[30] Most, but not all, of the contributors were from MCC-affiliated congregations. Forty-five of the named writers were men. Writers or interviewees came from thirty-two different countries and at least two indigenous nations in North America, not including the United States and Canada, where most of the writers were from. While the breadth of participants meant that reflections were often brief, it documents the way in which the *Report* freed many women's voices during these years. At the same time, the thematic focus provided some depth in educating and resourcing women and men who were in the midst of change.

The *Women's Concerns Report* ended with issue 176 in 2004. Patricia J. Haverstick, the editor of the last issue, noted that there were only five hundred people on its mailing list and that the Women's Concerns Desk decided to "look for new ways to reach broader constituencies." One way to do this, she wrote, "is to use the money we had been using to publish the *Report* to fund new projects and initiatives."[31]

The new Women's Desk staff person in Akron at that time, Linda Gehman Peachey, made such suggestions as:

---

29 A full list of *Report* topics appeared in the final issue, *Report* 176, Nov.–Dec. 2004, 20–22.

30 Some other interviewees and survey respondents were also not named. This number does not include those who submitted book reviews or who wrote letters to the editor.

31 *Report* 176, Nov.–Dec. 2004, 1.

- A peace justice publication that focuses on the intersection of sexism, racism and violence, immigration issues, and economic injustice. "We are not women only, but women within a particular history, economic class, ethnic group and nation. These dynamics also greatly influence our encounter with God and the world around us."
- Providing additional stories on the MCC web site, publishing small books, dramas, or documentaries that "communicate women's experience and wisdom."
- Hosting gatherings of women theologians from different groups and settings
- Organizing forums for discussion of theological and biblical issues important to women such as difficult biblical texts, power, violence, salvation, atonement, leadership, and the nature of God's love and justice
- Writing more articles in denominational publications
- Continuing to address sexism and internalized sexism
- Continuing to address child abuse, domestic violence, and professional misconduct in communities where this has received less attention
- Hosting local gatherings of women across racial, ethnic, and class lines for mutual enrichment, encouragement, and action[32]

A number of these ideas were implemented between 2004 and 2011 by the Women's Desk in Akron.

Concluding observations

The MCC women's concerns timeline (Milestones, Materials, Meetings) that Linda Gehman Peachy prepared in 2011 documents the many initiatives and projects the TF/CWC took from 1974 until then. In addition to the specific projects written about earlier, those involved in MCC Women's Concerns work pub-

---

32 These points are paraphrased from *Report* 176, Nov.–Dec. 2004, 4.

lished a significant collection of written material both in English and Spanish, helped to sponsor numerous conferences in cooperation with other Mennonite schools and organizations, and encouraged attention to women's concerns in projects such as the 1975 Foundation Series curriculum (through a letter encouraging stories and illustrations to accentuate wholeness rather than stereotypes) and the Don Kraybill and Conrad Kanagy 1985 survey of Mennonite and Brethren in Christ churches (through a request to include data on sexual violence). A primary focus in the later years was on sexual harassment, violence, and abuse. A first conference on violence and abuse took place in California in 1990, followed by a number of training events and publications.

The contrast between today and 1972 is striking. Then there were very few, if any, women in major leadership roles in MCC or as ordained pastors or heads of institutions in Mennonite, Mennonite Brethren, and Brethren in Christ conferences. Today the leadership situation in these places has changed substantially to incorporate more women—though likely not yet enough. In addition, teaching about sensitive questions related to sexuality has begun. Awareness of and action to prevent sexual abuse is much clearer. Examples of greater mutuality in men-women relationships in marriage and parenting are more prevalent. Gender models in curricula and promotional materials have been broadened. In these ways, one can say that the Peace Section decision to adopt "women's concerns" as part of its agenda, and to support the TF/CWC in pursuing its goals, to some degree helped transform attitudes, policies, and practices in MCC-related groups.

The question of causation is always complicated. We are well aware that what the Peace Section agreed to undertake was part of much larger cultural and religious transformation. Within the MCC constituency there were many other groups and individuals encouraging change in this direction. However, we believe the work of the TF/CWC contributed to major changes in MCC practices and program initiatives and in its constituent churches. How to apportion credit (or blame) more precisely would require a much broader and more extended study of the wide variety of factors influencing these changes. The Task Force *Reports* remain a valuable and largely overlooked resource in documenting a wide range of activity on women's concerns from 1973 to 2004. Additional research could benefit the self-understanding and growth of Mennonite-related churches in relation to women's concerns toward its further changing future.[33]

---

33 Mennonite theologian Carol Penner has analyzed and evaluated the way in which the *Report* expressed theological content and method important to women during those years. See Carol Penner, "Jesus and the Stories of Our Lives," in *Liberating the Politics of Jesus: Renewing Peace Theology through the Wisdom of Women*, ed. Elizabeth Soto Albrecht and Darryl W. Stephens (New York: T&T Clark, 2020), 33–52.

4

Blinders and power
Women of color proclaim

*Iris de León-Hartshorn
and Regina Shands Stoltzfus*

Editors' introduction

As the roles for white Mennonite women expanded in the 1970s and 1980s, the voices of women of color were largely confined to local congregations and women's auxiliaries (see chapter 9). With the 1960s just over, the early 1970s were marked with the Vietnam War, civil rights campaigning by primarily Black (male) leadership in southern cities of the United States (but also on college campuses, in urban settings, and in churches), and new legislation regarding voting rights in the Congress of the United States. Concurrently, the smoldering issue of women's rights, which burst onto the scene in the 1960s, was fueled by an earlier 1920 watershed decision to allow women (led by white suffragettes) the right to vote. Racism, then, was baked into the culture by defining whose voice could be heard and whose vote could be counted. "Women's liberation" became a rallying cry in the secular world with the publication of Ms. *Magazine*, for example, and editor Gloria Steinem's voice. In the halls of Congress, the thundering voice of Barbara Jordan, African American Democrat from Texas, revealed a new advocate for justice.

In the world of North American religion, publications by women also exploded. Feminist seminary professors and biblical and evangelical voices were arguing for new roles for women in the church, both local and institutional. The 1970s saw significant biblical studies that, again, echoed early twentieth-century American women scholars, teachers, and preachers like Quaker Lucretia Mott and Antoinette Brown Blackwell, all white suffragettes and religious leaders. Also in the early 1970s, Mary Daly wrote *Beyond God the Father* (1973) and challenged sexist language and theology. Rosemary Radford Ruether published on themes of community and expanding roles for women and challenged religious hierarchies (*The Radical Kingdom*, 1970). Georgia Harkness, a Methodist, traced historical attitudes toward women and presented hope for the inclusion of women in religion in her book *Women in Church and Society* (1972). It was clearly white feminists who dominated the religious and theological conversation.

Meanwhile, Mennonite women, mostly white, were joining their voices and proclaiming that Jesus was the model for affirming Christian women's leadership. The first Conrad Grebel Lectures by a woman, Lois Gunden Clemens, were published in 1971 (*Woman Liberated*). The struggle to ordain women for pastoral leadership began to show progress with the first Mennonite ordinations in North America in the 1970s. (See chapters 5 and 6.)

But did the expanding role for women include Mennonite women of color? Often, attitudes toward women outside the dominant culture reflected general cultural prejudices about women. It is hard to understand why, for example, Wilma Bailey, who was licensed by the Indiana-Michigan Conference (Mennonite Church) at Grace Chapel, Saginaw, Michigan, on February 7, 1980, as the first African American Mennonite woman to be credentialed in the United States, was never ordained.

This chapter features the voices of two women of color who were ordained a full twenty years after the first (white) women's ordination in the Mennonite denomination. While no one woman speaks for all in her class, ethnicity, or church, this chapter reveals the story of two women of color who have become prominent leaders in the (now) Mennonite Church USA.

Iris de León-Hartshorn was ordained September 11, 1994, by the Western District Conference (GCMC) and South Central Conference (MC) at Houston Mennonite Church (Texas), a dual-affiliated congregation. Her story reflects her journey from outside the Mennonite denomination into a Mennonite world—as a Latina, married to a pastor, sensing a call to ministry. Breaking into a largely white, male-dominated Mennonite religious body required passion, commitment, education, and supportive people along the way. Her reflections are based on responses to questions we asked her regarding her experiences in leadership in Mennonite spaces as a Latina woman.

Regina Shands Stoltzfus was ordained November 7, 1999, by the Ohio Conference (MC) at the Lee Heights Community Church, Detroit, Michigan. Her story is grounded in the Anabaptist theology and African American reality of an urban setting. Her talents and gifts were honed in the Mennonite church, and her story reflects both the resolve of her faith and also the resistance and prejudice that accompanied her faith journey. Her valued and persistent story in this volume reflects the power of a congregation committed to service, peace, and the encouragement of others along the way.

A Latina Mennonite experience: Iris de León-Hartshorn

My contexts from 1972 to 1989 to 2006

In 1972, I was attending Moorpark College in California, and I was twenty-one years old. I was attending a Southern Baptist church with my sister at the time. I was not part of the Mennonite church. I do remember one specific incident during my time with the Baptist church. During an altar call, I went forward because I was being called to serve the church, but it was not clear to me in what specific way. Immediately the male pastor told me I was being called to be a missionary. Now, if anyone knew me, they would know that, no, I was not being called as a missionary, but I soon learned that was one of the few acceptable choices a woman could be called to in the Baptist church. I have often wondered if it was also true at that time with the Mennonite church.

In 1989, I was living in Houston, Texas. My husband was pastoring Houston Mennonite Church, and I was working part-time with Pueblo to People, a nonprofit group. I also started taking courses part-time with Austin Presbyterian Theological Seminary (APTS). I remember contacting Associated Mennonite Biblical Seminaries (now Anabaptist Mennonite Biblical Seminary) about some type of arrangement doing studies long distance. They were not open to the idea at the time, and so I kept studying at APTS. I was very involved at Houston Mennonite Church and especially in worship. We, as a church, worked hard at using inclusive language in both our music and our sermons. For the most part, people accepted the change and participated in making it happen. We did have a few people who could not understand why it was important to use inclusive language. I had one man tell me that when he used the term "brothers," that included me. I told him I did not feel included when he used the word "brothers." I still felt in the late 1980s and early 1990s we had made a lot of progress in terms of using inclusive language.

In 2006, I found myself transitioning from working with Mennonite Central Committee (MCC) for eleven years as director of peace and justice to being on the cabinet of Mennonite Church USA (MC USA) as director of intercultural relationships. In the church, I noticed, as women were moving up within the Mennonite work institutions, women were not as present on boards or in pastorates. There seemed to be a growing gap. Other people felt it also. At that time Marty Lehman hired an intern, Joanna Shenk. Joanna did a churchwide survey testing if the observation of women's decreasing presence in leadership roles in the church was true. The results indicated that, yes, overall women in leadership roles were decreasing. Also decreasing was the use of inclusive language in congregations. Words do matter, and when you erase women by the language you use, you also eventually erase them in other ways, like serving in leadership roles.

Ordination and leadership as a Latina

My ordination was a mixed bag, as for many women my age. I was ordained in 1994 by a dual pastoral committee of Western District Conference and South Central Conference. I was serving as a hospice chaplain. I saw ordination as a confirmation of God's call in my life and the affirmation of my community of faith witnessing that in my life. I knew there were other women also seeking ordination. I was lucky to be part of a conference that supported women, the Western District. South Central Conference was at a different place, which made me, as a woman seeking ordination, feel a bit awkward. I think one of the most disappointing aspects of the process was when I met with the ministerial committee. Near the end, one of the men asked why I had chosen to keep my maiden name in addition to my married name. I was confused by the question because no one had ever asked me that question. I explained that my father's name would end with our family of four daughters, and I wanted to keep my last name to honor my dad. Also, as a Latina, keeping your maiden name was acceptable. He asked if I was thinking of leaving my husband. I was stunned by the question. I wanted to cry but chose to stay as stoic as I could and answer him no. That left a sour taste in my mouth. The process was frustrating, but my ordination in my home congregation was a wonderful experience, and I was surrounded by people who knew me and loved me.

In my early days with MCC, I supervised the Women's Desk, and I was asked to defend an article in the Women's Desk publication to the binational MCC board. We had people who read our publication just looking for things they found unacceptable. For some reason, this complaint rose to the top. I had a wonderful role model, Lynette Meck. She went with me and gave me some helpful tips on how to best address the complaint. After much back and forth I gained the support of the board on why the article was important. I said, "Learning who we are and what we believe will give us greater understanding to what is important to us as a people. As a Mexic-Amerindian, I believe we have something to contribute that would help bring our world into balance, but we are unaware of the gifts our Mexican culture could bring."[1]

My ancestry is from Mexico, where the climate is much more temperate year round and at times can be very hot. Our work ethic is one of moderation with an emphasis on relationships. Our survival was not dependent on time since we had plenty to eat year round. Our time was spent cultivating relationships and strengthening familial and communal ties. Can we see times where a Mexican work ethic would be a gift to those consumed with producing at the expense of their families? Can we see there will be times when working with time limits is essential? When we are asked to live by only one standard all the time, we discount the gifts of another culture that is just as valid and is desperately needed to give balance.[2]

Many times, the anti-racism work of the church has been under threat of going away, being watered down or assumed with another agenda. I have worked on several fronts in keeping the analysis we use intact. I have been heard on this matter many times in both MCC and MC USA. Recently I had influence in a sexual abuse case when MC USA promised the church that we would make an investigative report public. I was not alone in advocating for this to happen, but I felt my voice was important. When you are trying to change how an institution responds to something, like sexual abuse, that is different from how it was handled in the past, it is like trying to turn a huge freight tanker around in stormy waters. But I felt I was heard in this situation.

Being silenced or ignored in the church

I am silenced or ignored way too many times. What might be worse is when I share an idea, and it's ignored, but a man or a white woman repeats my idea and takes credit for it. Sometimes

---

[1] Iris de León-Hartshorn, "Continuing the Journey: Dispelling the Myth," in *Set Free: A Journey toward Solidarity against Racism* (Scottdale, PA: Herald, 2001), 74.

[2] De León-Hartshorn, "Continuing the Journey," 75.

that person is even asked to head up a project that was my idea. It is so hurtful.

I have co-facilitated various events with men. I felt powerless and ignored when I started to explain something, and my co-facilitator decided he could do a better job and just took over. This is a constant experience I have as both a woman and Latina. It's never ending.

Changes in and disappointments with the Mennonite church

I have seen a back and forth with women's leadership in Mennonite churches. Right now, it looks like we are headed in the right direction of utilizing women's gifts in the church and recognizing how they can enrich the church as leaders. I think the work that both the Women's Desk in MCC and Women in Leadership Project did was important to get us where we are. I supervised both but did not do the day-to-day gritty work. What I did do was to encourage, protect the space needed to do the work, defend the work when needed, and be there for the women doing the day-to-day work.

My biggest disappointment is that we did slip back, and it feels like a lot of work was lost. As a woman of color, I sense that we are heading in the wrong direction. People of color are under attack in various places in society, and it is impacting the church. Women of color are finding it hard to stay in leadership roles. The few that have "made it" are often seen as the exception, too liberal and not representative of all brown or Black people—and the list goes on. The diversity within our own groups is not recognized and is often used against us. I am not feeling as hopeful on the anti-racism front.

Counsel to women and people of color in Mennonite churches

In my experience within Mennonite churches, I have often seen churches of color try to model the white church in worship. I have often heard churches of color referred to as not being Mennonite because of their form of worship or how they operate as a church. Often, decisions are made on resources according to how they fit the standard of what is viewed as Mennonite. Resources are also allocated with the assumption that the group receiving the resources will operate in a manner consistent with the dominant culture's viewpoint.

I am not advocating doing away with accountability structures, but I hope that we can find many ways of being accountable that will be inclusive of other worldviews about time, relationships, work, and money. People of color must start to think outside of what has been presented to us as the norm and start presenting, with confidence, alternative ways of doing things. People of color need to provide viable alternatives—or at least a place to start a conversation.

As people of color, we are beyond complaining about what we do not have. We need to identify what we need to be healthy human beings. I believe we can find some creative alternatives for ourselves and our society.[3] When working on systemic change, whether it is sexism or racism, there are four things to remember. First, you cannot do the work alone. Know the pieces you can do and do them well. You are not responsible for doing everything. Second, you cannot let up on the work. When things seem to be going well, be aware that systems will revert as soon as they can. Be vigilant! Third, take care of yourself. Take time to enjoy the beauty around you. Sometimes working for change can get dark; keep your soul open to the beauty that life also offers. Finding balance is crucial. Fourth and finally, know at the end of the day that God's reconciling work will prevail.

An African American Mennonite experience: Regina Shands Stoltzfus

Experiences in church

I cannot think about my experiences in the Mennonite church as a woman without qualifying that I am a Black woman. My experience of being a gendered person goes hand in hand with being a person who is raced. These identities have absolutely shaped my

---

3 De León-Hartshorn, "Continuing the Journey," 76.

experiences—not only in how I see but also in how I am seen. W. E. B. Du Bois's notion of double consciousness is still a fitting explanation for the ways in which African Americans navigate life. In the US context, my identity as a Mennonite provides yet another filter, another way in which I see and am seen. Donna Kate Rushin's "The Bridge Poem" expresses it perfectly when she describes the ways she is always explaining one group of people to another group; "then I've got to explain myself to everybody."[4]

My experience of being a bridge was nurtured in my home congregation, an urban and primarily African American church in Cleveland, Ohio. It is the church in which I was baptized and where many years later I became the first woman to serve as a pastor.

My mother was raised in the South and attended Baptist churches as a child. Our family was part of the Great Migration of African Americans who moved from the South for better opportunities. Most of the kids I grew up with also had southern relatives that we visited in the summers, and our families temporarily housed series of relatives that continued to move north. We were invited to church by neighbors and quickly made Lee Heights Community Church our home church.

My mother once said one way to tell where people in our mixed-race, mixed-tradition church came from was by the way—and by how loudly—they talked: people from Baptist and Methodist traditions sang and talked louder. Mom said the Mennonites were quiet, and our church was a good place for people (like her) who were looking for something a bit in between. She, in particular, liked the quieter preaching of our pastor, but she missed gospel music and the call-and-response tradition of the Black church. She and others got their wish for gospel music when a youth choir was formed; I sang in that choir from the time I was thirteen years old. Music was one of the ways our congregation developed its own hybrid culture. We did not have just one choir; at times there

---

4 In *This Bridge Called My Back*, edited by Cherrie Moraga and Gloria Anzaldua (New York: Kitchen Table: Women of Color Press, 1981), xxi–xxii.

were as many as five. Music was a way of beautifully blending the many streams we had come from into one.

My congregational context prepared me to have an analysis of race and class. I also learned some things about gender. During my childhood and teen years, official church leadership positions were filled by men, even as women were heavily involved in many ministries and provided significant financial support.

The Black women in my neighborhood were champions of their communities. Most of them worked outside the home and still did countless hours of volunteer work, much of it in the church. My mother got involved in local politics because of the conditions in our Cleveland neighborhood. She and other moms went to PTA meetings together, participated in the local homeowners association, and started attending ward meetings to decide on issues to be taken to the local councilman: making sure streetlights were replaced, reporting when garbage was not being picked up, and addressing lots of other things that tended to get neglected. The women of the street clubs had to keep reminding local government that we were part of the city. And the church became an extension of this kind of advocacy, even from the pulpit. Mom said things like, "We weren't told who to vote for. We *were* told power was in the ballot, and if we didn't vote we didn't have power. *Everything* is political. Even though we weren't told who to vote for, we were also told not to vote for people who promised not to raise taxes, because taxes pay for things a society needs and care for poor people. We have to have taxes, or our system won't work."[5] This was in the 1960s and 1970s.

Despite this kind of activism in the neighborhoods, women's official leadership roles in the churches were unsurprisingly limited to stereotypical "women's work": working with children in Sunday school and boys' and girls' clubs, raising money for various ministries, and providing hospitality (and food) for church functions. When barriers to other leadership roles were broken, it was generally because men were not available or not stepping up. For instance, women could be on the usher board, but their roles

---

5 Phone interview with Joyce Collie, August 15, 2014.

were restricted. According to my mom, "There were all these strict rules that the men had to be the ones at the door, and that the men would take up the [offering] collection. It seemed silly even then, but we did it. When we [women] asked about it, we were told that it reflected the beginning of the church. Those rules were eventually phased out—men weren't around, and people forgot. They were just happy to have an usher!"[6]

As for a woman in the pulpit, this was unheard of in the first decades of the church. The polity of the denomination restricted women from serving as pastors. This began to change in the 1970s with the ordination of the first woman in the Mennonite church.

Historically, the day-to-day experiences of Black women did not allow them to ignore the salience of both race and gender as important parts of their identities. The complexity of their lives was in their creative expressions and political involvement. The church offered a place where their artistic leanings could emerge and flourish in service to intertwining their religious and civic identities. My mother's experience is one such example. Her initial attraction to our church was to children's activities. My mother was and continues to be interested in the arts, especially theater and writing. She was consistently and actively engaged in Afrocentric cultural pursuits, both preserving them and passing them on.

Her participation in a local theater company and establishing a Black women's writing group were tangible indications of her love of Black culture and art forms and her belief in the importance of African American culture as a means of progress and resistance against domination. Mom wanted Black people, especially children, to see themselves represented in literature and theater, and she set about making that happen in her community and in her church. This extended into the political realm, and as she noted, everything is political. Politics in the church was not a bad thing; it was perceived as necessary. While she did not campaign for the end of "silly" rules around gender regarding leader-

---

6 Phone interview with Joyce Collie, August 15, 2014.

ship in the church, she and others worked around the rules to get things done.

Most of my working adult life has been in Mennonite institutions. In most of those positions, I have spoken and written about structural and institutional violence, primarily the violence of racism. I have had many opportunities to make people uncomfortable and even angry. Talking about racism does have a tendency to make people's inner sexism rear its ugly head. Here are some of the things that have happened to me:

- In the third week of a seven-week course, a white man stood up in the middle of the classroom and erupted angrily during a discussion of racism.
- At the end of a seminary class I was teaching, a white male pastor made a racist statement to an African American female student.
- At a break during an anti-racism training, a white man asked me how it was that I developed a work ethic.
- In an anti-racism training, a white male trainer shouted at me more than once when I did not immediately respond to a request he made.
- I am often told I do not understand my own experience or context.
- In far too many meetings and other settings, I am talked over by white men and women, and ideas that I contribute are attributed to men who share my ideas moments later.

I lift up these examples because they are the kinds of experiences that have become somewhat normal to me, and I wonder if these experiences are shared by my white sisters.

To be Black in a white context means being simultaneously invisible and hyper-visible. At one churchwide assembly some years ago, I was looking for the registration area in the large convention center. I came upon a group of convention staff (identified by their convention T-shirts) and asked for directions. One of the workers looked at me and said, somewhat condescendingly, "This is a *Mennonite* convention." I responded that I was a *Mennonite* pastor, and I still needed to know where the registration area was.

Experiences in the pastorate

In the mid-1970s, a young African American woman filled the pulpit at Lee Heights Community Church in Cleveland during our pastor's sabbatical summer. Wilma Bailey would later become one of my professors at Goshen College and eventually went on to teach Old Testament and Hebrew at Christian Theological Seminary in Indianapolis. As a teenager, I did not have my sights set on a career in the church, but Dr. Bailey's presence at least let me see something I had not seen up to that point: an African American woman in the pulpit. The notion did not seem impossible to me; I had certainly seen women in several roles at church, though not as a pastor. Indeed, I later learned that a few people did not attend church that summer because a woman was serving as pastor. Eventually that barrier was eliminated—but not until the mid-1990s—and the church hired me as associate pastor. The congregation supported licensing and ordination (November 7, 1999, by Ohio Mennonite Conference), but an initiative to install a woman as co-pastor still could not get enough congregational votes to pass. It would be nearly another decade before that would happen.

Additionally, in our neighborhood ministerial alliance, some churches and pastors openly opposed women in the pastorate. This made things like the monthly breakfast meetings painful and awkward for me. For instance, it was not unusual for the group to be greeted with a hearty "Good morning, men of God!" I was not the only woman pastor in the neighborhood, but I was the only one attending the monthly breakfast meetings. I did eventually stop attending because I decided that particular battle was not one I wanted to fight. One specific experience demonstrated the interplay between the worlds I navigated as a leader in my congregation and in the neighborhood alliance. Every Thanksgiving, the alliance hosted a Thanksgiving Day worship service at one of the local churches. I had never attended the service before becoming a pastor because the holiday usually meant out-of-town travel to visit extended family. The first year I participated in the worship service as a pastor, the event was hosted at a neighboring church. I knew that the practice in other churches was for all the clergy to sit on the platform, facing the congregation. Our family arrived at the service a little late, and I was prepared to sit with my family instead of going up front and taking a seat after all the other pastors were seated. As we were getting settled, I noticed the pastor of the church in the front, making a "come forward" gesture with his hand. Surprised, I made my way up the aisle to the front of the church, prepared to sit with the others. But when I got to the front, the same pastor looked at me with surprise and said, "Oh, no. We don't do that in this church." The gesture was not for me but for another late arriving (male) pastor. I felt my face grow hot with embarrassment. I do not know if other people noticed, but I felt as if I had been called out for daring to think I could sit with the men—the real clergy. Before I could make my way back to my family, I noticed out of the corner of my eye our congregation's pastor emeritus. As a retired (male) clergy, he still had the right to sit on the platform with the others. He had witnessed this little display and, in a movement of solidarity, came down from the platform and sat with me.

Experiences with anti-racism work

Before my time in the pastorate, I had been doing anti-racism work in the Mennonite denomination—speaking in churches, doing workshops, writing curricula, and more. I clearly recognized the necessity of intersectional anti-oppression work, yet fighting sexism (and other *isms*) in the church seemed like more than I could take on at the time. This is a classic dilemma for Black women and other women of color, finding the time, energy, and resources to work against both racism and sexism, leaving barely any resources or energy to fight against other systems of domination. Yet these structures are interrelated, are interconnected, and feed off of one another. In the midst of all of this, I was building my commitment to working in the larger peace movement as a person of faith—yet the larger peace movement during my coming of age was not dealing seriously with its own racism and sexism.

The racialized history of the church in the United States means that the church has not escaped the impact of race and racism on its mission. The dependence of the southern economic system on chattel slavery made it well within the interests of policy makers, including Christians, to keep the system alive. Enslaved Blacks were evangelized in part to support and uphold the unjust system. Preachers and slaveholders tightly controlled and shaped the Christianity offered to enslaved Blacks in order to make them more docile and obedient. The notion of Manifest Destiny supported the Indian Removal Act and other government policies designed to "kill the Indian and save the man."

Religious communities must deal with this past in order to understand the present and live into the future. Acknowledging complicity with racism, past and present, must be faced in order to create authentic relationships. This truth-telling is not to force people to feel bad about a past they were not there for and did not orchestrate; instead, acknowledging "this happened, and it affects the way we live now" paves the way for building something new. There are models for the kind of work that needs to be done.[7]

This is an important teaching task for the church that can build on prior efforts. In 1995, the Damascus Road project was initiated. In March of 1995, over 250 Mennonites and Brethren in Christ gathered together in Chicago for "Restoring Our Sight." This conference for those seeking to challenge racism in the Anabaptist community examined the biblical basis for anti-racism work, the history of racism in the Anabaptist tradition, and insti-

---

7 Models for doing collective anti-racism work include SURJ (Showing Up for Racial Justice), https://www.showingupforracialjustice.org; the Equal Justice Initiative, https://eji.org; and Roots of Justice (formerly Damascus Road, described below). These organizations and others like them operate as collectives of white people and people of color educating and organizing for racial justice in local communities. The work is grounded in the belief that learning racialized history and its aftermath is critical.

tutional racism. One of the clearest calls to resist racism coming out of the gathering was to provide anti-racism training for long-term institutional change. Participants in the planning meetings made the following statement: "Together we have noted the biblical call to reconciliation. We believe that planning for long-term intentional anti-racism holds the promise of a renewed anti-racist multicultural church. Recognizing that this will not come by individual will or personal intent, we call for a process to equip our Mennonite and Brethren in Christ institutions to do the work of anti-racism."[8]

In response, a training and organizing model was created, and over the next fifteen years, nearly every Mennonite church institution, including denominational offices, colleges and universities, and mission boards, sent individuals and teams for training. The program was housed in Mennonite Central Committee (MCC), the service and relief agency of the family of Anabaptist churches. Many organizations required their entire staff and all new hires to take the training, with more than 1,800 people and sixty teams.[9] Eventually, due to philosophical differences and a group discomfort with not using an intersectional analysis that connected the oppressions of racism, sexism, and heterosexism, the Damascus Road program separated from MCC and reestablished itself as the Roots of Justice Anti-Oppression Process.[10] Due to this process, many across the church were able to use a common language and gained a growing ability to name institutional racism. Damascus Road was not the first attempt, nor should it be the last.

The by-laws of MC USA, approved by delegates at the churchwide assembly in July 2003, include a goal for the denomi-

---

[8] "Damascus Road Anti-Racism Core Trainer Manual, Introduction to Damascus Road: History" (unpublished, 2007), 1.

[9] Donald B. Kraybill, *Concise Encyclopedia of Amish, Brethren, Hutterites, and Mennonites* (Baltimore: Johns Hopkins University Press, 2010), 175.

[10] Damascus Road Transition, "Informing Constituents about Damascus Road's Transition to Independence," https://drtransition.wordpress.com/faqs/.

nation to "be anti-racist in all areas of church life and program."[11] Racial/ethnic groups that are officially recognized by the Executive Board of the denomination may appoint three delegates plus one for every one thousand members to the Delegate Assembly.[12]

Conclusion

Current events reveal that the anti-Blackness that propelled US history for most of its existence has not dissipated. There is pushback to gains made by Black African Americans. While laws have changed, systemic institutional racism operates in ways that continue to be death-dealing for Black people. African American women still need to resist racism and sexism and to fight for the survival of their communities. As social justice movements recognize the need for an intersectional analysis on which to base their justice work, it seems historic peace churches lag severely behind. Christian ethics should not only analyze "existing practices that inhibit and assault the social and spiritual well-being of persons"[13] but also consider and give leadership to the transformation of those practices, particularly within the Christian community but ultimately for the sake of transforming oppressive practices that harm all marginalized peoples.

---

11 "Mennonite Church USA Bylaws," II.1.k, https://www.mennoniteusa.org/resource-portal/resource/mennonite-church-usa-bylaws/.

12 "Mennonite Church USA Bylaws," V.2.c.

13 Traci West, *Disruptive Christian Ethics: When Racism and Women's Lives Matter* (Louisville: Westminster John Knox, 2006), 38.

5

The great hurdle
Women are ordained

*John A. Esau, Nancy Kauffmann,
and Karen Martens Zimmerly*

The social context of change

Bob Dylan's 1963 "The Times They Are A-Changin'" was the song of a new generation in society and church. Visions of a new world flooded the hearts and minds of many. Young writers spoke about renewal. Passions increased. Dreams of what might be filled the souls of those who saw a new day coming.

Beginning in the 1960s and extending forward for another decade, two issues dominated the world of North American society: the struggle for civil rights and the war in Vietnam. The experience of launching new visions of what might be gave birth to other hopes. Eras of social or religious change do not happen in a vacuum. Dreams of equality among peoples and races give rise to new hopes of equal opportunity and equal roles based on gender and sexuality. Idealistic youth and young adults called for an end of the status quo in every realm of society, including the church. Protests around the Vietnam War, civil rights, and women's rights pushed society and the church to do some hard soul searching. The system was shaken, and there was resistance to any change.

Feminist writers have described four distinct waves of working on issues of women's rights and concerns during the twentieth century in American society. The first wave was the early twentieth-century women's suffrage movement, which culminated in the Nineteenth Amendment to the United States Constitution, granting women the right to vote. It was a significant but limited victory.

The second wave of the women's movement during the 1970s called for women to be given more equal access to vocational equality and equal opportunity in society.[14] During this second wave, women within the church also gave voice to their sense of God's call to serve the church in ways and roles that, until that time, had generally been limited to men. In the United States, the Equal Rights Amendment was introduced in 1972 and would continue to call for American society to respond once again; it failed ratification in the state legislatures in 1982. On March 8, 1975, the United Nations declared the first International Women's Day, an annual event that continues to be recognized.

During the last third of the twentieth century an issue that rose to prominence among Mennonites—but also among many other Christian denominations—was the role of women in church ministry and leadership. Could the church welcome women with the rite of ordination, a credential long accepted as the symbol of ministerial service and authority? In the 1970s women would first claim and then gain support for being ordained to multiple roles of ministerial leadership in many churches including Mennonite denominations. Yes, the times were changing.

Some parts of the church held a great deal of mistrust toward the women's movement. There was some fear that the movement could affect the sanctity of marriage and cause chaos in the family and the church. In the "Reader's Say" column of the *Gospel*

---

14 Journalist Martha Lear coined the term "Second Feminist Wave" in a *New York Times Magazine* article, March 10, 1968, Section SM, 24. She wrote: "In short, feminism, which one might have supposed as dead . . . is again an issue. Proponents call it the second Feminist Wave, the first having ebbed after the glorious victory of suffrage and disappeared." A third wave began in the 1990s and focused on the removal of gender roles and stereotypes, particularly related to race and class. The fourth wave of the twenty-first century is characterized by the "Me Too Movement," dealing with sexual abuse and sexual assault.

Herald (former Mennonite Church denominational publication) in 1975, one male wrote, "Is it not odd that the concern seen for redefining women's role in the church is simultaneous with the women's lib push in American society? This raises the question, Who is leading and who is following?"[15] Katie Funk Wiebe, in the 1976 *Gospel Herald* article "Another Kind of Feminism," wrote about attending an Evangelical Women's Caucus in Washington, DC, commenting, "I know that for some individuals 'feminist' is a dirty word. Attaching 'evangelical' or 'biblical' doesn't make it any easier to accept. The stereotype of a feminist is a raging, hostile, aggressive, anti-male female with lesbian, pro-abortion attitudes. . . . What a relief to find the stereotype did not hold true."[16]

The church gave mixed signals to females in the late 1960s and early 1970s. As a young person, I (Nancy)—along with other women—was invited to test my gifts and participate in the life of the church. I was encouraged to listen to God's call on my life to serve others and the church. My baptism sealed my commitment to God and the church. As time passed, I realized that the church's interest in me was more as a young person than a young woman, and I became aware of the limitations on what a woman could and couldn't do, all supported by scripture. A month after I was married in 1972, an article by Ella May Miller, of the Heart to Heart radio program, appeared in the *Gospel Herald* addressing parents of high school graduates. She wrote, "I believe your daughter should first experience practical domestic work before considering college or professional training. Regardless of her talents and capabilities, she should learn the ABCs of housekeeping. . . . For after all, all normal girls anticipate marriage. Homemaking is the career for which they should be educated."[17]

In Canada, the questions of women in ministry and the possibility of ordination were on the national agenda of a number of

---

15 "Readers Say," *Gospel Herald*, July 1, 1975, 488.

16 Katie Funk Wiebe, "Another Kind of Feminism," *Gospel Herald*, Jan. 20, 1976, 44.

17 Ella May Miller, "Commencement," *Gospel Herald*, May 23, 1972, 455.

denominations besides Mennonites during the 1970s, except for the United Church of Canada, which had ordained its first woman in 1936 and by 1975 had twenty-four women out of fifty-three total candidates for ordination.[18] In 1973, the Toronto Anglican diocese urged the national denomination to delay the ordination of women to the priesthood until 1975 in order to allow further study.[19] In 1974, the Pentecostal Assemblies of Canada rejected a motion to ordain women.[20] That same year the Canadian Mennonite Brethren annual conference also discussed women in ministry. A leader stated that opening the door to women in leadership would lead to theological liberalism. The resolution that passed stated that they were not in favor of the ordination of women for preaching and pastoral ministry.[21]

Whether denominations voted yes or no, the possibility of female pastors was entering the imaginations of the church across the Canadian landscape. Within the Mennonite conferences that would eventually form Mennonite Church Canada, the path to ministry and ordination of the first women would span three decades. The decade and the regional context of the conference would influence the responses of the congregations and the struggles and joys that these first women faced.

Context is significant. Only as we understand the significance of the social revolutions that were occurring in North America can we begin to understand the religious changes that happened in the churches. Likewise, only as we perceive the significance of the feminist movement in this era will we be able to interpret how and why women within our churches claimed the right to

---

18 "Items and Comments," *Gospel Herald* 68, Aug. 12, 1975, 723.

19 "Delay Ordination of Women," *Gospel Herald* 66, July 31, 1973, 599.

20 "Reject Ordination of Women," *Gospel Herald* 67, Oct. 8, 1974, 264.

21 "Role of Women in Life of Church, Continuing Concern of Leadership," *Gospel Herald* 68, Aug. 12, 1975, 566.

roles in ministerial leadership and with it the church's affirmation through the rite of ordination.[22]

How did this change come about when the scriptures, tradition, and experience seemed to offer a strong wall of resistance to change? There appeared to be biblical texts to support male leadership. There was a long tradition extending back many centuries that worked to maintain patterns that barred women from ministerial roles. Perhaps most important, the experience of only males in pastoral roles over many generations reinforced emotional assumptions against women in ministry.

Mennonite back stories

For many, the question of whether women could be considered for positions of pastoral ministry and leadership seemed like a new and controversial issue. Traditionally the rite of ordination was reserved for men only. However, there was an awareness that, in the sixteenth-century Anabaptist reformation, women often played a significant role. Many of their stories are recorded in the *Martyrs Mirror*. Among the earliest martyrs was Anna of Freiburg. It is recorded that she "suffered many torments, [was] sentenced to death, and drowned in the water, and afterwards burned with fire."[23] Before her death she prayed, "I commend myself to God and His church; may He be my Protector today, for His holy name's sake. Amen."[24] About a third of the martyrs named in *Martyrs Mirror* are women. Court records contain numerous cases of women accused of holding illegal worship services and distributing communion. In Schleiden-in-the-Eifel,

---

22 To reflect further on the meaning and significance of social change, see the book by Robert A. Nisbet, *Social Change and History* (New York: Oxford University Press, 1969), 166–82. There he writes, "Change is natural. Change is directional. Change is immanent. Change is continuous. Change is necessary. Change proceeds from uniform causes."

23 Thieleman J. van Braght, *The Bloody Theater, or Martyrs Mirror*, 5th English ed. (Scottdale, PA: Herald, 1950), 434.

24 van Braght, *The Bloody Theater, or Martyrs Mirror*, 435.

some women were called ministers or even apostles.[25] Anabaptist women prophets abounded in Anabaptist congregations in Strasbourg and elsewhere along the Rhine.

While women clearly played significant roles in the Anabaptist reformation, there are no extant written examples of ordination or similar rites of credentialing. There do exist a series of back stories dealing with the ordination of women in the Mennonite church that need to be remembered as important precedents leading toward the shift that happened beginning in the 1970s. Back stories are significant occurrences that anticipate the future, and without them the present and future cannot be fully appreciated or understood.

The Dordrecht Confession of 1632

Beginning with the Schleitheim Confession of 1527, all the early Anabaptist confessions spoke about the office of ministerial leadership as an important and essential part of the church. In the Dordrecht Confession of 1632, article 9 is titled "The Office of Teachers and Ministers—Male and Female—in the Church."[26] While most of the article assumes males will be given roles of leadership, one paragraph speaks of women: "Also that honorable old widows should be chosen as servants, who besides the almoners, are to visit, comfort, and take care of the poor, the weak, the afflicted, and the needy, as also to visit, comfort and take care of widows and orphans, and further to assist in taking care of any matters in the church that properly come within their sphere

---

25 Lois Barrett, "Women in the Anabaptist Movement," in *Study Guide on Women*, edited by Herta Funk (Newton, KS: Faith and Life, 1975), 35. See C. Arnold Snyder and Linda A. Huebert Hecht, eds., *Profiles of Anabaptist Women: Sixteenth-Century Reforming Pioneers* (Waterloo, ON: Wilfred Laurier University Press, 1996). See also Ernst Crous, "Anabaptism in Schleiden-in-the-Eifel," *Mennonite Quarterly Review* 34 (July 1960): 189. Crous identifies Bernhartz Maria as one such woman apostle.

26 Howard John Loewen, *One Lord, One Church, One Hope, and One God: Mennonite Confessions of Faith* (Elkhart, IN: Institute of Mennonite Studies, 1985), 66.

according to their best ability."²⁷ This text suggests that women in some official, if supporting, capacity are a part of the ministerial leadership envisioned for the church.

Virginia Conference deaconess movement (1861–1962)
One of the lesser known stories of women ordained for ministry occurred in the Virginia Conference—Middle District. Over the course of about a century (1861–1962), twenty-eight women were ordained as deaconesses "to assist ministers in providing for the pastoral care and physical needs of women and girls and to help facilitate services of baptism, communion, and foot washing."²⁸ It would appear that the original vision grew out of the provision for women in the Dordrecht Confession. One story reported is that of Elizabeth Shank Showalter, who was ordained as a deaconess in 1889. While the early vision was that these women would serve in a ministering role, over time the expectations changed to where they became the enforcers of conservative dress codes and so on. The conference finally concluded that such a task could as well be done by the pastor's wife, and the ordination of deaconesses ceased.²⁹

---

27 Loewen, *One Lord, One Church, One Hope, and One God*, 66. This text from the Dordrecht Confession is acknowledged in the document "Leadership and Authority in the Life of the Church" (Elkhart, IN: Mennonite Church, 1980).

28 Anna Schowalter, "Holding to the Jot and Tittle: Deaconesses in Virginia Conference," *Anabaptist Historians*, Nov. 17, 2016, https://anabaptisthistorians.org/2016/11/17/holding-to-the-jot-and-tittle-deaconesses-in-virginia-conference/.

29 The Mennonite Church *Minister's Manual*, contained within the *Mennonite Church Polity* (1952), has a footnote in the section dealing is the ordination of deacons which reads, "In the Confession of Faith (Dordrecht), there is provision made also for the choosing and service of deaconesses, or female deacons. This custom, however, has almost passed into disuse and there are now, so far as we know, only a few churches that have deaconesses," 114–15.

Deaconess movement in Kansas

Another example of using the language of ordination for women in the early part of the twentieth century was the development of the deaconess movement in central Kansas.[30] Beginning in the community of Goessel and its Bethesda Hospital, the movement was supported by Bethel College and became a significant group with the founding of Bethel Deaconess Hospital in Newton, Kansas. "Sister Frieda Kaufman, Sister Catherine Voth and Sister Ida Epp were ordained when the Bethel Deaconess Hospital was dedicated 11 June 1908."[31] Some deaconesses also served in Mountain Lake, Minnesota, and Berne, Indiana, where at least one had a role as a pastoral assistant. However, most served as nurses and other medical workers.

Anna Mankes-Zernike

Born in 1887, Anna Zernike studied theology at the University of Amsterdam and the Amsterdam Mennonite Theological Seminary. "In 1911 she became the first woman pastor in the Netherlands when she accepted the invitation of the Mennonite (Doopsgezinde) congregation in Bovenknijpe."[32] Thus she was the first Mennonite woman to be ordained in Europe who then served in a pastoral leadership role in a Mennonite congregation.

Ann Jemima Allebach

Ann Allebach grew up in the Eden Mennonite Church of Schwenksville, Pennsylvania (Eastern District Conference of the

---

30 For a longer and more complete history of the deaconess movement—Mennonite and ecumenical, European and North American—see the article "Deaconesses" in *Global Anabaptist Mennonite Encyclopedia Online*, www.gameo.org. See also Katie Funk Wiebe, *Our Lamps Were Lit: An Informal History of the Bethel Deaconess Hospital School of Nursing* (Newton, KS: Mennonite Press, 1978).

31 *Global Anabaptist Mennonite Encyclopedia Online*, s.v. "Deaconesses," gameo.org.

32 *Global Anabaptist Mennonite Encyclopedia Online*, s.v. "Anna Zernike," gameo.org.

General Conference Mennonite Church [GCMC]). She is thought to be the first woman ordained among Mennonites in North America. Following her formal education, she became active in a variety of roles and leadership positions in the greater New York City area. Her ordination took place at First Mennonite Church of Philadelphia, Pennsylvania, on January 15, 1911. Though she preached occasionally in Mennonite congregations following her ordination, she never served as a pastor among the Mennonites. In 1916, she was installed as pastor of the Long Island Sunnyside Reformed Church. She died of a heart attack at forty-three years of age, on April 27, 1918.[33] It was more than sixty years before another Mennonite woman was ordained to pastoral ministry in North America.

Ordination of missionaries and spouses of missionaries

One of the sources of official policy regarding ordinations is the series of publications known as minister's manuals. The GCMC *Minister's Manual* (1950) contains several statements and suggestions that, while ordination was normally the prerogative of men, an exception was made in the case of the missionary. In a series of "Designations and Definitions," it states, "The missionary usually also assumes all of the above privileges and duties, with the exception that women missionaries do not generally exercise the distinctive duties of the elder nor do they officiate at marriage ceremonies."[34] This meant that women missionaries could bury, but they could not marry.

Annie Funk, a single woman missionary, is claimed to be the first Mennonite woman missionary to be ordained in North America in 1906. This occurred at the Hereford Mennonite Church in Bally, Pennsylvania, preparing for her foreign service. Annie is most remembered for having died with the sinking of the *Titanic* while returning home from India. A news story reported

---

33 Mary Lou Cummings, "Ann Jemima Allebach, Ordained 1911," *The Mennonite*, Jan. 18, 1977, 34–35.

34 *Minister's Manual* (1950), 96.

that she gave up her place on a lifeboat for the sake of a mother and her children.[35]

In addition, spouses of male mission workers were given ordination certificates of their own. My (John's) own father, John J. Esau, was ordained as an elder in 1935, when he was called to be the founding pastor (*church planter* was not a term then used) of First Mennonite Church of Lima, Ohio. In that role he was considered a missionary. I have in my personal possession the original certificate of ordination given to my mother on the occasion of my parents' ordination; it reads as follows:

> Certificate of Ordination of the General Conference of Mennonites of North America in the name of our Lord, Jesus Christ, the great head of the church: To all to whom these Presents may come, Greeting: Be it known that Mrs. Elvina (Augsburger) Esau, after having given sufficient evidence of his (her) Christian character and literary and Biblical knowledge and having declared his [sic] willingness to consecrate his (her) service to the Lord Jesus Christ and the church was solemnly set apart and ordained as a Christian worker according to the rites and customs of the church at Lima, Ohio on the 24 day of November A.D. 1935. In Witness Whereof, we have hereunto subscribed our names this 24th day of November A. D. 1935. P. A. Kliewer, Pastor, Ebenezer Mennonite Church; Edgar E. Toevs, St. John Menn. Church; Rev. Jacob Haas.

A similar story is reported by Richard Friesen regarding the ordination of his parents, Arthur and Viola Friesen, for missionary service with the Native American community. Following the service of ordination some persons were heard to exclaim: "Two persons were ordained today!"[36]

---

35 *Global Anabaptist Mennonite Encyclopedia Online*, s.v. "Funk, Annie C. (1874–1912)," gameo.org.

36 Conversation with Dorothy Nickel Friesen, April 2019.

In the 1950s Mennonite churches in Canada also had the practice of ordaining missionaries. What church leaders could not imagine at home seemed acceptable for women who would be sent far away. Esther Patkau, ordained as a missionary in 1951, returned to Canada as a seasoned pastor from Japan. In 1976, she began as associate pastor at First Mennonite Church in Saskatoon, where the early years of ministry were challenging, as many congregants were not comfortable having a woman pastor.[37] In 1980, when I (Karen) was twenty-one years old, Esther officiated at my grandmother's funeral. This was my first experience of a woman as pastor. I remember the warmth of her voice. She knew and had cared for my grandmother, and her love and hope in God was evident. I was comforted by her presence.

Women in church vocations—seminary support for women in ministry

A final back story anticipating the coming development of support for women in ministry and for their full credentialing through ordination was a unique program of Mennonite Biblical Seminary (MBS). MBS had several women studying in its various programs through its years in Chicago. Eleanor (Wismer) Kaufman enrolled, anticipating a ministry of music position, which she eventually found at Eden Mennonite Church in Moundridge, Kansas.[38] Others enrolled in the Master of Religious Education degree program, hoping for positions in Christian education. Finally, the seminary took a significant step in identifying a special program for women who were vocationally open to Christian service through the church. While it did not promise ordination, it tendered the belief that women could find a meaningful role following theological training in a graduate-level seminary program. The seminary called it Women in Church Vocations. The first four women enrolled in Women in Church Vocations were

---

37 Donna Schultz, "The Lord Has Been My Guide," *Canadian Mennonite*, 22, no. 6, https://canadianmennonite.org/stories/'-lord-has-been-my-guide-through-life'.

38 Conversation with Eleanor and Don Kaufman, May 1, 2019.

Virginia Claassen, Marion Keeney Preheim, Justina Neufeld, and Onale Stucky. Begun during the seminary's final years in Chicago and carried to its new campus in Elkhart, Indiana, in 1958, Women in Church Vocations was an open invitation for women to enroll in graduate seminary education.

Though individually women were sometimes given mixed messages within their seminary experience, the seminaries should be credited for their eventual strong support to women in ministry and for their right to the rite of ordination. Associated (now Anabaptist) Mennonite Biblical Seminary and Eastern Mennonite Seminary have been sources of inspiration and discovery for women open to the call of God in their lives. The seminaries helped lead the way.

The meaning of ordination

A number of questions are raised when discussing the ordination of women: What does ordination mean? What happens when a person is ordained? Is there a difference between the ordination of men and the ordination of women? What is the covenant that is being made? Some of these questions begin to find answers in the articles on "Ordination" in *The Mennonite Encyclopedia* or its online version, the *Global Anabaptist Mennonite Encyclopedia Online (GAMEO)*. The first article was written by Harold S. Bender in 1959 for the original publication; the second article was written by John A. Esau for the supplemental fifth volume in 1989.[39]

The 1959 article makes only the briefest mention of women and essentially negates the possibility of their ministry in North America. Bender writes, "In the 1950s, normally women were eligible for ordination only among the Dutch Mennonites. However, some Mennonite groups in effect give ordination to wom-

---

39 *Global Anabaptist Mennonite Encyclopedia Online*, s.v. "Ordination," gameo.org.

en missionaries, and the consecration of deaconesses is akin to ordination."[40]

By 1989 things had changed; women's ordination was becoming more accepted and more widely practiced. This is reported in Esau's 1989 updated article:

> A major change among North American Mennonites has been the growing openness to the ordination of women within the General Conference Mennonite Church and the Mennonite Church; . . . In 1987, 44 women were in licensed or ordained for ministry positions in the General Conference Mennonite Church, either as pastors or as chaplains. In the Mennonite Church the issue is being debated on an area conference basis. Half of the conferences are ready to ordain women, and 34 women are serving in licensed or ordained ministerial leadership positions in the Mennonite Church. Included in the above numbers are 14 women who serve in dual-affiliated congregations (1987).[41]

Attempts were made to state more clearly the meaning of ordination. The *Minister's Manual* of 1998 included a statement that described what the church is doing when someone is ordained. Each of the statements applied equally to the ordination of both men and women. *A Mennonite Polity for Ministerial Leadership* defined ordination as (1) confirmation of the person's call to ministry, (2) affirmation of the person's leadership gifts, (3) the ordinand's "priestly" role, (4) affirmation of the person's authority to represent the church, (5) the calling to particular tasks associated with the office of ministry, (6) mutual accountability between

---

40 *Global Anabaptist Mennonite Encyclopedia Online*, s.v. "Ordination," gameo.org.

41 *Global Anabaptist Mennonite Encyclopedia Online*, s.v. "Ordination," gameo.org.

congregation and minister, and (7) credentialing acknowledged by church, state, and society.[42]

While the term "the office of ministry" is not new to Anabaptist ministerial theology, it came into renewed use during this era. The office of ministry belongs to the church, never to the person being ordained. In ordination, the church is giving permission to the woman or the man for the right to occupy the office, but it is not theirs; the office of ministry belongs to the church.

Ordination is also always a commitment of accountability for what it means to occupy the church's office of ministry and to represent the entire church on its behalf. Again, this applies equally to men and women, to those who serve as pastors in congregations or as chaplains in other institutions, or to those who serve in conference or denominational positions.

A chronology of change—documents and stories

What follows is a series of Mennonite documents dealing with ordination that reflect the church's changing understanding regarding the ordination of women. Interspersed with summaries of these documents are stories of Mennonite women who were ordained in that time period. This displays in chronological order what the church was saying and writing and what ordained Mennonite women were experiencing.

"Some Theses Concerning Ordination," by Cornelius Dyck (1962)

The purpose of Cornelius Dyck's 1962 unpublished paper "Some Theses Concerning Ordination" was to introduce the subject of ordination for the joint faculty of Associated Mennonite Biblical Seminaries as part of the total discussion of Christian ministry. Dyck was a member of that faculty. While there is much that is of interest and significance regarding ordination, it is fully clear that the operating assumptions in the early 1960s were exclu-

---

42 Mennonite Board of Congregational Ministries and Ministerial Leadership Services, *A Mennonite Polity for Ministerial Leadership* (Newton, KS: Faith and Life, 1996), 25–27.

sively masculine. References are to "the brother" and "the brotherhood," with no indication of any openness to gender equality or to women being part of the conversation about ordination. The document is significant for what it does not say or discuss at that time and place.

"The Fullness of Christ," by John Howard Yoder (1969)

Although John Howard Yoder's 1969 pamphlet *The Fullness of Christ: Paul's Revolutionary Vision of Universal Ministry* neither is an institutional or denominational item dealing with issues of ordination nor directly addresses questions of gender and ministry, it is historically significant in how it impacted the quest for women's ministerial roles and their validation through ordination.[43] The earliest publication of Yoder's work was in a series of pamphlets, generally referred to as the *Concern* documents, of which this was issue 17. That it was reissued as a small book nearly twenty years later under the above title speaks to its enduring impact on the church. The context for the second edition was for the Believers' Church Conference on Ministry in 1987.

Yoder begins, "There are few more reliable constants running through all human society than the special place every human community makes for the professional religionist."[44] From there he goes on to claim that, in contrast to the traditional division in the church between clergy and laity, Paul's vision is for a church in which all members share equally in the ministry according to the gifts each has been given. Yoder acknowledges that this understanding was missed in the sixteenth century, so we cannot claim any Anabaptist origins to this idea. In effect, Yoder claims that only the apostle Paul and Yoder himself got it right.

---

43 See chapter 1, note 30, for a discussion about referencing the work of John Howard Yoder in this volume.

44 John Howard Yoder, *The Fullness of Christ: Paul's Revolutionary Vision of Universal Ministry*, Concern 17 (Scottdale, PA: Herald, 1969), 1.

If there is no set-apart ministry, there is no need for ordination.[45] And if there is no ordination, there is no need to concern ourselves with questions about the ordination of women for ministerial leadership in the church. While not always stated in this absolutist form, elements of this ministerial theology have been pervasive and enduring throughout the decades since the original publication of Yoder's work. A common misinterpretation of this has been the linking of Luther's phrase about "the priesthood of all believers" to our understanding of leadership in the church.[46]

Ironically, during the decades in which women were seeking to find their place in the ministry of the church, Yoder's theology had its greatest impact. Added to this were the societal moves toward egalitarianism among all relationships, which also tended to undermine authentic leadership needs within church and society. At the very point that women were gaining access to the rite of ordination, there was male leadership making the claim that ordination was invalid, unbiblical, and meaningless.[47]

---

45 I (John) was present at the 1987 Believer's Church Conference at Bethany Theological Seminary in Oak Brook, Illinois; my memory recalls Yoder speaking at that conference and saying something to this effect: If one person is to be ordained, then all should be ordained. In other contexts, this has taken the form of interpreting baptism as the ordination of every Christian. One wonders whether this is a theology formed by mixing and merging metaphors.

46 For a more accurate interpretation of Luther's phrase, see *Global Anabaptist Mennonite Encyclopedia Online*, s.v. "Priesthood of All Believers," gameo.org.

47 I (John) have within my files copies of correspondence among John E. Toews, Loren Johns, and myself regarding these issues. In an email to Toews in February 2004, I wrote: "I said many years ago that it was the ultimate male put-down to argue at the very time that women were gaining access to ministerial leadership and credentialing that men would argue that ordination had no meaning and was unbiblical." This file contains two documents by John E. Toews that contributed to the larger context of these issues: "Rethinking Biblical Ecclesiology for the Mennonite Church" and "Toward a Biblical Theology of Leadership Affirmation: Rethinking the Meaning of Ordination."

"Women Liberated," by Lois Gunden Clemens (1971)

Fortunately, there were other voices of strong and gifted women in those early years that helped younger women find their footing. One in particular was Lois Gunden Clemens, who wrote the book *Woman Liberated* in 1971, based on her 1970 presentations for the Conrad Grebel Lecture Series, for which she had been the first woman to present. She found new ground for the role of women in Genesis 1, where both men and women are created in God's image, and in Jesus's example of treating women not only as persons but as equal in God's eyes. Gunden Clemens made the case that Jesus "was fulfilling the law by teaching a more complete understanding of it. Jesus opened to woman love and respect that reached beyond sexual encounters and gave her full human value outside of marriage."[48] She challenged the church for not taking women seriously in the decision making and strategy planning within the church and thus failing to use the talents given to the church. In the final chapter, "Using All Gifts Creatively," she writes:

> Today it is becoming more common in some of the denominations for women to be ordained to serve as pastors of congregations. If there is indeed no difference in Christ between male and female, then it might well be that some women would be called to serve in such capacity today just as they served as prophetesses in earlier times. . . . The crucial issue presently facing the church . . . is whether or not the church is ready to make full use of the gifts women members bring as resources for enriching its life and strengthening it message.[49]

For me (Nancy) as a young woman, her words were profound and encouraged me to continue to listen to God's call on my life and to be faithful to that call. Her book later had a role in the ordi-

---

48 Lois Gunden Clemens, *Woman Liberated* (Scottdale, PA: Herald, 1971), 21.
49 Gunden Clemens, *Woman Liberated*, 128.

nation of the first woman for pastoral ministry in the Mennonite church in 1973.

The church began to slowly see expanded leadership roles within congregations to include women. I (Nancy) witnessed the election of Dora Shantz Gehman as the first woman to the elder board at Prairie Street Mennonite Church, Elkhart, Indiana, in the late 1970s. The congregation previously had studied the issue of women in leadership. Even though there were members opposed to women in that role, the vote was unanimous. At seventy-five years of age, with all her gifts and her spiritual life, she was considered the exception to their opposition, and the congregation believed she would serve them well. This scenario played out in other settings across the church where a respected and gifted woman became the exception to the opposition. In the end, the selection was based on the person's character, spiritual life, and gifts, which was the biblical intent all along. Each incident moved women closer to fuller participation in the church.

"Report of Study Committee on the Ordination of Women," by the Illinois Conference Leadership Commission (March 26, 1973), and "The Role of Women in the Church," by the Mennonite Board of Congregational Ministries (June 1973)

The "Report of Study Committee on the Ordination of Women," by the Illinois Conference Leadership Commission (March 26, 1973), and "The Role of Women in the Church," by the Mennonite Board of Congregational Ministries (June 1973), were both written in response to the request of the Lombard Mennonite Church of Lombard, Illinois, to ordain Emma Sommers Richards, whom they had called to be a pastor in their congregation in 1972.[50] Both ultimately recommended the ordination of Richards, making her the first North American woman to be ordained by any Mennonite denomination in the modern era (1970 and following).

---

50 See James E. Horsch, John D. Rempel, and Eldon D. Nafziger, eds., *According to the Grace Given to Her: The Ministry of Emma Sommers Richards* (Elkhart, IN: Institute of Mennonite Studies, 2013), 142.

An ordination account: Emma Sommers Richards (1973)
Emma Sommers Richards had served as a missionary in Japan with her husband, Joe Richards. She preached regularly during her time there. Back in the United States she taught in school, while Joe was a school principal and part-time pastor at Lombard Mennonite Church in Illinois. Eventually it became too much, and so Joe considered ending his time as pastor. When the congregation asked what could change his mind, he suggested calling Emma to co-pastor with him. She accepted, although she reminded the congregation that Mennonites do not ordain women. Emma loved the church and felt that, when invited by the church to do something, one should say yes. The congregation approached the Illinois Mennonite Conference (Mennonite Church [MC]) with a request for Emma's ordination. The conference in 1972 appointed a study committee made up of representatives from the congregation, the Illinois Mennonite Conference, and Mennonite Board of Congregational Ministries. On March 26, 1973, the study committee recommended to the conference delegates that Emma be ordained because of her sense of call and the congregation's affirmation of her call and her gifts. There was some vocal opposition, mainly by two men, one of whom pushed the presenter of the report aside and took over the podium to protest. In spite of their protests (or because of their behavior during their protests), the delegates voted to allow the Lombard congregation to ordain Emma to pastoral ministry but did not open the door for other women to be ordained.

By first calling her to the pastoral position and then subsequently calling for her ordination, the church created an occasion akin to that described in Acts 10 and 11. In both of these situations, experience came first, and then theology followed and was formed by the experience. The documents reviewed the biblical writings that appeared to be relevant and then looked at alternative models of how to live these out in the church and called on the church to continue to engage in this discernment. Finally, they "recommended that Emma Richards be ordained to the ministry."[51] She was ordained on June 17, 1973, for pastoral ministry. The day following the ordination, Ivan Kauffmann sent a report of the ordination service to the Mennonite media journals and to church leadership persons. These study documents and the subsequent ordination represented a major move in the direction of the church becoming more open to women in the ordained ministry.[52]

"Understanding Ordination," adopted by the GCMC upon recommendation of its Committee on the Ministry (1974)

Led by Jacob T. Friesen as director of ministerial leadership, the GCMC was quick to act so as to also be on record as supporting the ordination of women. The October 1972 issue of *The Mennonite* reported that the Committee on the Ministry was bringing its study on the ministry to congregations: "In its September meeting, the General Conference Committee on the Ministry made final plans for the study and discussed a number of other issues concerning the ministry: divorce and remarriage, ordination of women."[53] According to the report in *The Mennonite*, the document stated, "Affirming that in Christ there is neither male nor female, and that God is no respecter of persons, there are no barriers as to who may be called to serve as a pastor. Neither age, race, nor sex is a proper criterion. The sole criterion is whether the person has the necessary gifts to serve the church."[54]

Bringing such a bold statement to the denominational binational delegate body would put the entire denomination in support of the ordination of women. It would be a distinct advantage for the GCMC, making it so that area conferences would not be left to make conflicting decisions. As *The Mennonite* wrote, "But

---

51 Report of Study Committee on the Ordination of Women, by the Illinois Conference Leadership Commission, Mar. 26, 1973, 4.

52 For more on the ordination of Emma Sommers Richards, see Horsch, Rempel, and Nafziger, *According to the Grace Given to Her*.

53 "Study on Ministry Ready for Distribution Soon," *The Mennonite*, Oct. 31, 1972, 635.

54 "Study on Ministry Ready for Distribution Soon," 635.

one question was not settled: If a local church requested the ordination of a woman, would the district conference have the authority to deny this?"[55]

In August 1974, the GCMC approved the document "Understanding Ordination," which included slightly revised wording to the section supporting women in ministry: "Affirming that in Christ there is neither male nor female and that God is no respecter of persons, neither race nor class nor sex should be considered barriers in calling a minister."[56]

An ordination account: Marilyn Miller (1976)

Two years after the approval of the "Understanding Ordination" document, the first woman was ordained in the GCMC. Marilyn Miller had pursued theological study at Iliff Theological Seminary in Denver, Colorado, and following graduation, she was called to serve as a co-pastor of Arvada Mennonite Church in suburban Denver. She was ordained there on September 19, 1976. She said at the time, "For me, the way I can best live my Christian life at this moment is to be in the pastoral ministry."[57]

In an interview I (Nancy) had with Marilyn Miller, she talked about having sensed a call since she was a little girl, preaching often to her siblings and even to the chickens. She remembers the time her pastor shared the need for more pastors and encouraged the congregation to pray that men would respond to the call. Later outside alone with God, she asked why she had not been made a man if more pastors were needed. She had a deep longing to serve. She decided that, if pastoral ministry was not an option, then she would consider another field of study. Fortunately, the need for the family to move due to her husband's work moved her close

---

55 "Study on Ministry Ready for Distribution Soon," 635.

56 This document was printed in the revised *Minister's Manual* of 1983, edited by Heinz and Dorothea Janzen, as Appendix C, 173–77; quote from 177.

57 See Jan Lugibihl, "Celebrating a Woman's Gift," *The Mennonite*, Jan. 18, 1977, 35–36; Laurie Oswald Robinson, "Pioneer Pastor," *The Mennonite*, March 1, 2013, 12–16.

to a seminary and to opportunity. Eventually she was called to the pastoral team at Arvada Mennonite Church within Western District Conference, which was open to ordaining a woman pastor. Unlike in Emma Sommers Richards's story, there was no study or discussion about ordaining her. She continues to serve the Mountain States Mennonite Conference by mentoring young pastors, both male and female, with wisdom and grace.

Ongoing resistance to women's ordination

For male pastors the path to ordination was a uniform and predictable process across the church. But for most women pastors in the 1970s and 1980s, the path often had a messy or complicated story that included struggle, pain, endurance, and a strong faith in God. Richards once had a man walk out when she was the guest preacher. She stopped wearing a name tag at churchwide conventions to avoid being confronted. Miller remembered a man, in public, calling women pastors "wolves in sheep's clothing." She also heard a man in a workshop say women could not be preachers because they did not have the ability to confront. She confronted him by informing him that she was a pastor, and he shut up. Miller said she felt the most resistance when she headed east for church meetings and felt the women there had it harder than she did. Richards once told a group of pastors that a woman had to be twice as good at every level to be accepted.

Other women pastors, especially through the 1980s, had similar stories, whether it was criticism about the clothes they wore (in one case a male complaint was about a white cotton long-sleeve blouse with a high-neck collar that "revealed too much") or that women's voices did not sound as good over the mic. Women pastors were often confronted by people with the Bible in hand. Many women experienced having their remarks being dismissed, ignored, or assigned as a male contribution. At one point in the late 1980s, an anonymous person from Pennsylvania mailed to some of the women pastors across the church a pamphlet quoting a late 1770s sermon on the appropriate role of women in the church. Criticisms came from both men and women. When asked about how she dealt with conflict, Richards said she took heart that the criticism was directed only to the fact that she was a woman and was never directed to her integrity, spirituality, or gifts. That was usually true for women pastors in those early days. The important thing was for women pastors to keep focused on their call and their spiritual life and not be surprised about what might come out of people's mouths. A little sense of humor helped. Once when I (Nancy) was introduced as a woman pastor, the man's response was, "I didn't know they allowed women to do that," to which I replied, "I guess I just slipped through."

An ordination account: Kenneth and Anne Neufeld Rupp (1976)

One of the ways in which some women gained access to ministry positions and to ordination was by presenting themselves with their male spouse as a pastoral team. Kenneth and Anne Neufeld Rupp met as students at Mennonite Biblical Seminary in the 1960s. Through their early years together, Anne was not the typical pastor's wife; she occasionally preached and shared with Ken in various ministry roles. Finally, in candidating for the single pastoral position at the Pleasant Oaks Mennonite Church in Middlebury, Indiana, they came as a team sharing one full-time position. Neither of them was lead pastor; both shared in the preaching and otherwise using their gifts as called on or needed. Anne Neufeld Rupp was ordained in Middlebury on November 7, 1976, the first woman ordained by the Central District Conference (GCMC). Erland Waltner, president of Mennonite Biblical Seminary at the time, led in the ordination service.[58]

"Do the Scriptures Support or Oppose the Ordination of Women?" by Alvin Beachy (1979)

Former pastor and then professor of Bible and religion at Bethel College in North Newton, Kansas, Alvin Beachy wrote a paper titled "Do the Scriptures Support or Oppose the Ordination of Women?" in 1979 at the request of the Western District Con-

---

58 Personal conversation with Anne Rupp, May 8, 2019.

ference Ministerial Committee. The introduction reflected that, by that time, several women were already serving in pastoral positions within the district conference. However, there was continuing debate and disagreement from other congregations, often centering on biblical quotations that seemed contrary to the increasing acceptance of women in ministry. Using the best of biblical scholarship, Beachy systematically worked through the extensive biblical texts dealing with women. Adding quotes of scholars to his own scholarship, he made a strong case that there is nothing in the biblical text that ultimately prevents the ordination of women. Shaping his argument most clearly by the Synoptic Gospels—in true Anabaptist form—Beachy made the claim that Jesus stands with and for women in a patriarchal society: "If there is any scriptural basis for refusing to ordain women to the Christian ministry, simply because they are women, it cannot be found, in our opinion, either in the recorded teachings of Jesus or in the attitudes which the Gospels record that he displayed toward them."[59]

An ordination account: Doris Weber (1979)

Doris Weber grew up in the Western Ontario Mennonite Conference, which had Amish roots. When she was a child in the 1930s and 1940s, her parents took the family to many musical events in churches beyond the Mennonite fold. In one congregation the female pastor of the church introduced the musicians. The next morning Doris asked her mother if she thought Doris might be able to be a pastor someday. Her mother did not think so, but Doris never let go of that possibility.

After her sixth child began school, Weber returned to school to receive her Bachelor of Arts and Master of Divinity degrees. During these years she began pastoral ministry with her husband, Rod, at Avon Mennonite Church in Stratford, Ontario, in the early 1970s. Rod received the original invitation but insisted that Doris

---

[59] Alvin Beachy, "Do the Scriptures Support or Oppose the Ordination of Women: An Inquiry Based upon a Christological Interpretation of the Bible" (1979), 15.

be included in the pastoral call. Her ministry was built on a strong foundation of God's love and welcoming arms for the people she served. Preaching and pastoral care became opportunities to practice listening and loving. Bringing a woman's perspective opened a broader way to understand God and to address concerns that specifically impacted women. Co-pastoring with a spouse meant navigating differences in gender, differences in style, and the risk of ministry taking over family time. At times co-pastoring led to comparisons that created stress in the marriage.[60]

On March 8, 1979, Doris and Rod were both commissioned at Avon Mennonite Church. The conference minister was supportive of women in ministry, and in an era when ordination was downplayed, he thought commissioning would be more acceptable to the congregation. A short time after the commissioning, the commissioning document was replaced by an ordination certificate from the conference.[61]

Doris would go on to pastor numerous congregations on her own. She readily accepted interim ministry roles with the conviction that, if congregations had an experience with a pastor who was a woman, their fears would lessen.[62] In 1984, Doris and I (Karen) met as students at Associated Mennonite Biblical Seminaries (AMBS). I was twenty-five years old and became engaged that year, and Doris and Rod did our premarital counseling. My memory of Doris is one of a warm yet fearless pastor who was forthright and transparent. Marital issues were interwoven with reflection on the challenges and opportunities of co-pastoring, something we were considering. A possibility that had emerged within Doris more than forty years prior was taking hold in a new generation.

---

60 Mary A. Schiedel, *Pioneers in Ministry: Women Pastors in Ontario Mennonite Churches, 1973–2003* (Kitchener, ON: Pandora; Herald, 2003), 24–31.
61 Phone conversation with Doris Weber, April 2019.
62 Schiedel, *Pioneers in Ministry*, 117.

114 • John A. Esau, Nancy Kauffmann, and Karen Martens Zimmerly

"Leadership and Authority in the Church," by Mennonite Board of Congregational Ministries (1980)

Several things were happening among Mennonites during the decades between 1970 and 2000. Two Mennonite groups, one known simply as the Mennonite Church (MC), and the other as the General Conference Mennonite Church (GCMC), were finding their way with increasing levels of cooperation and collaboration, which eventually resulted in the merger on February 1, 2002, that formed Mennonite Church USA and Mennonite Church Canada. Throughout this time both groups worked separately and sometimes cooperatively on common agenda. For instance, issues of pastoral leadership were coming under intense scrutiny. Mixed into this was the separate but not disconnected question of women in ministry. Finally, there were major challenges concerning what the church believed about and how it practiced the rite of ordination and credentialing for servants of the church. Each of these issues was taken on by representatives of the MC who prepared the 1980 study guide *Leadership and Authority in the Church*.[63] The group was led by Ralph Lebold, who served as the task force chairman, and the study guide was written by Harold E. Bauman, staff person for the leadership office of Mennonite Board of Congregational Ministries. Session 4 was titled "Women in Church Ministries." Participants were invited to consider both the "limiting passages" in scripture and those passages concerning both Jesus and Paul and their "positive teachings" in "the relation of men and women in the church." Finally, the guide asked the question for the present, "What are the implications of the New Testament teachings and examples for women in church ministries today? Some congregations are selecting women to serves as elders, some as ministers (pastors), most often in a team setting."[64]

---

63 Mennonite Board of Congregational Ministries, *Leadership and Authority in the Church: A Study Guide and Study Report* (Scottdale, PA: Mennonite Publishing House, 1980).

64 Schiedel, *Pioneers in Ministry*, 31.

This document represented a bold effort to move the conversation and developing policies forward, but more was to come.

An ordination account: Joyce Shutt (1980)

At the request of the Fairfield Mennonite Church of Fairfield, Pennsylvania, the Ministerial Committee of the Eastern District Conference of the GCMC agreed to interview Joyce Shutt for ordination. Evidently the interview had gone well, but the committee did not agree to carry out the ordination event. Instead, representatives of the larger General Conference were called by the congregation to carry out the ordination service on May 18, 1980. Jacob T. Friesen, representing the denominational ministerial leadership office, and Marvin Zehr, representing the denominational Committee on the Ministry, were present to conduct the service of ordination of Joyce Shutt. Friesen interprets this as a legitimate appeal from the area conference level to the denominational level to resolve the disagreement about the ordination of women.[65] Shutt later said she was moved when people from across the United States and Canada came and laid hands on her, forming one long chain throughout the whole congregation. Almost a year later at the Eastern District Conference annual session, debate continued over the conference's response concerning the ordination of women and specifically concerning the ordination of Shutt. Unresolved were questions of denominational authority versus conference authority versus congregational autonomy. Shutt, however, brought a moment of grace when she stated before the assembly: "I wish to express my deep appreciation to the [district conference] Ministerial Committee for the loving, caring way they have related to me."[66]

An ordination account: Martha Smith Good (1982)

Martha Smith Good studied at AMBS in the early 1970s, when female students were finding their voice as leaders in gatherings

---

65 Personal interview with Jacob T. Friesen, April 30, 2019.
66 "Shutting Out Division over Women's Ordination," *The Mennonite*, May 19, 1981, 314–15.

outside the classroom. By the time she came to Guelph Mennonite Church in Guelph, Ontario, she had already served in several Mennonite congregations in both Canada and the United States. Smith Good was well acquainted with the joy and sacred trust of being a pastor. She had also experienced church structures and male colleagues that assumed male power and leadership. When an all-male elder board expected her to serve the snacks, she gently declined and stated that the one who brought the snacks should serve them. She learned to set boundaries and claim her position as equal.[67]

The struggle for ordination was painful. Initially the conference denied the request of Smith Good's congregation, without giving clear reasons.[68] Smith Good persisted and asked to meet with the conference personnel committee. The chair, who was the only woman on the committee, abdicated her role and invited Smith Good to lead the meeting. When Smith Good asked for transparency regarding their decision, she was met with silence. She courageously named that they had not spoken to her directly about an earlier experience of stress in ministry and made assumptions leading to the ordination denial. Since she met the qualifications of the current ordination guidelines, Smith Good let them know she expected to hear from them shortly for an ordination interview and then left.[69] In April 1982, she became the first woman ordained in the Mennonite Conference of Ontario and Quebec. In joyful worship and celebration with the congregation and her family, she was able to offer forgiveness for what had taken place earlier.

---

67 Schiedel, *Pioneers in Ministry*, 34.

68 Schiedel, *Pioneers in Ministry*, 35.

69 Martha Smith Good, *Breaking Ground: One Woman's Journey into Pastoral Ministry* (self-published, Pandora Printshop, 2012), 129–31.

"Resolution on the Ministry of the Women in the Church," Mennonite Brethren (1981)

The Mennonite Brethren represent a third major body of Anabaptist faith and heritage; they have spoken to the question of women in ministry and the further question of ordination of women with unusual clarity, albeit from a more conservative theological orientation. Before 1957, both married and single women missionaries were among those ordained by the Mennonite Brethren Church, so Mennonite Brethren do have an earlier history of ordaining women. Then in 1957, they addressed the credentialing of women for missionary service: "That in view of the fact that we as an M.B. Church, on the basis of clearly conceived Scriptural convictions, do not admit sisters to the public Gospel preaching ministry on par with brethren, we as Conference designate the fact of setting aside sisters to missionary work a 'commissioning' rather than 'ordination.'"[70]

However, the issue remained alive concerning women serving congregations in North American settings. In 1981, the denomination passed the "Resolution on the Ministry of the Women in the Church." It recognized the many significant contributions of women in the life of the church; nevertheless, it concluded in the following manner: "We do not hold that the passages in the New Testament (such as 1 Corinthians 14 and 1 Timothy 2), which put restrictions on the Christian woman, have become irrelevant, even though they were given in a different cultural context and, therefore, do need to be re-applied. And while we recognize that women played a significant role in the early church—something we would encourage them to do in our day as well—we do not believe that the Mennonite Brethren Church should ordain women to pastoral leadership."[71] The issue would not go away. Even-

---

[70] "Rules Concerning Ordination," in "We Recommend . . . Recommendations and Resolutions of the General Conference of Mennonite Brethren Churches," compiled by A. E. Janzen and Herbert Giesbrecht (1978), 177–80.

[71] "Resolution on the Ministry of the Women in the Church" in *Yearbook, 55th session, General Conference of Mennonite Brethren Churches, August*

tually the Mennonite Brethren permitted women to hold any position other than lead pastor,[72] and the Canadian Mennonite Brethren opened the door to women for all ministry positions in 2006.[73]

Ordination accounts: Dorothy Nickel Friesen, Lois Barrett, Patty Shelly (1985)

Church polity can create complex realities. Dorothy Nickel Friesen was called to serve as pastor of the Manhattan Mennonite Fellowship in Manhattan, Kansas. Attempting to reach broadly to the largest body of Mennonite support, this university-related congregation was jointly sponsored by the Western District Conference (GCMC), the South Central Conference (MC), and the Southern District (MB). There was considerable difference concerning the ordination of women among these three bodies. Some in South Central Conference were caught off guard when their reciprocal agreement with Western District Conference concern-

---

7-11, 1981 (Winnipeg, MB: Kindred, 1981), 46–47, available online at the Online Anabaptist Mennonite Library, www.anabaptistwiki.org.

72 In recent years, Willow Avenue Mennonite Church of Clovis, California, named Audrey Hindes as their "pastor" and avoided the language of "lead pastor."

73 Paul Schrag, "U.S. MBs Discuss Women in Pastoral Ministry," *Mennonite World Review*, Feb. 4, 2019, 2. In January 2019 the U. S. Mennonite Brethren called together a study conference on "The Bible and Women in Pastoral Ministry." Reports of the conference in the Mennonite media suggest that the issues remain unresolved. Retired Mennonite Brethren pastor and professor Larry Martens concluded: "An ongoing pastoral task for each generation is to engage in this kind of conversation about what holds us together and what are the issues where we have freedom and can bless one another as we live out the gospel." For a history of the Mennonite Brethren and women in ministry, see Douglas J. Heidebrecht, *Women in Ministry Leadership: The Journey of the Mennonite Brethren, 1954–2010* (Winnipeg, MB: Kindred Productions, 2019). The book notes that no other issue received the same level of attention in the church in the last half of the twentieth century. See also Dora Dueck, ed., *On Holy Ground: Stories by and About Women in Ministry Leadership in the Mennonite Brethren Church* (Winnipeg, MB: Kindred Productions, 2022).

ing ministerial credentials meant that South Central Conference suddenly had its first two women pastors, their credentials processed by Western District. Approval came down to a critical vote to jointly support Nickel Friesen and Lois Barrett by the South Central Conference—following a conference survey, a special conference session in Oklahoma City, and a final processing of Nickel Friesen's and Barrett's calls to ministry. The Mennonite Brethren Southern District agreed simply to list Nickel Friesen as "other" and withdrew their financial support of the Manhattan congregation.[74] Nickel Friesen and Barrett were ordained in 1985 in separate services—Barrett at Mennonite Church of the Servant in Wichita, Kansas, a dually affiliated congregation of GCMC and MC. Also ordained that year at First Mennonite Church, Denver, Colorado, was Patricia (Patty) Shelly by Western District Conference (GCMC) and Rocky Mountain Mennonite Conference (MC).

Ordination accounts: Rachel Fisher and Nancy Kauffmann (1986)

Rachel Fisher's pastoral journey began in 1975, when she was called to the pastoral team at College Mennonite Church in Goshen, Indiana. Indiana-Michigan Mennonite Conference was not credentialing women at the time and instructed the congregation to commission her. At least one male on the team was later ordained. In 1977, the congregation began its own study on the ordination of women, which eventually morphed into whether the practice of ordaining anyone was "suitable to the Mennonite tradition; and whether rituals of consecration should include all members, not just leaders."[75]

When I (Nancy) arrived on the pastoral team in September 1981, the study had concluded that the entire congregation accepts the call to ministry and mission from God instead of ordaining any pastor, male or female. The pastors would be commissioned along

---

74 Dorothy Nickel Friesen, *The Pastor Wears a Skirt* (Eugene, OR: Resource Publications, 2018), 16–20.

75 Ervin Beck, ed., *College Mennonite Church 1903–2003* (Goshen, IN: College Mennonite Church, 2003), 10.

with the whole congregation. During my interview, the conference's Church Life Commission raised questions about the path the congregation was taking. The commission then questioned Arnold Roth, the pastoral team leader, about the congregation's decision not to follow the conference's protocol for credentials, which had changed since their 1975 protocol of not credentialing women pastors. The conference's concern, as reported in their September 23 minutes, was twofold: (1) what College Church's departure from the usual procedure would say to the rest of conference and (2) whether College Church was using the term *commissioning* so not to license or ordain a woman. Arnold explained the congregation's process and stated that the congregation may be prophetic in the move to not ordain anyone.

On September 27, 1981, I and the other pastors, congregational leaders, and members were all commissioned in the same service. A several-page bulletin was developed scripting out everything to the smallest detail that was to be said and by whom. There was no designated leader, but one person stood at a small lectern off to the side to begin reading when it was the congregation's turn to respond. The result of the worship service brought on a great deal of strong negative feedback from members. A number of challenges arose with the decision to move in this direction. In the leadership's attempt to be prophetic, they had complicated that intent by choosing a word, *commission*, that already had its own meaning in the church and attempting to give it a different meaning. The concept never caught on within the conference, nor was it well understood by most congregational members. One example of the difficulty in the word choice was when I was denied access to the county jail during pastor-designated hours. A letter from the congregation stating that I was "duly recognized as a Christian minister and should be granted those privileges normally granted to a Christian minister" finally gave me access to visit.

When Roth resigned in 1985, the leadership had a dilemma. Some members were calling for an ordained pastor and were concerned that a new pastor joining the team would not want to be referred to as commissioned rather than ordained. By then the conference had recently affirmed "Guidelines for Certification for Ministry," which outlined "common usage in the Mennonite Church in order to foster continuity and unity."[76] Because of members' concerns and the conference's recent clarification, the board of elders decided that College Mennonite would fall into step with the conference. In March 1986, the congregation—with conference participation—held a recognition service for Rachel and me. From that point on, the language of our credential was changed to "ordained," and for two newer pastors, Phil Clemens and Rosemary Widmer, was changed to "licensed toward ordination." Later that year within the conference several other women pastors were moved from commissioned to ordained.

An ordination account: Margaret Richer Smith (1986)

Some women held off ordination because of their own personal beliefs. Margaret Richer Smith was licensed in 1979 and formally ordained in 1986. She reflects,

> The reason it took so long was because I had a strong belief in the priesthood of all believers. I felt baptism was an ordination for all followers of Jesus. I had both congregations and conference ministers nudging me to think otherwise, and I finally gave in on 1986, because Willis Breckbill [Indiana-Michigan Conference Minister] did not know what to do with me and asked me to please just comply. Then I did find it meaningful when those I had pastored for several years literally laid hands on me and prayed over me as I knelt. So humbling! I came to understand that being a pastor is a specific calling in the Body of Christ and to be ordained for that makes sense now. But I still like the idea of all of us who have said yes to baptism being ministers together.[77]

---

76 "*Recommended Guidelines for Certification for Ministry,*" Indiana-Michigan Mennonite Conference Assembly book (July 1985), C-10.
77 Email, Margaret Richer Smith to Nancy Kauffmann, May 3, 2019.

"Calling and Confirming Particular Ministries in the Church" (1986)

The Mennonite Church perceived that it had unfinished business on the larger subject of ordination and hence called for the consultation with that focus in May 1986. A significant footnote appears regarding women in their final convergence document, "Calling and Confirming Particular Ministries in the Church":

> A majority of participants in the Waterford consultation favored equal eligibility of men and women for all the ministries of the church. There was some dissent, however, from inclusion of women in ministries usually confirmed by ordination. The majority agreed on several words of exhortation to the church including: (a) We acknowledge that we have not used full the gifts of women in our church life. (b) We encourage conferences who have not studied the issue of women in ministry to do so. (c) We encourage conferences to approve the ordination of women for congregations requesting the same. (d) We encourage our congregations and conferences to respect each other in their decisions regarding the ordination of women.[78]

"Ordinal: Ministry and Ordination in the GCMC" (1986)

When I (John) assumed the position of director of ministerial leadership for the GCMC in January 1985, the Committee on the Ministry gave me one specific assignment along with a larger job description. They perceived that it was time to come to some greater sense of unity in our theology and our policy and procedures related to ministry in and for the church. The result of that assignment was the 1986 document "The Ordinal: Ministry and Ordination in the GCMC," or simply, the "Ordinal." By that time women were making significant strides toward acceptance as

---

78 This appears as a footnote in "Calling and Confirming Particular Ministries in the Church," the final document from the Consultation on Ordination in the Mennonite Church, which took place May 14–15, 1986.

fully ordained ministers and chaplains in and for the church. The "Ordinal" was written with the full understanding that women were eligible candidates for every position of ministry, from conference ministers in what we called "the bishop tradition" to pastors of "the elder tradition" to various forms of lay or special ministry in "the deacon tradition."[79] The World Council of Church document *Baptism, Eucharist, and Ministry* was one of the sources for the "Ordinal," including its stance on women in ministry.[80]

An ordination account: Ruth Boehm (1992)

Ruth Boehm began in 1989 as youth pastor at Bethel Mennonite Church, Winnipeg, at the age of twenty-five. She was a second-generation woman in ministry as she had experienced vibrant female pastoral leadership and mentoring in Ontario where she grew up. Her focus at Bethel was growing into being a pastor, whereas the congregation's issue was women in ministry. She received good support from her male colleagues. She also sensed she had better not "screw up" since this would reflect on the senior pastor and the risks he was taking with this issue.

Boehm delayed to her second term the ordination process that Bethel had established for its ministers. The ordination committee was assembled and invited the conference into the process. This was different from what Boehm had experienced in Ontario, where the conference took the lead with a two-year licensing process. The committee was extremely careful and clear that this was a church issue and not a personal issue, knowing there was some opposition to having a female pastor. Some of those most opposed were women who had experienced significant leadership in infor-

---

79 "Ordinal" (1986), 15–18.

80 *Baptism, Eucharist and Ministry*, Faith and Order Paper No. 111 (Geneva: World Council of Churches, 1982). Concerning women, it states: "Those churches which practice the ordination of women do so because of their understanding of the Gospel and of ministry. . . . They have found that women's gifts are as wide and varied as men's and that their ministry is fully blessed by the Holy Spirit as the ministry of men. None has found reason to reconsider its decision" (21).

mal roles. The committee recommended to church leadership that Boehm be ordained based on the thorough process of discernment that had taken place rather than a vote. Boehm and a large gathering, including family and many congregations, celebrated her ordination on November 1, 1992.[81]

Ministry seemed more difficult after ordination. Many in rural, southern Manitoba congregations were still against women in church leadership. Boehm felt she was on display now that she had made this ordination commitment. She wondered how well she spoke and whether she was competent. Then at a Women Doing Theology conference the critique came from the other end of the spectrum. There was open criticism that women who served as pastors had sold out to patriarchy. Fortunately, by this time she had a peer in Ardith Frey, a commissioned pastor in the Evangelical Mennonite Church conference. Her response was to stay calm and stay the course like a middle C or E in music that you return to.[82]

An ordination account: Karen Martens Zimmerly (1993)

From 1987–1992, I (Karen) was co-associate pastor with my spouse, Terry, at West Abbotsford Mennonite Church in the Fraser Valley, British Columbia. We were young seminary graduates and eager to test our gifts for ministry in a congregation that was open to both of us. Within days of our installation, we discovered that many in the congregation had understood my role in the traditional wife of a minister who would actively support her husband and be involved in the congregation but not have a pastoral job description or a paycheck. I was frequently asked what I could possibly do when I was in the church office. How could I

---

81 At the ordination service, Boehm wore a simple yet classy green dress sewn by her mother, and to express her feminine and fun sense of self, Boehm painted her toenails purple and wore purple undergarments. Mennonite Women Ordination Questionnaire, personal notes of Karen Martens Zimmerly, spring 2019.

82 Mennonite Women Ordination Questionnaire, personal notes of Karen Martens Zimmerly, spring 2019.

biblically defend pastoral ministry for women? Being a pregnant pastor would raise even more concerns, so we felt we needed to discuss this with the leadership before it became a reality.

Ordination was highly valued and seen as necessary to preside over communion. At one point when the senior pastor position was vacant, they wanted to ordain Terry. The conference minister discouraged Terry from accepting, as then the congregation would be less likely to struggle with accepting my ministry role. Terry said no. Congregational leaders, the majority who were male, struggled between restricting my pastoral duties to appease those who were strongly opposed and forging ahead with a study series that looked at seven areas of permissible leadership roles for women, including preaching and ordination of women. There seemed to be consensus, and the leadership developed a position statement that women could be ordained. A petition by twenty-six members opposed the consensus and requested that the issue "be brought to a congregational meeting, and be dealt with properly by a two-thirds majority vote."[83] A vote proceeded on each of the seven statements that had been studied earlier. The seventh statement permitting women to be ordained did not pass.

Despite challenge, opposition, and anxiety, these years were also meaningful. Younger adults were hungry for our love of biblical study and interpretation. They saw our co-ministry and co-parenting model as good news. I was also invited to preach and teach in other Mennonite congregations and serve on conference committees, putting me in touch with a wider circle that welcomed greater leadership from women. In 1992, we headed to Saskatchewan and became co-pastors at Grace Mennonite in Regina, where I was ordained on November 28, 1993.

"Confession of Faith in a Mennonite Perspective" (1995)

As the MC and GCMC moved toward merger, it was perceived that several unified statements might lend credibility to the union. The first of these was the 1995 *Confession of Faith in a Menno-*

---

83 West Abbotsford Mennonite Church membership meeting, Nov. 29, 1989.

nite Perspective. Article 15, "Ministry and Leadership," contains a brief statement of gender inclusiveness in ministry: "The church calls, trains and appoints gifted men and women to a variety of leadership ministries on its behalf. These may include such offices as pastor, deacon, and elder as well as evangelists, missionaries, teachers, conference ministers, and overseers."[84]

"A Mennonite Polity for Ministerial Leadership" (1996)

Though both the MC and GCMC had worked aggressively on questions dealing with ministry and ordination, it was perceived as necessary to bring this work together into a single document for the future church. A joint polity committee was established that worked for several years on what became the 1996 *Mennonite Polity for Ministerial Leadership*. Although there are several statements in the document regarding the inclusion of women, the following summarizes the commitment for the future:

> While women were active in key leadership roles in the Anabaptist reformation, we have for generations been influenced by patriarchal systems which assumed that only men could be ordained and provide ministerial leadership. Today, both denominations are moving together to affirm that God calls, gifts, and empowers both women and men for leadership positions in the church."[85]

---

84 *Confession of Faith in a Mennonite Perspective* (Scottdale, PA: Herald, 1995), 59.

85 *A Mennonite Polity for Ministerial Leadership* (Newton, KS: Faith and Life, 1996), 69. In 2014, a revised statement of ministerial polity was issued by Mennonite Church USA, *A Shared Understanding of Church Leadership*. By this time, gender inclusion was nearly assumed. However, the following statement appears to have been taken from the 1974 GCMC document "Understanding Ordination": "Affirming that in Christ 'there is no longer Jew or Greek, there is no longer slave or free, there is no longer male and female; for all of you are one in Christ Jesus' (Galatians 3:28), gender, race, social standing, or ethnic/cultural/national identity will not determine who is acceptable for ordination" (21).

An ordination account: April Yamasaki (1996)

In 1993, April Yamasaki attended Emmanuel Mennonite Church in Clearbrook, British Columbia, while teaching at the nearby Mennonite Bible College and writing and publishing materials on Christian living. When the pastor left suddenly, Yamasaki was asked to plan and lead four Advent worship services. After the first service, a woman asked, "How would you like to be the pastor of this church?" Yamasaki laughed it off, but she continued to be asked the same question by others, and finally the chair of the search committee called. The congregation had already done some good biblical study on the role of women in the church, and so they were ready to consider calling a woman.

God took Yamasaki from no thoughts about pastoral ministry to reluctantly meeting with the search committee to curiosity and finally to excitement. The initial call was for an interim period, but within that first year she was invited to become the lead pastor. The conference was ready to move forward with ordination. Yamasaki, however, was still getting used to the idea of being a pastor. She was aware that the wider church was adopting a two-year licensing process and suggested they follow that path. With ordination she was saying, "I've tested it, I've explored it, and I understand it now as an ongoing ministry for me." On October 27, 1996, she was the first woman ordained to pastoral ministry in the Conference of Mennonites in British Columbia.[86]

*Ordination accounts: Women as pastors
of Asian refugee churches*

In the 1980s and 1990s, Asian refugees arrived in Canada. Chinese, Laotian, Vietnamese, and Korean Christian leaders, with the help of Mennonite conferences, established fellowships and congregations across the country. Pastors in these groups were predominantly male, yet there were some women. Jean Hung was assistant pastor at Markham Chinese Mennonite Church in Ontario from 1993 to 1996, and Young-Jee Na served as co-pastor

---

86 Yamasaki would go on to serve the congregation for twenty-five years.

at the Valleyview Mennonite Church, a Korean congregation in London, Ontario, from 2001 to 2004.

Anna Dyck, who was ordained in 1953 as a missionary, became a church planter and pastor of three congregations in Japan. When she retired, she helped establish a fourth congregation in British Columbia, with the sponsorship of the Japanese churches.

Grace Mennonite Church in Regina, Saskatchewan, established Chinese and Laotian fellowships in 1988 within the congregation as a result of sponsoring refugees. Magdalena Widjaja, an Alliance-trained pastor, became the second pastor of the congregation's Chinese fellowship. She came from a large evangelical Indonesian congregation with understandings of the pastor being in charge. She had many adjustments to becoming a Mennonite pastor in the Canadian context. The fellowship was small, and the majority of attenders were Chinese university exchange students navigating a new culture, who would leave after four years of study. Accepting that decisions were shared with congregational leaders was new to Widjaja, yet she also learned to appreciate this support and accountability during challenging times of ministry. She was ordained in 1997.

Documenting change in the church

At the beginning of 1970, neither the *Handbook of Information* of the GCMC nor the *Mennonite Directory* of the MC had any women pastors listed. By 1980, the *Handbook of Information*, in the "Directory of Ordained/Commission Leaders" section, listed eleven women, both licensed and ordained, carrying official duties in the congregation, and four women as the congregational leader. The *Mennonite Directory* listed three women as licensed ministers, one woman as commissioned, and five women as lay leaders in a congregation. Emma Sommers Richards was still the only ordained woman pastor named.

By 1990, the *Handbook of Information* listed nineteen women licensed toward ordination, thirteen women ordained in a lead pastoral role, two women ordained as an associate pastor, ten women ordained for special ministries, six ordained women between assignments, and thirteen women commissioned to ministry. Listed in the *Mennonite Directory* were twelve women licensed toward ordination, twenty-four women ordained in a lead pastoral role, seven women ordained as an associate, ten women ordained for special ministries, eight women ordained between assignments, and five women commissioned. These numbers reflect some growth in the church's attitudes.

In 2000, the *Mennonite Directory* became a joint directory for the GCMC and the MC. By then there were seventy-six women licensed toward ordination, sixty-nine ordained women in a lead position, twenty-two ordained women in an associate position, forty-five ordained women for special ministries (including some on conference staff teams), thirty-two ordained women between assignments, forty-eight women licensed for special ministries, and eleven women listed as lay ministers. New additions to the listing of women ministers included twenty-six ordained women who were marked retired, four ordained women who were serving as conference ministry staff, and one ordained woman who was serving in a denominational ministerial leadership office. While there was significant growth in the number of women ordained across the church since the first woman had been ordained twenty-seven years earlier, there were still regional conferences and congregations that refused to ordain women for ministry.[87]

When I (Nancy) began as a conference regional minister for Indiana-Michigan Mennonite Conference in 2000, following Charlotte Holsopple Glick in that role, I discovered that some congregations had never had a woman preach in their congregation. Many of those same congregations were still using the 1963 *Mennonite Confession of Faith* (MC) rather than the 1995 *Confession of Faith in a Mennonite Perspective* (MC-GCMC). I also discovered that, when talking to a search committee about their openness to a woman pastor, the response back was sometimes something like this: "Well, yes, we are open to a woman [then a pause], but we want to make sure we get the best possible person." I have

---

[87] See the appendix in the present volume for a list of US and Canadian Mennonite women ordained between 1973 and 2005.

observed in the past thirty-four years that the women ordained to pastoral ministry were women of deep faith who loved God and the church and chose, in spite of the obstacles, to respond faithfully to God's call on their life. And the church was blessed. God will continue to call women and men into ministry to complete the purposes God has for the church.

In Canada, from the first few Mennonite women in pastorates in the 1970s, by 1985 there were twelve women in a diversity of Mennonite conferences that would eventually form Mennonite Church Canada. By 1990, there were twenty women, and by 2000 the number doubled to forty. By 2006, there were seventy-two women on the ministerial registry list. The denomination was growing in gender diversity among its pastors. Some of the women who began ministry in the 1970s and 1980s had given leadership in several congregations by 2006. After an initial experience with a female pastor, a number of these congregations would again hire a woman. But by and large the women in this era were the first in the congregation that called them. Thirty years since the first woman began as pastor, there were still approximately two-thirds of Mennonite Church Canada's 235 congregations that had not experienced the widening ways of understanding God and faith that come when women's voices and perspective are part of pastoral leadership.[88]

An enduring change

The move toward the ordination of women in the Mennonite church was not some short burst of enthusiasm but was an example of generational change. It has happened in our lifetime. In the perceptions of those women most involved in the earliest decades, the change appeared to be slow in coming and was often born out of conflict and controversy. Nevertheless, the move forward has been persistent and enduring. But it would be too hasty to conclude that, given the change that has occurred by the increasing acceptance and strong affirmation of the ordination of women

---

88 *Global Anabaptist Mennonite Encyclopedia Online*, s.v. "Mennonite Church Canada," Jan. 2018, gameo.org.

for ministerial leadership roles in the church, everything is now fine and there are no longer issues to be addressed. There is still the need to draw together issues of race and gender and invite the work of feminist and womanist theologians as we seek a more inclusive future. Nevertheless, it is encouraging to see that Mennonite women are today serving small, medium, and large congregations across North America. They are associate pastors, pastors of faith formation, and most often simply pastors. They are chaplains in institutions of care for the elderly and for various medical facilities. They are theologians and biblical scholars, teaching in church colleges and seminaries. They are administrators of the denomination and serve as area conference or area church ministers. Ordination as a three-way covenant among God, the church, and the ministering person continues to be a spiritual rite filled with meaning for women and men in ministry. Usually its impact catches the one being ordained as a surprising gift of grace, affirmation, and empowerment.

6

Surveys and conversations
Women pastors speak
Dorothy Nickel Friesen
and Diane Zaerr Brenneman

The preacher has breasts

and prays in liquid
voice, breathing
tenderness into the world.

Her words shake
the rocks packed hard
in my guts, melting them
smooth and clear to glaze
the glaring glass stains.

Now her voice slides
contours sand hills
and valleys,
curves,
landscaping scarred terrains.

It molds my will
with worn hands
telling me the story of the world
firming my listless spirit

to stand upright
on its finger-pressed base.

And then, coaxing,
the womanvoice pulls
at the plug which grips
itself at the pit of my being,
loosening, now plucking it
to release the thrashing currents
and still my soul.

—Raylene Hinz-Penner, May 23, 1990[1]

As the role of the ordained pastor in the Mennonite church emerged with "first" women's ordinations in 1973 and 1976, the floodgates broke open. Mennonite women attended seminary in greater numbers, and area conferences in both Canada and the United States extended ordination to women upon their congregations' requests. By 1992, the two largest Mennonite denominations, General Conference Mennonite Church (GCMC) and Mennonite Church (MC), recorded 10 percent of pastors were women.[2] Those twenty years were times of momentous change.

Change was happening not only in the secular culture in North America but also in the sacred halls of many Protestant, Catholic, and Jewish denominations. The movement for women's liberation was affecting congregations and seminaries, and sexism was recognized as prevalent in religion as in scores of other disciplines.

---

1 This poem was inspired by a female pastor's poetic prayers. Hinz-Penner reflected, "I began to believe that the poetic image, the female voice, even the female body in a pulpit, was having some effect on me." This poem was originally published in *Window to Mission*, June–July 1990, W-3, published by Women in Mission, General Conference Mennonite Church, and republished by permission of the author. Hinz-Penner now lives in North Newton, Kansas, after she retired from teaching at Washburn University, Topeka, Kansas.

2 Paul Schrag, "Acceptance of Women Pastors Varies in Different Conferences," *Mennonite Weekly Review*, Jan. 14, 1993, 1.

Mainline denominational study

Three sociologists, Barbara Hargrove (Iliff School of Theology), Jackson W. Carroll (Hartford Seminary), and Adair T. Lummis (Hartford Seminary) conducted a massive two-year research project in the early 1980s of more than thirteen hundred women and men clergy, seminary faculty, church executives, and lay people of nine major Protestant denominations (but not Mennonite). Their book contained in-depth and up-to-date information into the insights of clergywomen's new visibility, changing role, and impact on their church.[3] The reports of these interviews relayed experiences of women entering traditional male roles and offices. Several major findings were identified.

Two or three years into the 1970s, the numbers of women began to double and triple at most seminaries each year. In 1980, women made up about half of the MDiv students at most of the mainline seminaries.[4]

The strongest factor in women's decisions to be ordained was their belief that they had a call from God to the ordained ministry, like men. Less than a third of the women were seeking ordination in order to change the sexist nature of their denominations.[5]

Of the 635 clergywomen interviewed, 31 percent were married to a clergyman.[6]

While clergywomen acknowledged that the fact they were women probably entered into misunderstandings with laity and with senior pastors, their gender was not as important as other differences such as value, style, theology, and personality.[7]

---

3 Jackson W. Carroll, Barbara Hargrove, and Adair T. Lummis, *Women of the Cloth* (New York: Harper & Row, 1983).

4 Jackson W. Carroll, Barbara Hargrove, and Adair T. Lummis, "Women of the Cloth: New Opportunity for the Churches," *JSAC Grapevine* (Nov. 1982), 3.

5 Carroll, Hargrove, and Lummis, "Women of the Cloth," 3–4.

6 Carroll, Hargrove, and Lummis, "Women of the Cloth," 4.

7 Carroll, Hargrove, and Lummis, "Women of the Cloth," 5.

Women pastors seemed to have slightly more difficulty than men in negotiating these role demands on their time and activity, partly because they had less experience in the pastoral ministry than the vast majority of men, and no doubt also because the expectations of how women ministers should balance their professional and private lives were murkier than for men in pastoral ministry.[8]

Women's commitment to the parish ministry was less tied to their perceptions of ease of career mobility than those of young clergymen. Instead, their commitment to the parish ministry seemed more closely related to feeling challenged and effective in their parish work and not overly bored or isolated.[9]

Mennonite women pastor survey (1992–94)

For Mennonites, who were not part of the nine denominations studied or reported in *Women of the Cloth*, it was time to take the pulse of their women pastors to see what their experiences were as the "firsts" in Mennonite congregations, whether their experiences were similar to those from the other nine denominations, whether there were contexts that supported women in leadership, what the barriers were for women pastors in Mennonite congregations, and so on.

Renee Sauder, who had been associate pastor of Bethel College Mennonite Church, North Newton, Kansas, from 1983 to 1990, began a two-year role as coordinator of women in leadership ministries for the Mennonite Board of Congregational Ministries (MBCM) of the MC before assuming the lead pastor position of Erb Street Mennonite Church, Waterloo, Ontario, in 1992.[10] As

---

8 Carroll, Hargrove, and Lummis, "Women of the Cloth," 5.

9 Carroll, Hargrove, and Lummis, "Women of the Cloth," 6.

10 Sauder is a 1983 graduate of (now) Anabaptist Mennonite Biblical Seminary and was ordained in 1985. She has served in long-term and intentional interim pastorates in Kansas and Ontario over the last thirty-seven years. She has been an instructor in preaching and worship through the AMBS Pastoral Studies Distance Education Program, reflective of her passion for the spoken word. In May 2020, she retired from pastoral ministry at Stir-

coordinator of women in leadership ministries, her assignment was to survey women pastors who had served in GCMC and MC congregations in Canada and the United States from 1972 to 1992. Her twenty-two-page survey, modeled after the earlier nine-denomination survey, was sent to 186 women, and 134 surveys were returned, representing a 72 percent response rate.[11] Sauder wrote, "The high rate of return was an indication to me that the survey provided a forum for women to speak openly and candidly about their experiences, and of their desire to add their voice to understanding and determining the future role of women in leadership in our denomination."[12]

Major findings

The chances that a Mennonite church in North America would have a woman serving as its next pastor increased rapidly throughout the 1970s and 1980s.[13] One indicator of the pace of that change was the increase in the number of women enrolled in theological seminaries; 82 percent of the respondents had seminary training.[14]

In answer to the question, "What influenced you the most in your decision to pursue pastoral ministry?" 82 percent identified

---

ling Avenue Mennonite Church in Kitchener, Ontario, where she and her husband, Fred Loganbill, live. Poet and Bethel College Mennonite Church member Raylene Hinz-Penner reflected on Pastor Renee's effect on her in the poem that introduces this chapter.

11 See "Women in Pastoral Ministry Survey: General Conference and Mennonite Churches (1972–1992)," available online at https://archive.org/details/mennonite_women_in_ministry.

12 Renee Sauder, "A Survey: The Experience of Women in Pastoral Ministry," *Report* 114, May–June 1994, 10.

13 For complete survey findings, summarized here, see "Women in Pastoral Ministry Summary (1994)," available online at https://archive.org/details/mennonite_women_in_ministry. Also, see Renee Sauder, "Women in Pastoral Ministry Survey (1972–1992): Observations and Assessments," Pastor's Week, Elkhart, Indiana, Jan. 25, 1993.

14 Sauder, "Survey," 11.

"inner call" as the most important factor, far outweighing external factors such as "shoulder tapping" or congregational call.[15]

Fifty-one percent of respondents found a pastoral assignment within six months or less of graduation. The data suggested that first placements, which often represent entry level or stereotypically "female" positions (52 percent of respondents had worked as associates or assistants), are easier to acquire than second or third placements. What mattered to women who served as associates was that their ministry was taken seriously. Forty-two percent said they were not receiving enough feedback.[16] Forty-one percent of respondents expected that second or third placements would be difficult to find.[17] In answer to the question, "If you leave, do you think the congregation would call another woman?" 76 percent said yes. But when asked, "Did the congregation call another woman?" only 47 percent said yes. Women pastors said their congregations thought: "We've done our mission in hiring a female," or "This congregation has compromised with alternating male and female staff," or "I think my congregation really prefers male leadership."[18]

In their first placements, 71 percent of respondents said they were the first woman to have filled a pastoral position in that congregation.[19] One said, "It took 10 years of processing for the congregation to decide whether or not to ordain me. They did ordain me, with the stipulation that I do not preach."[20]

I (Dorothy) was the first woman to serve in a pastoral position when I was pastoral intern (credentialed in 1984) on the staff of Rainbow Boulevard Mennonite Church in Kansas City, Kan-

---

15 Sauder, "Survey," 11.
16 Sauder, "Women in Pastoral Ministry Survey," 4.
17 Sauder, "Survey," 11.
18 Sauder, "Women in Pastoral Ministry Survey," 3.
19 Sauder, "Women in Pastoral Ministry Survey," 2.
20 Sauder, "Women in Pastoral Ministry Survey," 3.

sas (1982–1984).[21] Being the "first" or "only" was my experience during nearly all my professional career in Mennonite congregations and institutions—an experience of many women ordained in the Mennonite church in the 1970s and 1980s.

Ninety-one percent of respondents had previously had full-time non-pastoral employment. For many women, pastoral ministry was a second or third career, and they brought with them a wide array of experience in other professions.[22]

Twenty-five women (19 percent) said the church experienced internal strife because they were called; 11 percent reported persons leaving the congregation because of their being called. Thirty-six percent said there was some opposition from their congregation to their being ordained.[23]

The level of satisfaction for women in ministry was high, and their sense of vocational stability in the congregation was strong. Ninety percent said they "usually" felt accepted and liked by members of their congregation; 49 percent said their pastoral position offered them maximum opportunity for expression of their talents for ministry; 59 percent said they were "very satisfied" or "satisfied" with their pastoral role in the congregation.[24]

My (Dorothy's) experience as a congregational pastor was very gratifying, and I was one who answered "very satisfied" on my survey. Although I previously enjoyed nearly ten years as a high school English teacher, I experienced greater fulfillment in the multifaceted role of pastor. Not only could I teach, but I could preach, counsel, administer, and lead.

---

21 I was the first woman full-time solo pastor of Manhattan Mennonite Fellowship, Manhattan, Kansas (1984–1990); the first female senior pastor at First Mennonite Church, Bluffton, Ohio (1995–2002); and the first female lead (executive) conference minister (Western District Conference, 2002–2010) for any area conference in Mennonite Church USA.

22 Sauder, "Survey," 12.

23 Sauder, "Survey," 12. For a deeper discussion about ordination in the Mennonite denominations, see chapter 5 of the present volume.

24 Sauder, "Survey," 12.

Most often, women pastors are questioned about their assumed conflict regarding time for self, family, and congregation. Can a woman pastor lead a "balanced" life? In answer to the survey question, "Do you have adequate time to spend with friends and family?" 59 percent said yes, and 41 percent said no.[25] "The loneliest clergy were those whose spouses tended to resent the amount of time they devoted to their work."[26]

Although sexual abuse was a topic in the culture, Mennonite women pastors needed to share their experiences via this anonymous survey opportunity. Twenty-four percent of respondents reported being sexually harassed. If co-pastors with spouse were removed from the tabulation, the number was 34 percent. (It was evident that working with one's spouse was a deterrent to sexual harassment.) In answer to the harassment question "by whom," it was reported: congregational members, 43 percent; pastoral colleagues outside the congregation, 27 percent; other pastoral staff, 16 percent; other church staff, 5 percent; and other, 8 percent.[27]

Sauder summary

Sauder concluded with several observations. First, the evidence was overwhelming that the role of the conference minister was influential in shaping the number and quality of placements in congregations. The conference minister played a key role in the process, whether by using formal authority or informal (but powerful) influence.[28] Second, the attitudinal shift that allowed women to respond to a call to ministry did not guarantee that women were accepted in the profession by our churches. "The positive change is greater than most people think, but smaller than most women would hope for."[29] Third, Sauder wrote, "We are in a new era of defining what male-female partnerships in ministry can be,

---

25 Sauder, "Survey," 12.
26 Sauder, "Women in Pastoral Ministry Survey," 3.
27 Sauder, "Women in Pastoral Ministry Survey," 3.
28 Sauder, "Women in Pastoral Ministry Survey," 11.
29 Sauder, "Women in Pastoral Ministry Survey," 11.

where trust and knowledge will be generously shared to enhance each other's ministry."[30]

In a summary paragraph, Sauder declared, "Women as pastors is not a passing phenomenon. The respondents to this survey form a chorus that bears a powerful message of a new creation, of an outpouring of an all-inclusive love, of the gospel mandate for all to be part of the body of Christ."[31] She added that women seem to work from a "base of inner strength and gumption in their call to a vocation that still holds many roadblocks for them."[32] "I was surprised at the frequency with which women indicated their surprise at discovering their giftedness and adequacy for ministry," she wrote. "Beneath the surface is a deeply acculturated sense of inadequacy. This tension between inner call and inner ambivalence is one that needs further attention."[33]

It was an extraordinary effort of MBCM to ask women pastors to share their experiences—some joyful, some painful—during the first twenty years of ordained ministry in the two Mennonite denominations, and women responded. While the nine-denomination Protestant survey was done about ten years earlier, the trends reported there were also experienced by the much smaller (and less studied) Mennonite groups. This second wave of feminism was clearly changing the leadership of all churches.

Mennonite pastors' survey (2005)

The next official effort of Mennonite Church USA to revisit the experience of women pastors was just as ambitious. This time, the scope of the survey was much wider and included male pastors. The 2005 "Survey of Women and Men in Ministry" was administered under the direction of Diane Zaerr Brenneman, denominational minister for executive leadership of Mennonite Church USA, and

---

30 Sauder, "Women in Pastoral Ministry Survey," 11.
31 Sauder, "Women in Pastoral Ministry Survey," 11.
32 Sauder, "Women in Pastoral Ministry Survey," 1.
33 Sauder, "Women in Pastoral Ministry Survey," 1.

in partnership with Mennonite Church Canada.[34] Administration and analysis of this survey were made possible through funding from the Pathways to Mission and Vocation program at Bluffton University (Ohio) by generous financial support from the Lilly Endowment, Inc., and the two denominational bodies.

When I (Diane) became a pastor in 1991, I was acutely aware that this role for women was still relatively new. I wanted to learn from women who answered the call to pastoral ministry before I did. So it was that I found myself having lunch with Renee Sauder in an Elkhart, Indiana, diner in the mid-1990s. I was pastoring in Iowa City and had come to Elkhart for the AMBS Pastors Week. Renee was there as well, and I wanted to hear her experience of being single in the ministry. (I particularly remember asking her about dating within the congregation!) Little did I know I would later serve in a denominational ministerial role not unlike Renee's and would be tapped to conduct a follow-up to her 1972–1992 survey of women in ministry.

Survey features

The 2005 survey had a few distinctive traits: it was administered with assistance from Bluffton University faculty and students, and it added a sample of male pastors in hopes it would enrich our picture of women in ministry. By this time, the United States and Canada were separate denominations (Mennonite Church USA and Mennonite Church Canada), but staff from the two churches continued to work together, and we surveyed both US and Canadian pastors.

Survey response was lower in 2005 (40 percent) than in 1992 (72 percent). I (Diane) pondered that significantly lower response. Perhaps it was more common to know women serving as pastors and therefore was less imperative to study ourselves. Wise wom-

---

34 See "Women in Pastoral Ministry Survey: Mennonite Church USA (1992–2005)" for the survey instrument of women pastors. See "Pastoral Ministry Survey: Mennonite Church USA (1992–2005)" for the survey instrument of male pastors. Both are available online at https://archive.org/details/mennonite_women_in_ministry.

en pastors build on the work of the women who pastored before us. Perhaps even more than a decade and a half later, there are things about ministry we can learn from our sisters and brothers in 2005.

Using the prior Sauder study as a reference document, the 2005 survey was impressive in its scope with over one thousand detailed items in the questionnaire. There were duplicate questions from that earlier survey, but there were new items as well. With the intentional inclusion of male pastors in the survey process, the experience of women pastors was now set in the context of female and male experiences in ministry. Did women practice ministry in different ways and with different assumptions than male pastors? Did Mennonite congregations expect women pastors to occupy the office of pastor the same as men? Now, twenty years later, were women recognized as leaders? Finally, were there fewer barriers to ordination, the "great hurdle"?

Another impressive feature of the 2005 survey was the use of academic research tools for the complete tabulation and initial analysis. Bluffton College professor of psychology Pamela S. Nath produced survey results that totaled nearly fifty pages.[35]

Survey findings

The sixteen-page survey was sent to all 417 US and Canadian women pastors and to a similarly sized sampling of 450 male pastors. There were completed and returned surveys by 169 women (75 percent US, 25 percent Canadian) and 129 men (73 percent US, 27 percent Canadian).[36]

The sample. Respondents were almost exclusively white.[37] The average age was 50.3 years for women, and 52.6 for men. Ages ranged from twenty-three to ninety-two. (I, Diane, know surveys

---

35 See Pamela S. Nath, "Women and Men in Mennonite Ministry Survey Results (June 2007)," available online at https://archive.org/details/mennonite_women_in_ministry.

36 Nath, "Women and Men," 10.

37 Nath, "Women and Men," 11.

need to be anonymous, but I wanted to sit with that ninety-two-year-old and hear her answers to our questions in person!)

We asked women and men to classify their role. We noted that, as in 1992, women were more likely to serve as associate pastors than as lead pastors and that women were named chaplain almost as often as associate pastor.[38] Of those surveyed, 17.7 percent of women and 45 percent of men were lead pastor; 13.3 percent of women and 5.4 percent of men were associate pastor; 13.9 percent of women and 3.6 percent of men were co-pastor with a spouse; 9.5 percent of women and 2.7 percent of men were co-pastor with a person other than a spouse; 2.5 percent of women and 7.2 percent of men were interim pastor; 1.9 percent of women and 2.7 percent of men were lay minister; 1.9 percent of women and .9 percent of men were minster or director of Christian education; 12.7 percent of women and 2.7 percent of men were chaplain; 7.6 percent of women and 6.3 percent of men were in church oversight; and 4.4 percent of women and 3.6 percent of men were seminary professor.

Role	Women	Men
Lead pastor	17.7%	45.0%
Associate pastor	13.3%	5.4%
Co-pastor with spouse	13.9%	3.6%
Co-pastor with person other than spouse	9.5%	2.7%
Interim pastor	2.5%	7.2%
Lay minister	1.9%	2.7%
Minister/Director of Christian Education	1.9%	0.9%
Chaplain	12.7%	2.7%
Church oversight	7.6%	6.3%
Seminary professor	4.4%	3.6%

Figure 6.1: Roles of survey respondents

---

38 Nath, "Women and Men," 11.

Job satisfaction. Most pastors were "satisfied" or "very satisfied" (82 percent women, 77 percent men) in Mennonite ministry. The majority of respondents in 2005 said they "almost never" or "never" have experienced burnout (61 percent) and have "almost never" or "never" thought seriously about leaving ministry (67 percent).[39] Although it was encouraging to see the majority numbers, it was of concern that nearly one third had experienced burnout and thought of leaving. This does not speak well of a workforce in general.

Significantly more women (52.4 percent) than men (35.2 percent) "usually" felt like they were accomplishing things in their ministry. Many of both men (95.2 percent) and women (93.9 percent) "usually" or "sometimes" felt this. And there were greater levels of satisfaction related to serving congregations with fewer members aged fifty or over. This satisfaction was unrelated to social class or theological positions (conservative versus liberal) of congregations.[40]

Leadership style and use of power. A new section of questions asked about leadership styles and use of power. Would ministry positions call for new leadership styles? We were curious. The 2005 survey sought to discover this in two major ways: (1) repeating items from the 1992 survey and (2) using new items from a survey by Edward C. Lehman.[41]

The 1992 survey items asked respondents to rate their leadership style on a ten-point scale with the endpoints of the scale being labeled "visionary" (I enjoy envisioning future goals for the congregation/dreaming about new possibilities) and "maintainer" (I enjoy carrying out already established goals). The 1992 survey also asked respondents to indicate their preferred decision-making style on a ten-point scale, endpoints being "maintaining the principle" (I make decisions based on the principle of the issue at

---

39 Nath, "Women and Men," 12.

40 Nath, "Women and Men," 12.

41 Edward C. Lehman, *Gender and Work: The Case of the Clergy* (Albany, NY: State University of New York Press, 1993).

hand) and "maintaining the relationship" (I make decisions based on the desire to maintain harmony in the relationship).

The 2005 survey found no gender differences on the visionary versus maintainer scale. The average response was 4.1 on a 7-point scale, toward the "visionary" end of the scale. But there were significant gender differences on the principle versus relationship scale. On a 7-point scale, women answered 6.3 and men 5.5 with 7 being the "maintaining relationships" end of the scale.[42]

Questions from the Lehman survey

Just as the Sauder survey (1992) mimicked a nine-denomination survey, the 2005 survey was informed by a 1990s survey by Lehman that studied women and men as pastors in mainline denominations. Lehman studied mainline Protestants and examined various potential differences between men and women in their leadership styles. The 2005 survey only included those items for which Lehman found gender differences. It used a five-point Likert scale with the anchor points zero meaning "not like me at all" and five meaning "very much like me." The four categories of items included were use of clergy power, empowerment of congregations, emphasis on rationality in decision making and problem solving, and ethical legalism.

The Lehman survey categories showed differences in ministry leadership styles between women and men. The 2005 survey also revealed these gender differences. Women were more likely to empower their congregations rather than focus on clergy power. Women were less likely to use rational problem solving and ethical legalism in their roles. However, there were differences among women as well as between women and men. Seminary attenders were less likely to show ethical legalism. Seminary attendance did not stand apart in any other ministry style. Those serving more liberal congregations were less likely to endorse clergy use of power and ethical legalism and more likely to identify with maintaining relationships in decision making. Those serving in congregations with smaller numbers of older people (people over fifty)

---

42 Nath, "Women and Men," 22.

were more likely to endorse rational problem solving. And those serving primarily middle- or upper-class congregations were less likely to endorse ethical legalism and more likely to identify with maintaining relationships in decision making. Greater levels of job satisfaction were associated with maintaining relationships in decision making and empowerment of congregations and less associated with clergy use of power and ethical legalism.[43]

Challenges facing women in ministry. The pressing questions in the early twenty-first century focused on functioning in a previously nearly all-male profession. Both women and men were asked what they saw as the three major challenges facing them in ministry. Answers from male pastors were not concentrated. There was considerable agreement on the most significant challenges for women. The top three according to women pastors were (1) structural or attitudinal gender inequalities faced by women (64 percent); (2) difficulty with balancing one's ministry with other aspects of one's life (57 percent); and (3) finding the most appropriate and effective ministry or leadership style (33 percent).[44]

Additional women's concerns were the need for role models or support (17 percent); recognizing one's call and dealing with doubt (15 percent); developing spiritually (12 percent); responding to critics of women in ministry (11 percent); developing sound doctrine (9 percent); surviving financially (6 percent); ministering to men (5 percent); establishing appropriate boundaries (4 percent); and dealing with challenges in the culture (2 percent).[45] One female pastor wrote, "Females are expected to maintain all the traditional stereotypical roles [of women] in addition to providing leadership. I have not yet met a male who was asked to lead a funeral service and bring two pies for the fellowship meal afterwards."[46]

---

43   Nath, "Women and Men," 25.
44   Nath, "Women and Men," 12.
45   Nath, "Women and Men," 32.
46   Nath, "Women and Men," 14.

There was some thought that women had a harder time than men getting second placements, as if congregations have "done their woman pastor thing" and then gone back to traditional male pastors. But the survey showed that most women report they found second placements in less than six months (58 percent); fewer men reported that to be true for them (41 percent). When asked about finding a second placement within a year, women reported 73 percent and men 66 percent. The majority reported the second placement involved a significant increase in responsibilities.[47]

The 2005 survey asked if their calling to the pastoral role led to internal strife in the congregation, and 16.7 percent of women said yes (compared to 19 percent in 1992). But interestingly, 20.8 percent of men reported their call led to internal strife in the congregation—higher than the women reported. We asked if their call led to people leaving the congregation. For women, 13.7 percent said yes (compared to 11 percent in 1992). A significantly fewer number of men reported their call led to people leaving the congregation (4.9 percent).[48] These results may not have reflected the contemporaneous experiences alone. It is possible some of the women who said yes in 2005 were remembering a conflict they also reported in 1992. It is not at all uncommon for congregations to experience some amount of conflict surrounding pastoral transitions. But conflicts regarding women's calls may be more intractable, at least for a small proportion of church members.

Top challenge: Structural or attitudinal gender inequalities. The survey asked male pastors about their attitudes, beliefs, and feelings toward women in pastoral ministry. Sixty percent were very positive, 15 percent positive, 17 percent neutral, 4 percent negative, and 4 percent very negative.[49] I (Diane) wonder if more male pastors who felt very negative about women in ministry simply did not return a completed survey.

---

47 Nath, "Women and Men," 14.
48 Nath, "Women and Men," 15.
49 Nath, "Women and Men," 16.

Male pastors were asked how knowing that the lead pastor was a woman would affect their attraction to a pastoral opening. Twenty-five percent said a woman lead made the position "somewhat" or "significantly" less attractive; 63 percent said it would not affect their attitude either way; and nearly 12 percent said it would make the position "somewhat" or "significantly more" attractive to them.[50] Seminary attendance was associated with more positive attitudes, but age and country of citizenship or service were not.

In about thirteen years between surveys, not only had the number of women serving increased, but their time percentages increased as well.[51] In 2005, 37 percent of women were full-time (compared to 26 percent in 1992); 19 percent were three-quarters-time (compared to 12 percent in 1992); 31 percent were half-time (compared to 37 percent in 1992); and 13 percent were less than half-time (compared to 25 percent in 1992). (While men were not interviewed in the 1992 survey, their numbers in 2005 were 62 percent full-time, 14 percent three-quarter-time, 14 percent half-time, and 11 percent less than half-time.) And yet, even with the increases in numbers and time percentages of women serving in ministry, the inequalities in attitudes and structures were still listed as the greatest challenge to women in ministry in 2005.

Employment status	2005 Women	2005 Men	1992 Women*
Full time	37%	62%	26%
Three-quarter time	19%	14%	12%
Half time	31%	14%	37%
Less than half time	13%	11%	25%
*Men were not surveyed in 1992.			

Figure 6.2: Employment status

---

50 Nath, "Women and Men," 18.
51 Nath, "Women and Men," 37.

Regarding reasons for working part-time, the most frequent reason cited by both men and women was financial constraints or size of the congregation (men, 52 percent; women, 39 percent). Both women and men noted part-time was an explicit choice: working as a co-pastor, being part of a pastoral team, needing time for family, and having the flexibility to participate in other activities (women, 41 percent; men, 9 percent). There was a significant difference in genders who cited family as a reason for working part-time (women, 20 percent; men, 0 percent).[52]

Second-ranked challenge: Finding balance. Balancing ministry and family was identified by 48 percent of women or more because an additional 14 percent mentioned risk of burnout without explicitly mentioning family. Only 14 percent of men explicitly identified balancing work and family as a challenge.[53] One woman pastor said, "The temptation to think you have to pastor perfectly is enough. . . . When you add needing to mother perfectly, it can become overwhelming. There is a seductiveness about both vocations (pastoring and mothering) that can be hard to resist." Another said, "More than once I've heard myself say, 'I need a wife!'" One male pastor said, "I think women in ministry are in an excellent position to model healthy limits to pastoral work. In the past, many male pastors have been swallowed by their churches and have been unavailable to their children. I believe women pastors may have a stronger voice to advocate for healthy limits to ministry expectations."[54]

Marital status. The marital status and parental status of women were significantly related to the number of hours they worked.[55] Of those surveyed, 64 percent of single women worked

---

52 Nath, "Women and Men," 38.

53 Nath, "Women and Men," 27.

54 Nath, "Women and Men," 26.

55 Of those surveyed, 85 percent of women and 96 percent of men were married (although one should be cautious about claiming this as a representative sample of the marital status of all pastors in 2005). Specifically, 9 percent of women and 0 percent of men were single (never married); 81

full-time versus 31 percent of married women; 14 percent of single women worked half-time or less versus 49 percent of married women; 59 percent of women without children worked full-time versus 31 percent of women with children; and 23 percent of women without children worked half-time or less versus 51 percent of women with children.[56]

Marital status	Women	Men
Single (never married)	9%	0%
Married	81%	92%
Widowed	1%	3%
Widowed and remarried	1%	2%
Divorced	5%	0%
Divorced and remarried	3%	2%
Separated	1%	1%

Figure 6.3: Marital status

Marital stress. Men and women answered the same when considering the pastoral role placing stress on the pastor's marriage. On a five-point scale where one was "very stressful" and five was "no more stressful than another occupation," both genders averaged 3.5 ("sometimes stressful"). Likewise, the impact of the schedule of a pastor on the family was mentioned by approximately one-third of both men and women (men, 36 percent; women, 33 percent).[57]

Barriers for women pastors. In her interpretation of the survey, Nath was clear that there were still obstacles for women

---

percent of women and 92 percent of men were married; 1 percent of women and 3 percent of men were widowed; 1 percent of women and 2 percent of men were widowed and remarried; 5 percent of women and 0 percent of men were divorced; 3 percent of women and 2 percent of men were divorced and remarried; and 1 percent of both women and men were separated.

56 Nath, "Women and Men," 28.
57 Nath, "Women and Men," 28.

pastors.[58] Acceptance of women was sometimes limited to certain positions, whereas other positions (e.g., lead pastor or conference leadership positions) were not available to them.[59] Women were more likely than men to experience sexual harassment, both in general and from members of their congregations.[60]

Women were more likely to describe external influences (e.g., uncertainty about being accepted by a church or family resistance) as a source of their doubts (although not always explicitly related to being a woman).[61] One respondent commented, "I had many doubts. With family, friends, and church uncomfortable with this, was I hearing God right? Was I made wrong? Did I have the wrong gifts for a woman?"[62] Another wrote, "It felt like I was working for 600 bosses instead of congregation members. I struggled with trying to please everyone. Did I really want my life to be constantly scrutinized with a microscope?"[63] Moreover, although female pastoral candidates were no more likely than male pastoral candidates to encounter congregational strife around their calling, more people left the church as a result of conflict over a woman being called into ministry.[64]

Significant improvement. There were many indicators of continuing improvement in the climate for women in leadership between the 1992 and 2005 surveys, as summarized by Nath. Women pastors reported high levels of job satisfaction. Indeed, in 2005, most men (77 percent) and women (82 percent) reported that they were "very satisfied" or "satisfied" with their pastoral

---

58   Nath, "Women and Men," 5.
59   Nath, "Women and Men," 34.
60   Nath, "Women and Men," 31.
61   Nath, "Women and Men," 42.
62   Nath, "Women and Men," 41.
63   Nath, "Women and Men," 43.
64   Nath, "Women and Men," 15.

role; this compared to only 59 percent of women who reported that they were satisfied in 1992.[65]

The majority of women pastors who sought second placements found them relatively quickly. In the 2005 survey, 58 percent of female pastors and 41 percent of male pastors reported that they found a second placement in less than six months after deciding that a move was desired. Although women are still significantly less optimistic (61 percent) about finding another placement as compared to men (81 percent), there was a great improvement since 1992 when only 39 percent of women thought finding a new place would be "somewhat" or "very easy" and 61 percent felt that it would be "somewhat" or "very difficult."[66]

The vast majority of women clergy (92 percent) felt accepted, liked, and appreciated by most members of their congregation, compared to 59 percent in 1992. There were no gender differences in this survey regarding acceptance.[67]

There was a slight increase in the proportion of women serving as co-pastors with their spouses who described their role as "equal" (67.4 percent compared to 66 percent in 1992) and a slight decrease who described their role as "subordinate" (27.9 percent compared to 34 percent in 1992). However, in 2005, 69 percent of women serving as co-pastors with their spouses reported that the congregation would not have called them if not for the spouse, which was down from 76 percent in 1992 but still troublingly high.[68]

Recommendations

Nath concludes her survey results with several recommendations.[69] First, she recommends that church leadership continue to work at advocating for women in ministry. "It's a risky job," she

---

65 Nath, "Women and Men," 12.
66 Nath, "Women and Men," 14.
67 Nath, "Women and Men," 15.
68 Nath, "Women and Men," 35–36.
69 Nath, "Women and Men," 9.

writes. "Would I get hurt? As a Mennonite minister, you don't have much protection compared to a more hierarchically organized denomination."[70] Second, she recommends that male pastors who are supportive of women in pastoral ministry should be encouraged to be in dialogue with their male colleagues who are not. She suggests, third, that the church would benefit from further conversations about different approaches to leadership including teaming styles, associates, co-pastors, various ministry styles, and so on. Fourth, she writes that pastors would benefit from continuing education on establishing boundaries between ministerial duties and family or private life.

Nath's fifth recommendation is that conference ministers educate both male and female pastors regarding normative experiences of those who are discerning a call and seeking a first placement. One example of a particular gift of a woman pastor was her question, "Should I pastor a Mennonite church? I have a charismatic bent."[71] Sixth, Nath recommends that the impact on single status on the call to ministry and the unique challenges faced by single pastors are worth investigation. Finally, she recommends that continued attention be given to educating pastors regarding the challenges of navigating sexual and emotional boundaries with congregational members.

When I (Diane) reflect on the recommendations, I wonder how well we took our own advice. I can only reflect from a denominational leadership perspective and remain hopeful that conferences and local churches put the recommendations into practice in various forms. I wonder if male pastors who were supportive of women were ever provided opportunities to be in dialogue with their male colleagues who are not, for example. Denominational staffs did work at clarifying different approaches to leadership (teams, associate, co-pastor, etc.). And our seminaries offered continuing education on setting up boundaries between ministerial duties and family or private life and navigating sexual and

---

70 Nath, "Women and Men," 42.
71 Nath, "Women and Men," 43.

emotional boundaries with congregational members. I remember hosting workshops for pastoral spouses but not ones for single pastors.

The attitudes toward women in ministry certainly improved from the 1992 Sauder study to the 2005 Zaerr Brenneman study. The overall satisfaction with the choice to be a congregational pastor, despite doubts and barriers, also showed great growth by women. Nevertheless, today Mennonite Church USA continues to need more qualified pastors than are available. Only 16 percent of pastors in Mennonite Church Canada and Mennonite Church USA are women. If God gives gifts regardless of gender, that figure should be at least 50 percent.[72] Advocating for hiring a woman as a pastor is not the search committee's job alone. These people are volunteers who rightly feel a lot of responsibility to find and act on the consensus of the congregation. Before we ever need a pastor, all of us in congregations need to be studying the scriptures about women in leadership, teaching our young people and ourselves what we believe about God's gifts, and developing a culture of calling young people of any gender to consider pastoral ministry.[73]

Mennonite Member Profile 2006

Mennonite Church USA invested in another major survey conducted by Conrad L. Kanagy called the Mennonite Member Profile 2006. Although this survey asked many other questions about the members, it included the same question regarding the ordination of women that previous Anabaptist surveys in 1972 and 1989 had asked (see chapter 1). While in 1972, 17 percent of respondents agreed that women should be ordained, and in 1989, that number had increased to 49, by 2006, Kanagy found a 67 percent favorable response.[74] Nevertheless, he cautioned, "Although there

---

72 Diane Zaerr Brenneman, "Pastor Shortage?" *Report* 178, Sept.–Oct. 2004, 5.

73 Brenneman, "Pastor Shortage?" 5.

74 Conrad L. Kanagy, *Road Signs for the Journey: A Profile of Mennonite Church USA* (Scottdale, PA: Herald, 2007), 78.

is greater openness to the ordination of women today than in the past, members still prefer male leadership. Fifty-eight percent prefer a man as lead pastor of their congregation, compared to 40 percent who have no preference and only 2 percent who prefer a woman."[75] Interestingly, he noted there were no significant differences between men and women in their gender preferences for pastoral leadership. This marked a positive change from 1972, when "traditional attitudes unfavorable toward increased participation by women in lay leadership and ministerial roles appear to persist among both male and female church members, with men evidencing slightly less traditional attitudes than women."[76] Likewise, in the 1989 survey—named Church Member Profile II, which duplicated the 1972 survey—sociologists J. Howard Kauffman and Leo Driedger found, "Male and female responses were similar [regarding the ordination of women] except that the proportion of males that favored ordination (47 percent) was slightly higher than the female proportion (42 percent)."[77]

While the three member studies showed an astounding attitudinal change toward the ordination of women (from 17 percent to 49 percent to 67 percent) in three decades, it was still clear that women faced barriers regarding ordination. What needed further examination was the attitude of women toward other women, including what structures in society create attitudes that are "normal" for women, where examples of discrimination could be found, and whether religion and its practices pose specific attitudes toward women by women.

Conclusion

In the 1990s, there was an effort to produce a new statement of faith by the GCMC and MC, and in 1995 the *Confession of*

---

75 Kanagy, *Road Signs for the Journey*, 78.

76 J. Howard Kauffman and Leland Harder, *Anabaptists Four Centuries Later: A Profile of Five Mennonite and Brethren in Christ Denominations* (Scottdale, PA: Herald, 1975), 198.

77 J. Howard Kauffman and Leo Driedger, *The Mennonite Mosaic: Identity and Modernization* (Scottdale, PA: Herald, 1991), 206.

Faith in a Mennonite Perspective was overwhelmingly supported and approved by both denominational bodies.[78] Article 15 of the *Confession* addresses women in leadership directly: "The church calls, trains, and appoints gifted men and women to a variety of leadership ministries on its behalf. These may include such offices as pastor, deacon, and elder as well as evangelists, missionaries, teachers, conference ministers, and overseers." Perhaps another survey is due to see what current attitudes and practices are and how well they align with this statement. Maybe women and men will report new ways to serve Jesus Christ. And maybe, just maybe, our daughters and sons will prophesy and dream dreams. May it be so.

A Prayer for Ministers

O Living Christ,
    in each of us you come to meet us.
Behind the steady pace of our lives,
    beneath the noise and detail, you dwell within us.
Here we find the interior peace
    and rest of your presence.
Here you bid us enter,
    to quench our thirst for all that is holy in life.
For your constant presence, we give you praise.
    For your constant guidance, we give you thanks.
        For your love and mercy without ceasing, we lift a song in our hearts.

Engage us, O Lord, among all the signs visible and invisible
    which discover your presence among us,
        so that we can enter into this day
            empty of our pretensions,
            unafraid of our fears,
            alert to every new possibility.

---

78 *Confession of Faith in a Mennonite Perspective* (Newton, KS: Faith and Life, 1995), 59.

Empower us to give our heart's love generously
 to all who need us.
Help us to honor the goodness in others,
 to put our arms around the sad ones
  that they might be comforted,
 to enter into the suffering of others,
 to speak the prayers and do the deeds
  that befit our vocation as ministers and servants of
   your church.
Grant to us, the power to speak your word faithfully, that
the good news of your gospel
 may prosper in us and through us.
Let it be your instrument of holy discontent
 wherever the world is unjust or calloused against your
 mercy.

Make of it a herald of your kingdom,
 speaking for the authority of your promise
  that your word, having gone forth with power,
  will not return to you empty.
Thus may we be good witnesses to your gospel,
 for which we daily give thanks.
In your presence let us be strengthened
 for the tasks to which you have called us.
Praise be to you, Lord God,
 who awakens us to this new day, filling us with grace
 overflowing.

    Amen.

—Renee Sauder, Associate Pastor,
 Bethel College Mennonite Church, February 1990[79]

---

79 Used by permission of the author.

7

Conferences and publications
Women do theology
Lois Y. Barrett

Before the 1970s, most Mennonites in North America simply assumed that ordained ministers would be men. In its European origins, Anabaptism arose in patriarchal cultures, and those patriarchal cultures made the ocean voyages to the New World in the seventeenth, eighteenth, nineteenth, and twentieth centuries along with Mennonite immigrants. Thus, the theology that many Canadian and American Mennonite women inherited in the last quarter of the twentieth century was done by men on behalf of the "brotherhood." Few other North American denominations had many women in ministry or doing theology. Although Pentecostal beginnings had often been led by women, by the 1970s even many of those church groups had accommodated to a male-dominated culture.

At the beginning of the twentieth century, the new theological movement known as fundamentalism strengthened the theology behind that male prerogative in the church. In one sense, fundamentalism was a reaction to the Enlightenment, the philosophical movement that honored only what could be discerned through reason and the five senses (in the early twentieth century, represented theologically by "modernism"). That seemed to leave little room for divine revelation or the authority of scripture. But fundamentalism also was a reaction to the women's suffrage movement. At a Mennonite women's history conference in 1995, Betty DeBerg summarized her research on the periodical

The Fundamentalist around 1900. Its articles gave evidence that a particular stance toward women's leadership in church and society came *prior to* a particular way of interpreting scripture. In other words, she concluded, the fundamentalist hermeneutical method was developed in order to solidify a lower rank for women.[1]

Mennonites, especially those groups that had immigrated earlier to North America, were influenced by fundamentalism and its attitudes toward women. In Lancaster Mennonite Conference in eastern Pennsylvania, contact with fundamentalism in the late nineteenth and early twentieth centuries seemed to make dress codes for women more rigid and more at odds with the surrounding culture than had been the case earlier.[2] Farther west, in the Mennonite Library and Archives in North Newton, Kansas, is a small book that had evidently been in some Mennonite leader's library: *Bobbed Hair, Bossy Wives, and Women Preachers*.[3] (The author was against all three.) Across the North American Mennonite church, fundamentalism had an influence, although it differed from conference to conference, from congregation to congregation, and from church agency to church agency. For example, in the General Conference Mennonite Church (GCMC), the Home Mission Board was much more fundamentalist in its leanings than the Foreign Mission Board in the first half of the twentieth century and became more so over the decades.

---

1 Betty A. DeBerg, *Ungodly Women: Gender and the First Wave of American Fundamentalism* (Minneapolis: Fortress, 1990).

2 See the story of Amanda Musselman in Louise Stoltzfus, *Quiet Shouts: Stories of Lancaster Mennonite Women Leaders* (Scottdale, PA: Herald, 1999), 20–23. See also Joanne Hess Siegrist, *Mennonite Women of Lancaster County: A Story in Photographs from 1855–1935* (Intercourse, PA: Good Books, 1996).

3 John R. Rice, *Bobbed Hair, Bossy Wives, and Women Preachers* (Murfreesboro, TN: Sword of the Lord Publishers, 1944). The book has been reprinted as recently as 2000. Rice was the pastor of the Fundamentalist (later Galilean) Baptist Church of Dallas, Texas.

By World War II, the Home Mission Board was not sending out single women at all.[4]

If Mennonite women were to serve the church as leaders, they needed to counter both the traditional theological and sociological arguments against this and the newer fundamentalist arguments by doing their own theology.

Publications

Beginning in the 1970s, Mennonite women's theology, history, and biblical interpretation appeared in numerous periodicals and books. In 1975, Herta Funk, staff member for the General Conference Commission on Education, edited a booklet with a dual purpose: to provide a study guide for the evangelical feminist book *All We're Meant to Be* and to commission five original essays on "women in the Bible and early Anabaptism."[5] The essays were "Woman's Place in the Creation Accounts" by Perry Yoder, "Factors to Consider in Studying Old Testament Women" by Dorothy Yoder Nyce, "Jesus and Women" by Dorothea Janzen, "Paul's Teaching on the Status of Men and Women" by John Neufeld, and "Women in the Anabaptist Movement" by Lois Barrett.

The Institute of Mennonite Studies published a volume in its Occasional Papers series titled *Perspectives on Feminist Hermeneutics*.[6] Numerous collections of Mennonite women's stories were published, including *Full Circle, Mennonite Women, Encircled,* and

---

4 Lois Barrett, *The Vision and the Reality: The Story of Home Missions in the General Conference Mennonite Church* (Newton, KS: Faith and Life, 1983).

5 Herta Funk, ed., *Study Guide: Part I: Women in the Bible and Early Anabaptism; Part II: Lesson Helps for All We're Meant to Be* (Newton, KS: Faith and Life, 1975). See Letha Scanzoni and Nancy Hardesty, *All We're Meant to Be: A Biblical Approach to Women's Liberation* (Waco, TX: Word, 1974).

6 Gayle Gerber Koontz and Willard Swartley, eds., *Perspectives on Feminist Hermeneutics*, Occasional Papers 10 (Elkhart, IN: Institute of Mennonite Studies, 1987).

She Has Done a Good Thing.[7] The evangelical feminist periodical *Daughters of Sarah*, published from 1974 to 1995, had considerable Mennonite input; selected articles from the magazine were published in the book *The Wisdom of Daughters*.[8] Both *The Mennonite Quarterly Review* and *The Conrad Grebel Review* devoted issues to papers from Women Doing Theology conferences.[9]

Gatherings about and for women in ministry

Mennonite women were not only writing; they were also meeting together to talk about women in the church and in society. Across the church, there were workshops, retreats, seminars at church assemblies, and regional women's meetings where women—and sometimes men as well—gathered to talk about theology and ministry. There were regional conferences like "Challenges Facing Black Mennonite Women Today," in October 1977 at Camp Hebron, Halifax, Pennsylvania, with ninety attendees, and a Mennonite Central Committee–sponsored conference in Canby, Oregon, in the 1970s on "A Biblical Understanding of Women and Men in the Church." There were also academic conferences, like a conference with papers at Associated Mennonite Biblical Seminary (AMBS) in Elkhart, Indiana, in June 1986 that resulted in the book *Perspectives on Feminist Hermeneutics*,[10] and "Quiet in the Land," a Mennonite women's history conference that took place June 8–11, 1995, at Millersville University in Pennsylvania.

---

7 Mary Lou Cummings, ed., *Full Circle: Stories of Mennonite Women* (Newton, KS: Faith and Life, 1978); Elaine Sommers Rich, *Mennonite Women: A Story of God's Faithfulness 1683–1983* (Scottdale, PA: Herald, 1983); Ruth Unrau, *Encircled: Stories of Mennonite Women* (Newton, KS: Faith and Life, 1986); Mary Swartley and Rhoda Keener, eds., *She Has Done a Good Thing* (Scottdale, PA: Herald, 1999).

8 Reta Halteman Finger and Kari Sandhass, eds., *The Wisdom of Daughters: Two Decades of the Voice of Christian Feminism* (Philadelphia: Innisfree, 2001).

9 *Mennonite Quarterly Review* 68, no. 2 (April 1994); *Conrad Grebel Review* 10, no. 1 (winter 1992).

10 Koontz and Swartley, *Perspectives on Feminist Hermeneutics*.

One of the primary sustained means of carrying on the conversation about women in ministry was through a series of conferences called "Women in Ministry." The first Women in Ministry conference was convened in 1976 by Emma Sommers Richards (who had been recently ordained) at the congregation she and her husband served, the Lombard Mennonite Church on the suburban outskirts of Chicago, Illinois. Some support for the meeting came from the Mennonite Central Committee Task Force on Women's Concerns and the General Conference Commission on Education. Sixty-five people, mostly women, came. They heard Nancy Hardesty, co-author of *All We're Meant to Be*, speaking about nineteenth-century women ministers in the Wesleyan tradition. One participant, Gloria Martin of St. Jacobs, Ontario, noted:

> Few congregations are presently open to affirming a woman's call to ministry. Are we to respond to the "urges within us" and the support of a few friends, as Nancy's nineteenth century women did? And if we do where are we to minister? . . .
>
> Some women are close to losing patience. It has become an issue of faithfulness that the church must be called to move on, now. Others were more inclined to call for patience lest our hurrying move congregational members to further and further poles. Probably most of us moved uncomfortably somewhere in between, hoping for both patience and movement.
>
> The conference did not solve anything. But somehow one person's bitterness mixed with another's humour, sharp-edged frustration was dulled by being shared, someone's hope touched another's weariness. Affirmations concluded the weekend. We would like a chance to

meet again; the need for emotional and spiritual support will continue.[11]

The Women in Ministry conferences did continue. Between 1976 and 2000, at least fourteen Women in Ministry conferences took place. The planning committees were ad hoc. Sometimes the conferences happened every year; sometimes they happened every eighteen months or two years. Congregations and Mennonite colleges and seminaries provided space. At most of the conferences, hundreds of Mennonites, overwhelmingly women, from across North America attended. A 1979 conference at AMBS in Elkhart, Indiana, attracted 250 participants. At Phoenix in 1988 there were 270 participants; at Harleysville, Pennsylvania, in 1991, 375 attended.[12]

---

11 Gloria Martin, "Conference Held for Women in Ministry," *Report* 11, July 1976, 4.

12 Women in Ministry conferences during the time period covered by this book include the following:

- April 30–May 2, 1976, Lombard, Illinois; speakers: Nancy Hardesty, Dave Augsburger, Emma Sommers Richards
- June 16–18, 1977, Sedalia, Colorado, "Persons in Ministry," speakers: Perry and Elizabeth Yoder, Lois Barrett, Marilyn Miller, Joyce Shutt, Patricia Shelly
- October 27–29, 1978, Akron, Pennsylvania, "Persons in Ministry," speakers: Arlene May, Willard Swartley, Ruth Brunk Stoltzfus, Dorothy Yoder Nyce, Emma Sommers Richards
- November 2–4, 1979, AMBS, Elkhart, Indiana, "Enabling for Action," speaker: Diane McDonald; 250 attended
- March 27–29, 1981, Bethel College, North Newton, Kansas; speakers: Dorothea Janzen, Emma Sommers Richards
- October 15–17, 1982, Kitchener, Ontario; speaker: Kathleen Storrie
- May 3–6, 1984, Harrisonburg, Virginia; speaker: Virginia Ramey Mollenkott
- Oct. 24–25, 1986, AMBS, Elkhart, Indiana; speaker: June Alliman Yoder; 64 attended

At the 1984 Women in Ministry conference at Harrisonburg (Virginia) Mennonite Church (lodging in the Eastern Mennonite College dorms), two hundred participants viewed sculptures created by women, created new worship rituals, and went to sixteen workshops on topics ranging from mutuality in marriage to inclusive language in worship, being heard in a committee, dealing with conflict, journaling, eating disorders, sexual abuse, and creative worship planning. Shirley Kohler Yoder reported after the event: "For weeks after the conference, it continued to impact the participants. Virginia Mollenkott's presentations evoked lively discussion and healthy controversy. She embodies the love of Christ for the outcasts and rejects in twentieth century society. We needed to hear her. It was good to have been there."[13]

Sometimes there were tensions. Should the conferences be titled "Persons in Ministry"? The 1977 and 1978 conferences did have that title. There was controversy. Some local Mennonite leaders successfully pressured Mennonite Central Committee British Columbia to withdraw its sponsorship of the 1995 conference at Columbia Bible College in Abbotsford. Was "ministry" defined so broadly that women pastors had no place to talk about their issues? At some conferences, there were separate workshops for women pastors to meet this need. There was at least one spe-

- Nov. 18–19, 1988, Phoenix, Arizona; speaker: Marilyn Miller; 270 attended
- Mar. 30–Apr. 1, 1990, Fresno, California, "Women Telling the Story"; speaker: Katie Funk Wiebe; 125 attended
- March 1–2, 1991, Harleysville, Pennsylvania, "Women at the Well"; speaker: Mary Schertz; 375 attended
- April 26–27, 1993, Conrad Grebel College, Kitchener, Ontario, "Women in Pastoral Ministry"; speaker: Cecilia Hahn
- May 26–28, 1995, Columbia Bible College, Abbotsford, British Columbia; 125 attended
- May 31–June 2, 2000, Goshen, Indiana; speakers: Martha Smith Good, Elaine Bryant, Juanita Nuñez, Jane Roeschley

13 *Report* 55, July–Aug, 1984, 8.

cial conference titled "Women in Pastoral Ministry" in 1993 at Conrad Grebel College in Waterloo, Ontario.

Beyond the tensions, the conferences were a welcome place for Mennonite women to share experiences, hear each other, do theology, and plan the future. The 1981 conference in North Newton, Kansas, included a mix of theoretical and practical workshops, including "Women in Seminary," "Women Learning Leadership Skills," "Peace Issues for Women," "Have Mennonites Sold Out to Consumerism?" "Interpreting Scripture," "Two-Career Marriages," "Coping with Depression," "Developing a Strong Self Image in Traditional Women's Roles," "Interpreting Difficult New Testament Passages," "History of Women in Religion," "Legal Questions for Women," "Sexism in Language," "The Pastoral Ministry for Women," "Women and Men Working Together in Church Institutions," and "Men and Masculinity."[14]

After the third conference, Joyce Shutt noted:

> Conferences are strange experiences. The speakers, so vital for the input and expertise they bring, shape the nature of the discussions. Yet the success or failure of such gatherings lies more in the extra-curricular conversations than in the presentations themselves. After the session—these are the times a shy stranger comes forward and says to another, "Thank you. Never before have I heard a woman dare to say openly, 'My goal is to be ordained.' That gives me hope and support in pursuing my own sense of call." Or friend hugs friend. "I couldn't make it without your support. It's so good to have you here today."[15]

Ruth Brunk Stoltzfus told the assembly, "For most of my life I thought I was weird because I wanted to use my mind and I loved

---

14 *Report* 35, Jan.–Feb. 1981, 10.
15 *Report* 23, Dec. 1978, 8.

to preach. In places like this, I discover many women who share those dreams and gifts."[16]

A more focused set of conferences was called "Women Doing Theology," where the emphasis was on more academic theology. Some of the topics like inclusive language and biblical interpretation had been part of the earlier Women in Ministry conferences. Now women wrote and presented papers on theological and methodological issues in the writing of the history of Anabaptist-Mennonite women, a new Rule of Christ for Anabaptist women, forgiveness, and the atonement. The Women Doing Theology conferences drew on resources from the increasing number of Mennonite women with seminary degrees and other advanced academic degrees. Between 1992 and 2003, six of these conferences were scheduled at Mennonite academic institutions.[17]

Mennonite women's ways of doing theology

From the presentations at the Women Doing Theology conferences—as well as the Women in Ministry conferences and various publications—it is possible to gain some insight into the varieties of theology among Mennonite women from 1972 to 2006, including how they understood biblical interpretation, the role of the community in doing theology, how to do theology differently from the traditions they had inherited, and how to use the extant theological methods for women's purposes.

---

16 *Report* 23, Dec. 1978, 9.

17 Women Doing Theology conferences during the time period covered by this book include the following:

- April 30–May 2, 1992, Conrad Grebel College, Waterloo, Ontario; 190 attended
- June 23–25, 1994, Bluffton College, Bluffton, Ohio
- May 9–11, 1996, Canadian Mennonite Bible College, Winnipeg, Manitoba
- June 25–27, 1998, Bethel College, North Newton, Kansas
- May 4–5, 2001, Conrad Grebel College
- May 16–18, 2003, Eastern Mennonite University, Harrisonburg, Virginia

Biblical and historical models

Mennonite women, like women in other church traditions, began looking for women in the Bible as models for contemporary times. The apostle Paul may have asked some women to be quiet in church, but there was plenty of evidence that Paul worked with women leaders on a regular basis, including Phoebe, Lydia, and Priscilla. This is especially evident in Romans 16, where Paul greets a long list of people, including Prisca, Mary, Junia (prominent among the apostles!), Tryphaena, Tryphosa, the mother of Rufus, Julia, and the sister of Nereus. Women noted that, in Romans 16:1, the word used to describe Phoebe as a "deaconess" in the King James Version is translated "minister" when applied to Paul and Apollos (1 Cor. 3:5) and as "deacon" referring to male officers in the church (1 Tim. 3:10, 12, 13).

Mennonite women lifted up Sarah, Hagar, Miriam, Deborah the judge, and Huldah the prophet in the Old Testament and noted the significance of Mary the mother of Jesus, Mary Magdalene, Joanna, Susanna, and other unnamed female disciples in the New Testament. Jesus told parables with women as the main characters, including the woman whose yeast leavens the dough and the woman who searches the house for her lost coin. Although the tradition of interpretation of 1 Corinthians 11 had focused on the husband as the head of his wife, the text instructs women to cover their heads when *prophesying*! The next chapter lists prophecy as a gift of the Spirit and assumes it is to be exercised publicly. Moreover, Mennonite women asked what it means that women were to have (a symbol of) authority on their heads "because of the angels" and what the significance was of covering one's head in first-century Mediterranean cultures.

In the history of the church since the first century, women served as models for the present. In a presentation at the first Women Doing Theology conference in 1992, I (Lois) asked, "If Bernhartz Maria of Niederrollesbroich served as an Anabaptist apostle and preacher in the 16th century, then why cannot Mennonite women in the twentieth century be preachers and evangelists?"[18] As in the New Testament, Mennonite historical writings often differed between prescriptions for women and descriptions of what women actually did. In the Dutch Anabaptist tradition, Menno Simons could admonish women to "be obedient to your husbands in all reasonable things";[19] yet the *Martyrs Mirror* (also in the Dutch tradition) reported that only eight years after Menno published his advice to women to stay home and mind the house, Elizabeth Dirks, a colleague of Menno, was arrested for being a teacher of many people.[20]

Anabaptist women were especially noted for prophecy, a role for women justified in the Middle Ages on the basis of Acts 2:17 (quoting Joel 2:28): "In the last days it will be, God declares, that I will pour out my Spirit upon all flesh, and your sons and your daughters shall prophesy." Anabaptist women followed in the steps of second-century Montanist prophets Maximilla and Prisca, twelfth-century abbess Hildegard of Bingen, medieval beguine Hadewijch of Flanders, and lay women Margarete Porete and Bridget of Sweden. In sixteenth-century Europe, where many people believed that they were living in the last days, it was no surprise that God was giving prophetic visions to Anabaptist women like Ursula Jost and Barbara Rebstock in Strasbourg, Aeffgen Lystyncx in Amsterdam, and Margaret Hottinger in St. Gall in the Swiss Confederation.

Anabaptist women could be prophets and were allowed leadership roles—such as Barbara Rebstock, who was evidently

---

18 Lois Y. Barrett, "Women's History/Women's Theology: Theological and Methodological Issues in the Writing of the History of Anabaptist-Mennonite Women," *Conrad Grebel Review* 10, no. 1 (winter 1992): 2; citing Ernst Crous, "Anabaptism in Schleiden-in-the-Eifel," *Mennonite Quarterly Review* 34 (1960): 189.

19 In Menno Simons, "The True Christian Faith" (1541), *The Complete Writings of Menno Simons*, ed. Leonard Verduin and J. C. Wenger (Scottdale, PA: Herald, 1956), 383.

20 Thieleman J. van Braght, *The Bloody Theater or Martyrs Mirror of the Defenseless Christians*, 13th English ed. (Scottdale, PA: Herald, 1982 [1660]), 481–483.

part of a leadership council in the Melchiorite congregation in Strasbourg—because these Anabaptists believed that the Age of the Spirit was imminent, and the church was called to live now according to the rules of the age to come. The old rules about the relationships between men and women no longer applied when people were inspired by the Holy Spirit. These were the last days when the Spirit was being poured out in new ways, on women as well as men.[21] A reduction in women's roles in the Anabaptist movement appears to have coincided with a reduction in reliance on the more visible gifts of the Spirit and an increase in routinization of leadership within congregations.

Inclusive language

Throughout this period of expanding women's experience in the church, a major issue was inclusive language, not only for humans but also for God. In 1977, Sally Dyck wrote in the *Report* that using only masculine imagery for God has excluded the possibilities of other imagery that can help men and women in their relationship with God, proclaim important attributes of God, and reach different people in different situations. She noted feminine imagery for God in the Bible: a woman giving birth, a woman comforting her children, a midwife. Like many other women, Dyck described how her experience of God changed with the change in language: "Imagery which is common to my experience as a woman has blossomed my interest and receptivity to the word of God. . . . The spiritual freedom to include feminine (biblical) images of God can catapult all of us into a whole new depth of relationship with God."[22]

Sixteen years later, inclusive language was still an issue. Jackie Wyse wrote in the *Report*:

> Who cries to us from the margins of scripture? If we listen, we will hear the rustling of the Spirit at the moment of creation, the birthing of the earth, the sculpting of both

---

21 See Barrett, "Women's History/Women's Theology," 8–9.
22 *Report* 15, July 1977, 2–3.

women and man in God's image. We will hear prophets and poets proclaiming the presence of the Divine in feminine, masculine, and non-gendered images: God as a rock, a shield, and a deliverer; a father and a knitter; a lover, a light, and a lion; a woman groaning in childbirth; a mother bird sheltering the vulnerable under her wings. Some of these metaphors dance on the margins of the biblical imagination, while others feel as familiar as an old, cherished hymn. Taken together, the sheer variety of images for God in scripture is breath-taking and boundary shattering.[23]

Furthermore, various Mennonite women noted that language can never fully describe God. God is bigger than our words. Every metaphor, every image for God—even father or mother—is a partial description of God. God as rock, God as redeemer, God as living water, God as mother bird—each tells us something about the nature of God, but none are a complete description of God. Is it right, they asked, to latch onto only a few images of God to the exclusion of all others? Any speech about God is not the whole truth. Lydia Harder wrote in a 1988 issue of *Report* on God-language:

> It is no surprise that the people who are calling for a new look at our God-imagery are persons who have been oppressed by Christian people and nations. Black people are rejecting a white god who condones slavery and apartheid. South American people are resisting obedience to a North American god who allows exploitation of the poor. Women are questioning a male god who calls forth structures that deny full personhood to women and justify patriarchal power of men over women.
>
> Jesus' words, "You shall know them by their fruits," (Matthew 7:16) can be a guide to testing our God-images. What actions, feelings and commitments do our images

---

[23] *Report* 169, Sept.–Oct. 2003, 7–8.

call forth? Legitimizing unjust social orders as God's will brings into question whether we have adequately understood God.[24]

Along with many other women in church and society, Mennonite women were recognizing that words have power. Words can communicate or cut off communication. They asked whether women feel included when the congregation sings, "Rise Up, O Men of God." Or whether women have any power when people refer to an omnipotent God with male-only language. Or whether God as Mother feels closer and more relatable than God as Father. Reta Halteman Finger wrote:

> Language is our way of presenting images and concepts to each other. When language is predominately masculine, women and the feminine are rendered invisible. It would appear, without saying anything explicitly, that the masculine is the more important gender. . . . I have two sons, now eight and ten years. Several years ago, in Sunday school they learned a mealtime song. After thanking God for the food, the song ended with, "We thank you, God, for being our Father." I suggested that sometimes we should sing, "We thank you, God, for being our Mother." It seemed more natural, since mothers usually do most of the food preparation in the family. This was met with great resistance by our boys, who insisted that God is not a mother. The text should not be changed; to them it was carved on tablets of stone. Besides, they insisted, God is a man because he looks like one. All the pictures portrayed God as a stately old man with gray hair, the elderly father of Jesus.[25]

Ruth Brunk Stoltzfus wrote:

---

24 *Report* 76, Jan.–Feb. 1988, 2.
25 *Report* 42, Mar.–Apr. 1982, 2.

> Women have had to do unending "translations" while reading all about "man" in the Scriptures and may not have gotten the precise meanings intended for them. Ephesians 4:22–24 (KJV) tells us to put off "the old man" and put on the "new man." Our dear men might try to imagine being taught to put off "the old woman" and put on "the new woman." The light breaks in the newer translations that say, ". . . get rid of your old self, . . . put on the new self." This happened to me.[26]

Moreover, language changes over time, as Gayle Gerber Koontz observed:

> At one time "man," from Old English *mann* was similar to the generic *Mensch* in German, could be used to say, "His mother was a good Christian man." The use of the word has clearly narrowed, heightening the question for women, when am I included? Ambiguity is particularly confusing to children who get the impression that woman is a "subspecies," included in man. As one child, Sylvia, put it in a letter, "Dear God, Are boys better than girls? I know you are one but try to be fair."[27]

If "mankind" no longer denotes all of humanity, we should no longer use words that exclude half of humanity, women theologians said.

Over twenty years, inclusive language for humans was moving toward becoming the norm. But there was diversity of practice on inclusive language for God. Questions like these remained: Should we use gendered language for God at all? Is Christ "he" and the Holy Spirit "she"? Do we edit scripture for inclusive language, not only where male translators used male language to translate neuter language, but also where the male language is in the Hebrew or Greek? Do we use the language of "goddess"? Are ancient religions that had female deities necessarily more

---

26 *Report* 42, Mar.-Apr. 1982, 4.
27 *Report* 15, July 1977, 1–2.

woman-friendly, particularly if a goddess is primarily a fertility symbol? The questions continued past 2006.

Experience

For a long time, biblical scholars had tried to look at scriptural texts in the contexts in which they were written and first heard, and it was becoming more common for scholars to look at their own contexts as interpreters and how their social locations influenced the ways they saw the text. Moreover, an understanding was growing among theologians that the gospel has always been clothed in a context. The Bible is not a set of disembodied timeless truths but a story of God's interaction with God's particular people in their particular contexts. Much of the New Testament tells of the struggle to move beyond an exclusively Palestinian context and to proclaim and embody the gospel in a new Greco-Roman context. Likewise, Mennonite women looked at how biblical interpretation and theology might be different if done from a woman's social location, with a woman's bodily experience. They asked questions like these: Did the fact that the interpreter had a woman's body make a difference? Did women's different experiences shed different light on the text?

For example, Lydia Harder not only looked at the story in John 13 of Jesus washing the disciples' feet from the perspective of status and power relationship, but she also juxtaposed it with the story in John 12 of Mary anointing Jesus's feet: "When the two stories are taken together we can clearly see the mutuality in the relationship of Jesus and his disciples. Mary, in her act of love for Jesus, overcomes any feeling of inferiority which the difference in status between her and Jesus would indicate. Jesus' insistence that he and the disciples are one in the act of footwashing overcomes any difference in status between himself and his disciples. Over/under relationships are not to be part of the Johannine community."[28] Instead of the traditional interpretations of these stories emphasizing humility, the texts from a woman's perspec-

---

28 Lydia Harder, "Biblical Interpretation: A Praxis of Discipleship?" *Conrad Grebel Review* 10, no 1 (winter 1992): 29.

tive are examples of valuing all people and challenging societal roles. She continued:

> The Jesus who serves has been separated from the Jesus who gratefully accepts the footwashing of a woman in his time of need. We have been blind to the fact that the objections to both footwashings center on the crossing of societal norms of acceptable relationships between people. . . . Allowing our feet to be washed and washing someone else's feet belong together as one symbolic act of mutual love and respect. This interpretation challenges both the powerful and the less powerful to act in love, overcoming barriers which tend to separate us, whether these barriers are between rich and poor, master and servant, teacher and students, or men and women.[29]

After a Women Doing Theology conference in 2003, Reta Halteman Finger reflected on hospitality as an integral part of Jesus's gospel—and particularly on the hospitable hidden women of Acts 2, 4, 6, and 16. Lydia, she said, is portrayed as both persuasive and manipulative. "Anyone who could prevail upon Paul to change his mind must have been forceful indeed."[30]

Women's bodily experience could change the experience of the text. In her interpretation of Matthew 9:19–22, the story of the woman who touched the hem of Jesus's garment and was healed of her constant flow of blood, Nancy Lapp wrote: "I'm in the story, longing for healing, wanting to be made whole, wanting to touch Jesus. Jesus looks at me. He's not afraid of my womanness. I'm not unclean to him. He sees me as a person. . . . The beginning of healing and wholeness took root in my soul. . . . I felt the unconditional love of God, pure grace, as never before. I saw the beauty of my own soul. I discovered that my faith was not

---

29 Harder, "Biblical Interpretation," 31.
30 *Report* 171, Jan.–Feb. 2004, 6.

grounded in the inerrancy of the scriptures. My security was not in words, but in the Word made flesh."[31]

Women discovered it made a difference who was doing the biblical interpretation. Women's experience mattered. That experience mattered not only in hermeneutics but also in theologizing. It mattered who was using theology to make decisions. Some Mennonite women resonated with Roman Catholic theologian Rosemary Radford Ruether's humorous piece on a fictional synod of mother superiors deciding on whether men could be priests. According to Ruether, the "Holy Mothers" in Rome drew up a decree disqualifying men from the priesthood because they were too violent and emotional, unqualified to represent the One who incarnates peace. Women were created last, the crown of creation. Men with their larger bodies represented the material, while women represented the spiritual. The article turned on their heads all the arguments barring women from ministry.[32]

Women's experience led them to question the separation of theology from biblical studies and the separation of knowing and doing that had begun with Peter Lombard, Thomas Aquinas, and the scholastics in the Middle Ages. They asked whether the practice of discipleship affects how we understand the Bible. They called into question systems of ethics and morality that saw decision making on the basis of principle alone. Women's experience demanded that relationships as well as objective, disembodied principles mattered in discernment.[33] Knowing involved the personal, the covenantal, and the concrete as well as the abstract. This is illustrated by a note about one Women Doing Theology

---

31 Nancy Lapp, "Matthew 9:19–22: Waiting to Touch Jesus," *Report* 49, May–June 1983, 6.

32 Rosemary Radford Ruether, "Can Men Be Priests?" http://www.womenpriests.org/teaching/ruether2.asp.

33 See Mary Field Belenky et al., *Women's Ways of Knowing: The Development of Self, Voice, and Mind* (New York: Basic Books, 1986, 1997). For a more recent and theological understanding of women's ways of knowing, see Esther Lightcap Meek, *Loving to Know: Introducing Covenant Epistemology* (Eugene, OR: Cascade, 2011).

conference that dialogical response to the presentations resulted in "thoughtful, experiential, and academic reflections."[34] Women said that all of these—reflection, experience, and scholarship—ought to be part of theology.

Liberation theology

Liberation theology came to prominence with the publication of *A Theology of Liberation* by Gustavo Gutiérrez, a Roman Catholic from Peru, in 1973, and liberation theology quickly became a theme of feminist theology in North America with Letty Russell's *Human Liberation in a Feminist Perspective—A Theology*, in 1974.[35] Mennonite women also began to use forms of liberation theology as well as seeing sexism in church and society as one of the principalities and powers. Moreover, they often saw sexism in conjunction with other forms of oppression such as racism, colonialism, and classism.

Toinette Eugene, a Roman Catholic theologian speaking at a Mennonite conference on feminist hermeneutics in 1986, stated, "All ideologies of dominance and subordination are intrinsically linked." Referencing Alice Walker's book *The Color Purple*, she said, "The oppressions which [the characters in the book] experience due to race, sex, class, and caste must be transformed together, not as separate problems which have some isolated impact on their human condition." A liberationist understanding of the Bible begins with analyzing social reality, not trying to take a neutral stance. "The biblical interpreter must make her or his stance explicit and then take an advocacy position in favor of the oppressed."[36]

---

34 Rhoda S. Glick, *Report* 171, Jan.–Feb. 2004, 8.

35 Gustavo Gutiérrez, *A Theology of Liberation: History, Politics, and Salvation* (Maryknoll, NY: Orbis, 1973); Letty Russell, *Human Liberation in a Feminist Perspective—A Theology* (Philadelphia: Westminster John Knox, 1974).

36 Toinette M. Eugene, "A Hermeneutical Challenge for Womanists: The Interrelation between the Text and Our Experience," in Koontz and Swartley, *Perspectives on Feminist Hermeneutics*, 21, 22.

A liberation approach to biblical studies and theology came most often from Mennonite women of color, who regularly referenced the stories of Hagar (Genesis 16 and 21). Hagar is described in Genesis as a woman who is Egyptian and a low-status servant of Sarah. Hagar bears a son, Ishmael, to Abraham and is banished to the wilderness. In a presentation to a Women Doing Theology conference in 1994, Wilma Ann Bailey cautioned that womanist hermeneutics looks different from white feminist hermeneutics:

> African-American women are in a different relationship to African-American men than Caucasian women are to Caucasian men. Anabaptist feminists must be conscious of this fact so that they may be sensitive to issues of race, class, and ethnicity as they relate to feminism. Anabaptist feminists who have truly believed that in Christ there is no male or female, but that all are one, must encourage the development of multiple models that reflect the living reality of the women of the world.... [These models] help to affirm the development and contribution of women and men of all racial and ethnic groups within their cultures. At the same time, they allow for a critique of that which diminishes women and men in each culture and in all cultures.[37]

Other Mennonite women took liberation theology in a political direction, analyzing patriarchal social structures and drawing on the theme of suffering as a common experience of those on the margins.

Suffering, forgiveness, and atonement

One of feminists' largest criticisms of Christianity during this period was the way that the church had often applied Christian teachings on suffering, humility, and forgiveness differently to women than to men. Women seemed to be the recipients of most of the teachings on meekness, forgiveness without accountabil-

---

[37] Wilma Ann Bailey, "Hagar: A Model for an Anabaptist Feminist?" *Mennonite Quarterly Review* 68, no. 2 (April 1994): 228.

ity, and suffering without complaint. For Mennonite women, this raised questions such as these: Was there a Christian theology of the cross that saw suffering in a different light? Could a woman be humble and still have self-respect? Should a sermon to men on humility look different from a sermon to women on humility? Is suffering necessary for salvation?

In a presentation to the 1994 Women Doing Theology conference, Gayle Gerber Koontz explored neglected aspects of Christian teaching on forgiveness: "What seems underdeveloped are the theological and spiritual resources which assume the point of view of injured ones—resources which help us see how God's grace heals violated trust and shame and how fellow Christians participate in that process. . . . It is wrong for Christians to recommend forgiveness for the sake of the debtor and to ignore the needs of the injured one."[38] Salvation, she noted, involves both forgiveness of sins and healing of injury and shame. Likewise, Christian forgiveness is not simply individual to individual; it involves the Christian community in calling the offender to accountability, acknowledging genuine repentance, and hearing and empowering those who cannot now forgive.[39]

At the same conference, Mary Schertz recognized that some feminists have rejected suffering and the cross as trapping women in an abusive cycle. Instead, she asserted that the cross represents "the suffering a disciple is expected to bear in the danger one may encounter in the vigorous and athletic pursuit of the mission of God. The texts [in Luke-Acts] do not value suffering in general. They do not glorify suffering for the sake of suffering. They do not acclaim victimization. They simply encourage the pilgrim through the hardships and dangers that the faithful may encounter as they proclaim and enact the kingdom of God."[40] For Luke,

---

38 Gayle Gerber Koontz, "As We Forgive Others: Christian Forgiveness and Feminist Pain," *Mennonite Quarterly Review* 68, no. 2 (April 1994): 176–77.

39 Koontz, "As We Forgive Others," 192.

40 Mary H. Schertz, "God's Cross and Women's Questions: A Biblical Perspective on the Atonement," *Mennonite Quarterly Review* 68, no. 2 (April

she said, the suffering and death of Jesus are salvific because he held true to the nonviolent reign of God that he proclaimed and enacted. Disciples who proclaim and enact this reign will also get themselves into trouble and suffer. But this suffering is different from simply accepting the suffering caused by disease, poverty, injustice, and cruelty.[41] This suffering is the consequence of participating in God's mission in the world.

Trajectory theology

For some women it was not enough simply to cite examples of women's ministry from the Bible or to reinterpret particular teachings applied to women. Such methodology did not pay enough attention to context and to direction of movement. For example, if the apostle Paul and the early church gave broader leadership roles to women than the surrounding society did, that set a direction, a trajectory. This raised the question: If that trajectory were continued into the present, what would it look like for the church today to keep moving in that direction in the expansion of women's roles and responsibilities in the church?[42] This trajectory theology assumed that the best question is not: Is this practice right or wrong for all time? But, given our present context, the question is this: Is this practice moving in the right direction toward maturity in Christ? Various theologians applied this theological method to the issues of slavery and warfare in the Bible, and it began to be applied to women in the Bible as well.[43]

Trajectory theology went beyond simply looking for examples of women to emulate in the Bible and church history because it took context and culture into account. Doing so raised new

---

1994): 205–206.

41 Schertz, "God's Cross and Women's Questions," 206–207.

42 In some theological circles, trajectory theology is also known as redemptive movement theology.

43 Willard Swartley, *Slavery, Sabbath, War, and Women* (Scottdale, PA: Herald, 1983); William J. Webb, *Slaves, Women & Homosexuals: Exploring the Hermeneutics of Cultural Analysis* (Downers Grove, IL: InterVarsity, 2001).

questions, like these: How can we understand what an admonition for women to cover their hair meant in the context in which it was written? And how can we apply the text in Western culture, where the practice of women's wearing of hats or headscarves on a regular basis has virtually disappeared? What is the direction of this trajectory?

Trajectory theology is also related to theories about stages of moral development, in that people cannot understand a moral stage more than two stages above where they now are. In a society where women are seen as possessions of men, then, a trajectory toward the empowerment of women might look different than in a culture steeped in Enlightenment ideas of individual rights.

Few Mennonite women wrote theology explicitly out of this particular methodology, but it was a subtext in some writings. Mary Schertz's drawing of an arrow from the cross to our engagement in the mission of God was a step in that direction.[44] Trajectory theology was also a major theme in an article by Gayle Gerber Koontz titled, "The Trajectory of Feminist Conviction."[45] In this essay Koontz explored a way to respect the authority of both scripture and feminist experience rather than choosing one or the other. In the Bible, she noted, there is a trajectory moving from the violent destruction of enemies to limited vengeance (an eye for an eye) to returning good for evil and loving enemies. In the same way, there is a biblical trajectory moving from violent patriarchy to benevolent patriarchy to Jesus's treatment of women that challenged basic patriarchal identities and the New Testament calls to mutual submission of men and women.

Within a patriarchal order, an ethic of mutual submission can be good news for the weak because the powerful are called to learn the meaning of submission. Koontz wrote, "This ethic calls the powerful to be radically responsible to the weak, begins to

---

44 See Schertz, "God's Cross and Women's Questions," 206–208.

45 Gayle Gerber Koontz, "The Trajectory of Feminist Conviction," in *Essays on Peace Theology and Witness*, ed. Willard M. Swartley, Occasional Papers 12 (Elkhart, IN: Institute of Mennonite Studies, 1988); previously published in *Conrad Grebel Review* 5 (fall 1987): 201–220.

challenge their categorization of others as marginal and inferior, and calls the identified 'powerful' to serve. In a patriarchal context men must learn to let go of some of their relative power and social status in relation to women and subordinate men."[46] While mutuality is possible in patriarchal societies, it is also right to welcome cultural and political systems that are more egalitarian and provide a broader arena for women's action. In such societies a Christian feminist ethic might call for "reciprocal servanthood." Koontz explained: "Commitment to reciprocal servanthood and nonviolent love offers a critical perspective on individualistic, predominantly rights-oriented ethics, and of violent or more coercive means of achieving fuller justice in relation to women."[47]

Thus, Koontz utilized trajectory theology as a way to value the biblical narrative of the ways God has worked with God's people in history—and to value more equality for women: "We can note, for example, that the seeds of feminist consciousness, which have come to fruition in the nineteenth and twentieth centuries, were present in the biblical story. We do not need to seek to demonstrate that the biblical materials exhibit and recommend the kind of equality envisioned by many modern feminists in order to recognize in the movement from violent to benevolent patriarchy to the mutual submission of men and women, the emergence of the seeds of feminist consciousness."[48] If the Bible can move along this trajectory, so can contemporary women.

Conclusion

Between 1972 and 2006, Mennonite women did theology in different ways. Their theologizing began as the lifting up of models of women in the Bible and the church's past. It borrowed from other Christian traditions and theological methodologies. It explored context. It paid attention to women's experiences. It asked hard questions that challenged patriarchal traditions and

---

46 Koontz, "Trajectory of Feminist Conviction," 163.
47 Koontz, "Trajectory of Feminist Conviction," 166.
48 Koontz, "Trajectory of Feminist Conviction," 174.

past interpretations. But most of these theological writings did not abandon the Bible. Perhaps there was a subconscious attempt to heal the split between biblical studies and theology that had characterized academia since the scholastics of the Middle Ages. Women did not attempt an "objective" interpretation of scripture but offered embodied interpretations that honored both the past and the present context. Who the interpreter was made a difference! Out of these theologies practiced by Mennonite women, new insights were emerging and pointing toward yet more theologizing to come.

8

Moving into church structures
Women govern
Lois Y. Barrett

In 1972 society at large was struggling with issues of women's representation. In the United States, the Equal Rights Amendment to the Constitution had been passed by two-thirds of the House and Senate and was winding its way through ratification by state legislatures. Women had the right to vote but few women were on the ballot. In 1973, only 3 percent of the seats in the US Congress and 8 percent of the statewide elective offices were held by women. By 2005, those percentages were 15 and 26.[1] In Canada, women made up 9.6 percent of Members of Parliament in 1984, compared to 20.8 percent in 2006.[2] Women's involvement in governance was shifting a little.

Women were seeking careers beyond those stereotypically assigned to women and looking for equal pay for equal work. But few heads of corporations or nonprofit organizations were women. In the 1970s, degree-bound women graduate students were a minority. Despite my spotless grade point average and research experience, the head of my university department discouraged me from applying for graduate school and was skeptical about wheth-

---

1 See Women in Elective Office 2020 at the Center for American Women and Politics, https://cawp.rutgers.edu/women-elective-office-2020.

2 See Sylvia Bashevkin, "Women's Representation in the House of Commons: A Stalemate?" *Canadian Parliamentary Review* (Spring 2011): 18, https://www.canlii.org/w/canlii/2011CanLIIDocs299-en.pdf.

183

er I would be a good fit for the most prestigious schools. Only a few women had sought graduate education in a Mennonite seminary. By 1978, over a period of about thirty years, a total of seventy-two women had received degrees from the four Mennonite seminaries in North America—sixteen of them in theology, most of the rest in Christian education. Mennonite Brethren Biblical Seminary had had thirteen women graduates; in the Mennonite Church (MC), Eastern Mennonite Seminary had had four women graduates, and Goshen Biblical Seminary twenty-one; and in the General Conference Mennonite Church (GCMC), Mennonite Biblical Seminary had had thirty-four.[3] Some of these women were beginning to make their way into the governance of the church and the staffing of its mission.

Congregational governance

Traditionally, many Mennonite congregations had been governed by the "brotherhood"—literally. Sisters in Christ had had no vote in congregational meetings. Not only were there no women pastors; there were also no women elders or deacons, and women were barred from many other church offices. By 1972, this was changing. Linda Matties noted that the decade of the 1970s was a watershed "between the striving to be good Marthas and surprising discovery that Marys could do a whole lot more than just sit and listen at Jesus' feet." As she described,

> With fewer babies at home, more women attended business meetings and many men prided themselves on pragmatic decision making. So, to the surprise of diehards and legalists, women got elected to some significant positions. Then, to everyone's continuing surprise, they did the jobs they were elected to as well as or better than their male predecessors. They conducted choirs and experimented with new and creative liturgies. They streamlined labor-intensive Christian Education programs. They dared to speak to the congregation from

---

3 *Report* 19, April–May 1978, 2.

behind the pulpit. They moved from their seats at the feet of Jesus to the chair held by the disciples who had been given the task of passing on those teachings.[4]

Two surveys, one in 1975 and one in 1985, illustrated the changes happening (and not happening) in congregations of Western District Conference (GCMC), South Central Conference (MC), and Southern District (Mennonite Brethren). While a student at Bethel College, North Newton, Kansas, Janette Zercher designed the 1975 survey on male and female roles in congregational committees. First, she asked a number of people to rank these committees according to importance, significance, and how essential it was to the local church's functioning. The ranking from most to least important was (1) board of elders or deacons, (2) administrative or church council, (3) education, (4) trustees, (5) music, (6) extension or outreach, (7) fellowship, (8) service, (9) peace and relief, (10) library, (11) nursery, and (12) flower.

The survey found that a larger percentage of men than women were on the committees at the top of the hierarchy, and a larger percentage of women were at the bottom. In addition, the higher-ranking committees had more members. Zercher wrote:

> The church elects or appoints more people—and more of those are men—to the committees at the top of the committee hierarchy. To the committees at the bottom of the hierarchy, fewer people are elected or appointed—and more of those are women. The smaller percentage of people serving on the library, nursery, and flower committees seems to further point to their less important status.

---

4 Linda Matties, "The Mary-Martha Complex in the Post-Modern Church," *Report* 102, May–June 1992, 10.

The middle committees—music, extension, fellowship, service, and peace—show a more equal representation of men and women.[5]

She found that congregations often had women as Sunday school teachers but chose men as Sunday school superintendents. Chairs of committees were usually male. Women played the piano and organ and directed children's choirs, while men were choristers and adult choir directors. Figure 8.1 reproduces some of Zercher's results:[6]

Committee	Female	Male
Trustees	1.0%	99.0%
Deacon/Elder Board	10.2%	89.8%
Administrative Board	18.3%	81.7%
Peace and Relief	23.3%	76.7%
Extension/Outreach	44.6%	55.4%
Service	50.0%	50.0%
Worship	55.6%	44.4%
Education	56.8%	43.2%
Fellowship	58.0%	42.0%
Music	65.6%	34.5%
Nursery	83.3%	16.7%
Library	94.0%	6.0%
Flower	97.0%	3.0%
All Committees	40.1%	59.9%

Figure 8.1: Committee roles

The 1985 survey of thirty-five South Central Conference congregations (in Kansas, Missouri, Oklahoma, Arkansas, and

---

5 Janette Zercher, "Women's Role in Church Committees Examined," *The Mennonite*, Aug. 19, 1975, 464–65.

6 "Women's Representation on Church Committees," *Report* 8, Jan.–May 1975, 3–4.

Texas), conducted by Leland Harder, who was then conference minister, had similar findings. Men represented 97 percent of trustees, 93 percent of ministers, 80 percent of elders or deacons, 75 percent of treasurers, 70 percent of council members, 61 percent of Sunday school superintendents, and 58 percent of committee chairs. Women represented 99 percent of flower committee members, 93 percent of library committee members, 91 percent of nursery committee members, 80 percent of social-fellowship committee members, 67 percent of secretaries, 60 percent of Sunday school teachers, 58 percent of song leaders and education committee members, and 56 percent of worship and music committee members.

These findings seemed to reflect the respondents' biblical interpretations. Regarding Old Testament teaching about the order of creation, 52 percent believed that man was fitted for a primary leadership role, while woman was fitted for nurture and service; 36 percent saw no distinction; and 12 percent were uncertain. With regard to New Testament teaching, the study found that 41 percent believed man was to be the leader, or head; 53 percent saw equality in function; and 6 percent were uncertain.[7]

A 1983 survey of more than one thousand people in Lancaster Mennonite Conference (MC) found that, in two out of three congregations, women led children's meetings in public worship or children's church, served as secretary for congregational meetings, spoke on an assigned topic, led singing, or were committee members for the nursery or children's church. In a few congregations, women were church council members, Sunday school teachers for mixed adult classes, speakers from the pulpit, church treasurers, Sunday school superintendents, or chairs of the congregational meeting.

The Lancaster survey found that education was a factor in whether people favored women being deacons ("deaconesses," in the terminology of the survey). Only 15 percent of those with no higher than a grammar school education favored this, 30 percent

---

[7] Printout provided by Leland Harder to South Central Conference congregations, April 27, 1985.

of those with no higher than a high school diploma, and 65 percent of those with at least a college education.

The unscripted comments at the end of the survey spanned a range of opinions: "I believe women's gifts should be used in the church, but I do not believe in ordination"; "Submission of women to men is the most Christian way of ordering responsibility"; "Selection of all leaders should be based on qualification and calling by the Holy Spirit, not on sex"; "Mutuality is the main theme in understanding relationships of women and men in the church"; "The Bible clearly teaches what women's place is and should be taught rather than asking people's opinion in a survey like this"![8]

Women's participation in congregational governance was a necessary precursor of women's participation in pastoral ministry. If a congregation would not choose a woman as a deacon or elder, it was unlikely they would choose a woman as a pastor. Or if a congregation would not choose a woman to sit on church council, it would not be likely to support a woman sitting on a denominational board or commission. Alternatively, as more women began serving as deacons, elders, or church council members, opportunities began emerging for them to serve at higher levels of church governance.

Women as board members for church institutions

A major shift in women in church leadership positions occurred between 1972 and 2006. At the 1980 triennial sessions of the GCMC in Estes Park, Colorado, a group of women attending Dorothy Nickel Friesen's workshop on feminism were dismayed that so few women were on the ballot. In response, they advertised a daily meeting for feminists in the Rustic Room coffee shop and developed a plan to nominate four women from the floor of the conference.[9] Kimberly Schmidt wrote in 2003: "If my memory serves me correctly, a man from Illinois stood with the wom-

---

8 *Report* 56, July–Aug. 1984, 9–10.

9 Anna Juhnke, General Board; Carol Suter, Division of Administration; Marjorie Ediger, Mennonite Biblical Seminary; and Anne Falk, Commission on Overseas Mission. See *Report* 33, Sept.–Oct. 1980, 8.

en; he echoed their sentiments and concluded by nominating a black woman from his church. Our candidates were elected, and I received a valuable lesson in feminist principles and organizing. Anger at established patriarchal customs spurred this overnight change in GC leadership. Since the meetings in the Rustic Room, women have gained top positions in churches, conferences, and at our institutions of higher learning. This change happened relatively fast, within one generation."[10]

The first woman elected to a major Mennonite board was Bertha Fast Harder, who in 1962 became a member of the Board of Education of the GCMC (later called the Commission on Education). She had already been a "first" in many parts of the church: she was the first director of voluntary service for the GCMC; she was the first woman instructor (part-time) on the faculty of Mennonite Biblical Seminary (one of the institutional ancestors of Anabaptist Mennonite Biblical Seminary). She noted that, during her first term on the Board of Education, the chair would address his letters to board members with "Dear Brethren and Bertha."[11] When you were the first woman to serve on a particular board, you were generally the only woman.

Still, by the mid-1970s few women served on boards and committees for Mennonite institutions in North America, either at the regional level or on the US and Canadian level. By 1977, the GCMC had a few more women on its boards than in 1962, but every board chair was male. Figure 8.2 below compares board seats held by women in 1977 and in 2000 (just before the denominational merger). It shows that, in the GCMC, women's represen-

---

10 Kimberly Schmidt, "You've Come a Long Way, Baby; or, Was the Anger Worth It?" *Report* 168, July–Aug. 2003, 9.

11 John D. Harder and James C. Juhnke. "Harder, Bertha Fast (1914–2008)," *Global Anabaptist Mennonite Encyclopedia Online*, https://gameo.org/index.php?title=Harder,_Bertha_Fast_(1914-2008). Also see Bertha Fast Harder, "Go and Teach Christian Education," in *She Has Done a Good Thing*, ed. Mary Swartley and Rhoda Keener (Scottdale, PA: Herald, 1999), 144–52.

190 • Lois Y. Barrett

tation at the churchwide level improved during these twenty-five years in all but one commission.[12]

GCMC Board or Commission	Women 1977	Women 2000	Men 1977	Men 2000
General Board/ Executive Board	4 (24%)	9 (45%)	13 (76%)	11 (55%)
Division of Administration	1 (11%)	2 (29%)	8 (89%)	5 (71%)
Commission on Education	7 (44%)	6 (50%)	9 (56%)	6 (50%)
Commission on Home Ministries	3 (19%)	6 (46%)	13 (81%)	7 (54%)
Commission on Overseas Mission	4 (27%)	3 (23%)	11 (73%)	10 (77%)
Seminary (GCMC reps)	2 (20%)	3 (33%)	8 (80%)	6 (67%)

Figure 8.2: Representation on GCMC boards or commissions

As figure 8.3 shows, in the MC, there was similar change over twenty-three years, with most churchwide boards increasing the percentage of women serving as board members, and one (Mennonite Mutual Aid) barely shifting. But even the 1977 total of fourteen women serving on churchwide boards was an improvement over 1973, when there were five women on the six boards, with no more than one woman per board.[13]

---

12 *Handbook of Information 1977/1978, General Conference Mennonite Church* (Newton, KS: Faith and Life, 1977) and *Mennonite Directory 2000* (Newton, KS: Faith and Life; Scottdale, PA: Herald, 2000).

13 *Report 5*, Apr. 1974, 6.

MC Board	Women 1977	Women 2000	Men 1977	Men 2000
General Board	2 (12%)	9 (45%)	15 (88%)	11 (55%)
Mennonite Board. of Congregational Ministries	3 (25%)	5 (42%)	9 (75%)	7 (58%)
Mennonite Board of Education	3 (25%)	5 (50%)	9 (25%)	5 (50%)
Mennonite Board of Missions	2 (18%)	5 (45%)	9 (82%)	6 (45%)
Mennonite Mutual Aid (MC reps)	2 (20%)	2 (22%)	8 (80%)	7 (78%)
Mennonite Publication Board	2 (18%)	6 (50%)	9 (82%)	6 (50%)

Figure 8.3: Representation on MC boards

For both the MC and the GCMC, it appeared to be hardest to elect women to boards that dealt primarily with money (Division of Administration and Mutual Aid). It was easier to elect women to a board dealing with Christian education, it seemed. In 1985, the overall rates of women's participation on organizational boards was 40 percent in the GCMC and 30 percent in the MC. But in the new combined US Executive Board in 2000, there was almost equal representation by intention.

A 1985 study of Mennonite Central Committee (MCC) board compositions showed some progress for most boards between 1975 and 1985, as seen in figure 8.4.[14]

---

14 Data were taken from the MCC Personnel Listings of June 15, 1975, June 15, 1980, and May 31, 1985. Summarized in *Report* 63, Sept.–Oct. 1985, 4–5.

192 • Lois Y. Barrett

MCC Board	Women 1975	Women 1985	Men 1975	Men 1985
MCC Executive Committee	1 (12%)	2 (17%)	7 (88%)	10 (83%)
MCC Board members	2 (6%)	6 (16%)	32 (94%)	31 (84%)
MCC Canada Executive Committee	1 (17%)	1 (12%)	5 (83%)	7 (88%)
MCC Canada Board members	2 (7%)	3 (10%)	28 (93%)	28 (90%)
MCC US Executive Committee	1 (11%)	2 (29%)	8 (89%)	5 (71%)
MCC US Board members*	4 (13%)	6 (23%)	27 (87%)	20 (77%)
MCC Canada Peace/Social Concerns*	4 (22%)	2 (22%)	14 (78%)	7 (78%)
MCC US Peace Section	4 (17%)	7 (37%)	19 (83%)	12 (63%)
West Coast MCC	2 (12%)	2 (12%)	14 (88%)	14 (88%)
MCC Central States	4 (19%)	8 (32%)	17 (81%)	17 (68%)
MCC Great Lakes	2 (14%)	7 (30%)	12 (86%)	16 (70%)
MCC East Coast*	3 (15%)	3 (13%)	17 (85%)	20 (87%)
Mennonite Disaster Service	0 (0%)	1 (5%)	6 (100%)	18 (95%)
Mennonite Mental Health Service	0 (0%)	2 (12%)	16 (100%)	15 (88%)
Mennonite Economic Development (MEDA)	0 (0%)	3 (14%)	20 (100%)	19 (86%)
Mennonite Indemnity, Inc.	0 (0%)	0 (0%)	14 (100%)	14 (100%)
*1975 data not available; 1980/81 data substituted				

Figure 8.4: Representation on MCC boards

The compiler, Emily Will, noted that the data in this table "left plenty of room for individual interpretation. Some will see great progress; others will see little. Some will see much hope for continued forward momentum; others will say women's increased participation has leveled out." While the total number of women on MCC boards increased from thirty to fifty-five over the decade, the total number of men was relatively steady (from 256 in 1975 to 253 in 1985). It appears that, on most boards, women were not replacing men, but the boards were simply being enlarged by adding women.

Yet, some women were elected to positions previously held by men. Irene Dunn was elected to the General Conference General Board in 1975. Florence Driedger was the first woman president of the GCMC beginning in 1987. She had been elected vice-president in 1986 and began as president the following year after the death of the previous president; she was re-elected president in her own right in 1989. In 1993, Donella Clemens became first woman moderator of the MC. In 2000, women were also moderators of six of the twenty-one conferences that would soon form Mennonite Church USA: Central District Conference (Janeen Bertsche Johnson), Franconia Conference (Donella Clemens), New York Conference (Constance Finney), Northern District Conference (Sharon Waltner), Pacific Northwest Conference (Pat Hershberger), and Western District Conference (Leann Toews).

In addition, women served on special committees—the Inter-Mennonite Confession of Faith Committee (1987–1995), the Integration Exploration Committee, and the inter-Mennonite committee for the new vision statement that produced "Vision: Healing and Hope." I (Lois) was one of several women on the twelve-member Inter-Mennonite Confession of Faith Committee, which was also staffed by a woman, Miriam Book. The resulting document, *Confession of Faith in a Mennonite Perspective*, used mostly inclusive language,[15] and Article 15, Ministry and Leadership, was clear on including women and men in ministry. And if

---

15 Compare, for example, the line "We believe that the church is called to proclaim and to be a sign of the *kingdom* of God" (42) with the line "We place our hope in the *reign* of God" (89) in *Confession of Faith in a Mennonite Perspective* (Scottdale, PA: Herald, 1995). Some male members of the committee refused to let the document use completely inclusive language.

a nominating committee needed suggestions of women willing to serve, MCC offered the *Resource Listing of Mennonite and Brethren in Christ Women*, which, by 1985, had more than two hundred brief resumes of US and Canadian women for institutions to consider.[16]

Women as staff for church institutions

Women were increasingly serving in upper-level administrative staff roles in Mennonite institutions. The following is an incomplete list of some of the women who were "firsts" in their category of assignment, along with the beginning date of their appointment:

- 1985, Alice Roth, vice president for administrative affairs, Goshen College
- 1986, Muriel Thiessen Stackley, editor, *The Mennonite*
- 1987, Norma Johnson, executive secretary of General Conference Commission on Education—first woman head of a Mennonite churchwide agency, other than women's organizations
- 1989, Pat Swartzendruber, vice president, Mennonite Board of Missions
- 1989, Lynette Younds Meck, executive secretary for Mennonite Central Committee US
- 1990, Gayle Gerber Koontz, academic dean at Associated Mennonite Biblical Seminary (acting academic dean, 1985–86; interim president, 1994)
- 1991, Mary Burkholder, executive secretary, Mennonite Conference of Eastern Canada
- 1994, Charlotte Holsopple Glick, conference minister for Indiana-Michigan Conference
- 1996, Shirley H. Showalter, president, Goshen College

---

16 *Report* 63, Sept.–Oct. 1985, 2.

- 1997, Lee F. Snyder, president, Bluffton College (1984, interim academic dean at Eastern Mennonite College)
- 2001, Lois Coleman Neufeld, director of Canadian programs for MCC Canada
- 2001, Janet Plenert, executive for Christian Witness, Mennonite Church Canada

In 1985, the MCC offices in Akron, Pennsylvania, did an audit of the types of staff positions held by men and women in 1985, compared to 1975. The audit found that women still made up most of the office staff in the level 1–3 salary grouping. But men and women were approaching equal representation in the 4–5 salary grouping. These mid-level positions, few of which were in existence in 1975, were an opportunity for women. Although no women were in the 7–8 responsibility level, significant numbers of women were in the 6 category. As summarized in a *Report* article:

> Perhaps the most dramatic shift in women's involvement has occurred away from [MCC] headquarters. Ten years ago, all country representatives and VS [Voluntary Service] unit directors were men. Today, the great majority of the overseas positions are shared by couples. In the United States, VS unit directors are equally likely to be men, women, or couples. . . . Couples who come to headquarters assignments after having worked side-by-side in overseas or VS settings, sharing the burdens and joys of responsibility, have sometimes been disappointed when such flexibility is not allowed at headquarters.[17]

Figure 8.5 below shows numbers and percentages for men and women at various levels and in various parts of the MCC organization in 1975 and 1985. A look at similar data in 2001 showed little change by percentage since 1985. In upper-level management positions in MCC Binational and MCC US head-

---

17 *Report* 63, Sept.–Oct. 1985, 4.

196 • Lois Y. Barrett

quarters and regions, women represented 25 percent in 1985 and 23 percent in 2001.[18]

Organization	Level 1-3 Women	Level 1-3 Men	Level 4-5 Women	Level 4-5 Men	Level 6-8 Women	Level 6-8 Men
MCC Canada 1975	11 (92%)	1 (8%)	1 (33%)	2 (67%)	0 (0%)	6 (100%)
MCC Canada 1985	24 (92%)	2 (8%)	8 (32%)	17 (68%)	1 (6%)	15 (94%)
MCC US 1975	4 (80%)	1 (20%)	0 (0%)	2 (100%)	0 (0%)	3 (100%)
MCC US 1985	15 (83%)	3 (17%)	7 (39%)	11 (61%)	2 (22%)	7 (78%)
MCC International 1975	26 (87%)	4 (13%)	1 (20%)	4 (80%)	1 (6%)	14 (93%)
MCC International 1985	28 (88%)	4 (12%)	7 (50%)	7 (50%)	4 (25%)	12 (75%)
Total 1975	41 (87%)	6 (13%)	2 (20%)	8 (80%)	1 (4%)	23 (96%)
Total 1985	67 (88%)	9 (12%)	22 (39%)	35 (61%)	7 (17%)	34 (83%)

Figure 8.5: Representation in MCC organizations in 1975 and 1985

While "equal pay for equal work" was a rallying cry for feminists, it was not a reality for many women. When I first started working for the GCMC in 1971 as news service director and associate editor of *The Mennonite*, the supervisor who hired me determined my pay by asking me what I had made in my previous job as a journalist and offered me twenty-five dollars a month more. After not too long in the job, I discovered that there was no consistent, formal pay scale for staff in the GCMC offices. People who did similar kinds of work were paid very differently, and most often the people with the lowest pay were women. To add insult to

---

18 *Report* 161, May–June 2002, 2.

injury, an additional two hundred dollars a year was paid to "heads of household," and only one of those "heads of household" was female—a widow with children at home. Never-married women did not count as heads of household, nor did any married women. I asked one of the executives how Staff Council (all men at that point) had decided whether I or my husband was the head of our household. He said that, if a husband was present, then the man was the head. But the topic had been raised and the inequalities brought to light. Shortly thereafter, Staff Council instituted a new pay scale based on responsibilities, tenure at the office, and education, and a little later the symbolic head-of-household bonus was done away with. Pay for women on staff generally increased, and for one woman pay almost doubled.

Issues around being the "first"

It was often difficult for women who were the first in their elected or staff position. Often they not only lacked other female mentors but also faced direct or indirect resistance to their leadership from men. Some women were calm and measured about the resistance they encountered; others were more concerned to correct the injustices they experienced. Florence Driedger wrote, "And what does it feel like to be in a predominantly male environment? Where there has been love, caring, and focus on the task, there has been a sense of team work and accomplishment. When persons have felt threatened there has been a need to respond as one does to anyone who is threatened."[19] Likewise, Marie Wiens remembered her experiences on an otherwise all-male board:

> At first it was awkward being the only women on a board or administrative staff that had been all male until then. . . . I confess I don't think of myself as being the only female on a board—*until* a man makes some remark calling attention to it, not out of malice, but because it is still a bit novel. There have, of course, been some humorous incidents, like the registration card which asked,

---

19 *Report* 63, Sept.–Oct. 1985, 7.

"Will your wife attend the Friday banquet with you?" To which I replied, "No, and neither will my husband." Or the management seminar I attended once where the name tags were made to anchor in a shirt pocket. I was the only person there without a shirt pocket![20]

Others remembered the emotions involved in the governance changes. Kimberly Schmidt reflected:

So have we come a long way? Yes and no. Ordination struggles in several conferences should encourage feminists to own their anger and to use it for constructive change. I well remember the nervousness that accompanied Marilyn Klaus' quest for more female leadership [at the 1980 General Conference sessions]. Nervousness, however, was soon replaced by relief and a giddy triumphal feeling when conference delegates voted in favor of our candidates.... Owning anger, admittedly a challenge for many of us, and using it constructively to overcome gender oppression in the church, can and has fostered change.[21]

Sometimes it was difficult to be taken seriously. Multiple women wrote about their experiences of not being heard in committee meetings. Emma Sommers Richards wrote:

About 15 years ago [1970] I was on a churchwide administrative committee as the only female. The male chair recognized me kindly during breaks, held the door for me and asked about my husband and children. But, as he led the meeting, he ignored my presence in the discussions and committee decisions. One occasion stands out vividly in my memory. During a meeting I expressed my opinion on the issue at hand. Then the chair turned to a male member of the committee and asked for his

---

20 *Report 63*, Sept.–Oct. 1985, 8.
21 Schmidt, "You've Come a Long Way," 10.

opinion. He responded by saying, "I like Emma's idea and would support it." The chair asked him, "Would you please state what you would support?" And the committee member simply turned to me and said, "Emma, would you please restate it since you can do so much better than I." So it was, after two years the chair was challenged to listen to the female member of the committee. Things have changed over the past 15 years.[22]

But maybe not. Iris de León-Hartshorn wrote in 2002:

> When communicating, more weight is given when white males speak. When I first came to MCC, we had a management meeting. I stood up and made a suggestion, and it was ignored. Jeannie commented, "It didn't seem like they heard you." So she stood up and said, "Iris brought up this suggestion. I think it is a valid idea, and we need to talk about it." Jeannie also received no response. Ten minutes later, a white male in the institution stood up and made the same suggestion. He was heard and praised for his great idea. Then a man of color stood up and pointed it out. He said, "You know, Jeannie and Iris made the same suggestion ten minutes ago and no attention was given to it. Now when a white male says the same thing, all of a sudden it is a great idea." That is very frustrating and many times, as a woman in leadership, I feel that I have a lot of ideas. I have things to contribute, but I am not taken seriously. Often I have to say something several times. Also, it has been really hurtful when men have used some of my ideas and gotten the credit. That's been difficult and demoralizing. But probably in many work places that happens a lot more.[23]

---

22 *Report* 63, Sept.–Oct. 1985, 13.
23 Iris de León-Hartshorn, "Barriers to Women of Color," *Report* 161, May–June 2002, 7.

Emily Will wrote, "At what point does the feminist, male or female, no longer focus on access into the system but rather on changing the system? In some cases, the very process of rapping on a closed door has led people to consider building a new house instead."[24]

Often women were assumed to be in stereotypical roles. LaVerna Klippenstein, a free-lance writer from Winnipeg, Manitoba, noted in several anecdotes the frequent lack of recognition of the value of her work.

> The man introduced himself and paid me what was meant to be a fine compliment. "Even men," he said, "read what you write." I should have been impressed. Instead I was puzzled. I do not see myself as a woman writer, but simply as a person who expresses concerns, ideas and insights. . . .
>
> "What are you doing?" asks the voice on the phone. "Writing," I answer. "Good. I hoped to catch you when you were free." She wouldn't understand that I'd sooner be interrupted while I'm painting the porch. . . .
>
> Anyone who has written has met those who say, "I read your article," only to look puzzled when you ask, "Which one?"[25]

As someone who has done freelance writing myself, I can understand her reactions. I have lost count of the number of times at churchwide meetings I have introduced myself to someone who then says, "Haven't you written Sunday school lessons for children?" I reply, "No, I have never written for children, but I have written several times for the *Adult Bible Study Guide* and for other adult study booklets." Some of these people have a hard time believing me.

---

24 *Report* 63, Sept.–Oct. 1985, 2.
25 *Report* 37, May–June 1981, 4–5.

Women and decision making

In 1985 a group of women from the Goshen-Elkhart, Indiana, area who had served on various Mennonite boards or in a variety of teaching and administrative roles in church agencies met in a living room to review their experiences. They agreed that more women were being hired for leadership roles by church agencies, thanks in part to encouragement by women board members. But most of the women present could vividly remember being the only woman present on a board or being one of two or three women in a room full of male executives. They recalled feelings of uncertainty, discomfort, and exclusion. One woman described being frustrated by men who made decisions in the restrooms during breaks and failed to inform her of their conclusions. A report on this women's group recalled:

> In their minority position, some of these women felt a need to justify themselves with male credentials in the male world. Their skills and experience outside the corridors of power seemed to count for little. They especially remembered hesitation to voice contrary views or support unpopular positions. They believed they would not be forgiven for mistakes. They sensed great pressure to be productive and successful. . . . All of the women reported that they had received no orientation whatsoever for their role as minority persons. They simply had to find their own way through difficult, uncharted territory.
>
> These women perceived Mennonite men to be ambivalent about women's roles in places of power. Men tend to reward women who play the game by male rules. Some reported that men are even more threatened by women now than earlier because the chances are much greater that women will be elected or hired. . . .
>
> Another crucial difference is women's view and use of power. Women want to use power to create; men tend to use power to control. Men, for example, may use their

board and agency positions as springboards to new, higher positions. They will delegate behind-the-scenes work to others and spend their time in public roles. Women are more likely to focus on the job that needs to be done than on the power plays or turf protection. They assume teamwork and cooperation and look for creative, people-oriented solutions to organizational problems.[26]

The group concluded with a list of needs for women in Mennonite institutions: orientation for new women appointees; training for confronting, expressing anger, and managing conflict; valuing of women's extracurricular, outside-of-employment experience; mentoring by both men and women; affirming men who share power with women; a new definition of teamwork; and a re-visioning of images of power and authority to conform to the model of Jesus Christ. "To gracefully meet the challenge without becoming cynical or weary is the task that lies ahead," they said.[27]

Noting the value in having women on leadership committees, Anna Kreider Juhnke wrote: "After observing the gracious leadership of men in MCC U.S. and General Conference, I cannot claim that women bring superior gifts of nurturance and group process. However, it seems to me that the committees I know with more equal male-female representation are more informally democratic and less solemn about themselves than those that are mostly male."[28] Similarly, Iris de León-Hartshorn expressed the need to revalue the more consensual way that women have traditionally made decisions: "We are not weak or indecisive. We make decisions differently."[29]

In the secular world, a variety of research has been done on women and leadership. The groundbreaking book in 1986 was

---

26 Marlene Kropf and Alice Roth, "Experiences Shared," *Report* 63, Sept.–Oct. 1985, 14–15.

27 Kropf and Roth, "Experiences Shared," 14–15.

28 *Report* 63, Sept.–Oct. 1985, 10.

29 *Report* 63, Sept.–Oct. 1985, 9.

Women's Ways of Knowing.[30] There, the authors went beyond Lawrence Kohlberg's identification of decision making by universal ethical principle as the top of the scale of moral development. Instead, in this study, women participants saw the highest level of moral development as making decisions that valued both principles and relationships.

In secular and religious settings, female executives, board members, and political candidates have been required to be both competent and likeable. How many male executives have been told, "You need to smile more"? Likewise, women have been socialized not to appear aggressive. Some women tried to make a distinction between aggressive and assertive behavior. Aggressive behavior stands up for one's own rights in a way that violates the rights of others, while assertive behavior stands up for one's rights in such a way that the rights of others are not violated. Aggressive behavior seeks to humiliate or dominate; assertive behavior is honest and direct and shows respect for the other person.[31] Given this distinction, the question remained: Could women be appropriately assertive? Or perhaps they would be told, "Watch your tone!" or "Don't be one of those angry women," as one seminary professor cautioned me when I was a student in 1981.

Conclusion

In this chapter we have seen how, between 1972 and 2006, women began populating the board rooms, executive offices, and classrooms of Mennonite institutions as well as congregational committees. While this expansion of leadership roles was a significant step for Mennonite women, it did not come without its challenges.

By 2006 many boards, committees, and executive offices still did not have equal numbers of men and women. When Mennonite Church USA was formed in 2001, not a single head of its agencies was female. The new Mennonite Church Canada had one

---

30 Mary Field Belenky et al., *Women's Ways of Knowing: The Development of Self, Voice, and Mind* (New York: Basic Books, 1986, 1997).
31 Sharon Molzen, "Understanding Assertive Behavior," *Report* 33, Sept.–Oct. 1980, 3.

woman heading a churchwide commission. Change had perhaps been more rapid at the congregational level, where many women were now deacons and elders, as well as members of the nursery committee.

In Mennonite structures, women sometimes had to adapt to male ways of doing things or face resistance to their own ways of doing things. Despite this resistance, women also began changing the institutions and modeling new ways of listening and decision making. Mennonite women were now a part of church governance.

9

Women are "adjunct"
Women serve and learn leadership
*Anita Hooley Yoder
and Marlene Harder Bogard*

In late 2014, I (Anita) was hired to write a book on the history of Mennonite women's organizations (published in 2017 as *Circles of Sisterhood*).[32] Since I had never been involved in a church women's group, nor really considered joining one, I was not sure where to begin. And I certainly was not sure what I would uncover in my research. I had no idea how women's organizations had affected the development of their larger denominations. Or how local women's groups contributed to the development of their congregations. Or how these groups had helped—or perhaps hindered—the personal development of the individuals involved in them.

What I uncovered was a complicated, creative story that started in local sewing circles well over one hundred years ago. By the early twentieth century, these sewing groups had formed strong and influential regional and denominational organizations, in both the (Old) Mennonite Church (MC) and the General Conference Mennonite Church (GCMC). These organizations have experienced ups and downs in participation, but their legacy endures today in Mennonite Women USA, the women's organization of Mennonite Church USA, and the women's organization

---

32 Anita Hooley Yoder, *Circles of Sisterhood: A History of Mission, Service, and Fellowship in Mennonite Women's Organizations* (Harrisonburg, VA: Herald, 2017).

of Mennonite Church Canada. Throughout their history, women helped each other find ways to proclaim God's good news of acceptance, value, and joy to people around the world and (perhaps just as importantly) to themselves.

During the years 1972–2006, Mennonite women's groups functioned as both the backbone of local Mennonite congregations and as a sort of appendage. In some contexts, women's groups—which were variously sewing circles, moms and preschoolers gatherings, or meetings for a specific fundraising effort—were vital forces of congregational life and ministry. In other places, women's groups were dying out. But as they were from their start, Mennonite women's groups continued to be places where women extended themselves in service to others and found meaningful avenues of personal spiritual development.

In the late twentieth century, local women's groups and the denominational women's organizations were sometimes easily dismissed. For some outside the groups, they were at best irrelevant and at worst a hindrance to women seeking leadership positions in the wider church and society. Women both inside and outside of the organizations felt their "adjunct" status. Participants sensed a perception that women's groups were somehow a supplement to the real work of the church, even while they witnessed the importance of the groups to their personal lives and to the functioning of many local congregations and their denominations.

Women's organizations and the development of their denominations

The early 1970s saw women's groups in both the MC and the GCMC shift their relationships to their respective denominations. In 1971, the MC reorganized its structure, and the women's organization became a commission of the newly formed Board of Congregational Ministries. To reflect the new relationship, the organization changed its name slightly from the Women's Missionary and Service Auxiliary to the Women's Missionary and Service Commission (WMSC). This change reveals two shifts for the women's organization. First, it became, in name at least, a more essential part of the denomination's work, replacing the term "auxiliary" and its evocation of a supplemental body that supports the main work of a restricted group. Doris Lehman was the WMSC board president at the time. Married to a dentist, she explained the name change using an example from her personal life. "I have no objection to being a member of a dental auxiliary, because I'm not a dentist," she said. "But some of us didn't think it was appropriate to be an auxiliary of the church. . . . I am a Christian along with my husband, and we're in the church together."[33]

The GCMC women's groups in the 1970s were also concerned about their relationship to their denomination—and the involvement of women in the work of the denomination. By 1973, the GCMC women's organization, then known as the Women's Missionary Association (WMA), had representatives on each of the denomination's three commissions (the commissions on Overseas Ministries, Home Ministries, and Education). However, these representatives were considered unofficial members and did not have voting privileges, except for the Commission on Home Ministries, which had two members from the women's organization and involved them as regular commission members. When the WMA executive secretary wrote to the GCMC General Board requesting a review of the status of the women's group representatives, the board referred the matter to the denomination's Constitution Committee. This committee replied with a recommendation to continue current practice, saying that the members appointed by the women's organization should not have votes, as they were a "special interest group." Perhaps wanting to avoid further discussion of the matter, the commissions on Overseas Ministries and Education dropped their WMA representatives.[34]

In February 1974, GCMC commissions and boards were gathered for their annual meeting, a time when the leaders of the

---

33 Quoted in Helen Good Brenneman, *Ring a Dozen Doorbells: Twelve Women Tell It Like It Is* (Scottdale, PA: Herald, 1973), 126.
34 Gladys V. Goering, *Women in Search of Mission* (Newton, KS: Faith and Life, 1980), 90–92.

women's organization gathered as well. Gladys Goering, who had recently begun as executive secretary of the women's organization, went before the GCMC General Board with two other women to deliver a statement on behalf of the WMA that argued for voting representation within denominational bodies. Elsie Flaming, who at that time was president of the Ontario women's organization, remembers sitting in a side room with other women and praying together while their leaders spoke to the board. "They went to this meeting with a lot of apprehension," Flaming said in a 2015 interview, pausing with emotion at the poignant memory. "And they came back and they were just beaming, that they had been accepted."[35]

Goering's statement outlined several reasons why the women's organization should be granted voting representatives in the structure of the denomination. First, the organization had 10,692 members, two-fifths of whom were Canadian, a bond that helped unite the binational GCMC. Second, women's groups were significant contributors to the denomination, giving well over half a million dollars annually to projects at various levels. Third, being part of the commissions would enable the women to be more informed about the denomination and its programs. The fourth point mentioned that, ideally, the percentage of women elected to commissions would be much higher, but that this was not likely to happen soon.[36] Finally, as the women's organization was in the process of reassessing its future direction, being part of the commissions could be a real help. "To be shut out will say something to us also," the statement noted.[37]

The General Board unanimously granted the request, and the Mennonite Biblical Seminary board also made changes to accommodate a representative from the women's organization. Naomi

---

35 Elsie Flaming, interview by Anita Hooley Yoder, May 20, 2015.

36 At that time, the commissions on Overseas Ministries and Education had women members not connected to the women's organization, though women made up a very small percentage of the commissions, and there were no measures to ensure their representation.

37 Goering, *Women in Search*, 92–93.

Lehman, board president of the women's organization, recalled the "gratefulness and celebration" that followed the General Board's decision. "We experienced the joy of being full-fledged partners in the mission of the church, accepted for ourselves as well as for the financial and material aid contributions we have made for so many years," she wrote in the magazine of the women's organization.[38]

Besides being involved in the work of their denominations, women's group participants were central to the interdenominational agency Mennonite Central Committee (MCC). At first the women mainly provided material items made by their sewing groups. They quilted and tied comforters, but often these groups also initiated the collection of school kits, layettes, Christmas bundles, and a variety relief kits for MCC from their congregations and beyond. In the late twentieth century, women's organizations started to provide the labor necessary for the functioning of MCC Relief Sales and MCC thrift stores. Many women's groups undertook impressive efforts for the sales. For example, the women's group at Zion Mennonite Church in Pryor, Oklahoma (now part of the Conservative Mennonite Conference), has organized congregation members to annually make vast quantities of food for the Oklahoma Relief Sale since the sale's inception in 1978. Each year they can hundreds of quarts of apple butter. One year they made 319 angel food cakes, and another year they made 845 pounds of noodles.[39] Large MCC stores like the Et Cetera Shop in Newton, Kansas, utilize hundreds of volunteers. One of these volunteers, Lela Mae Sawatzky (also a former secretary for the GCMC women's organization) described the shop as "a place of inter-Mennonite and community cooperation."[40]

---

38 Naomi Lehman, "Which Way Are We Heading?" *Window to Mission*, April 1974, 3.

39 Christine Scheffel, email to Anita Hooley Yoder (information from Zion Mennonite Church's 2011 centennial book), Dec. 5, 2015.

40 Paul Schrag, "Kansas Thrift Shop Celebrates Forty Years, Honors a Founder," *Mennonite World Review*, May 9, 2016, 14.

During the late twentieth century, women's groups also became more involved in their own mission projects and international support. In the MC context, the women's organization provided modest scholarships for young women at Mennonite colleges and seminaries who planned to do service or church-related work. Barbara Reber, WSMC executive secretary during the 1980s, started a project called "A Nickel a Day . . . a Prayer a Day." The women's organization distributed small banks for people to deposit coins into as they remembered to pray for mission projects. "It was a very good feeling when I presented $15,000 raised through this project to Mennonite Board of Missions during General Assembly," Reber recalled.[41] The WMSC also contributed smaller amounts to other church women's events, such as Women in Ministry gatherings or the emerging Hispanic Mennonite women's conferences. And rather than simply supporting mission workers in faraway places, the organization began making international connections itself, sending Jocele Meyer and Grace Slatter to a gathering of Mennonite women in India in 1977.

The GCMC women's organization, then called Women in Mission, sent two representatives to the All-India Mennonite Women's Conference in 1977. When they returned, these women traveled around the United States and Canada sharing about their experience with the women who had supported them. In 1978, a twenty-four-member women's choir from Taiwan came to North America, primarily to attend the Mennonite World Conference assembly in Wichita, Kansas. Women in Mission arranged for the choir to make more than thirty additional appearances in five provinces and eight states, taking care of most of their lodging, food, and travel needs. This visit led to personal connections with women from a part of the world where the GCMC had several missionaries and to a reciprocal trip by two Women in Mission leaders, who visited women's groups and missionaries in Taiwan, Japan, and Hong Kong in 1981.[42]

---

41 Quoted in Saralyn Yoder, "Barbara Reber: Happy with Women's Changing Roles," *Voice*, Oct. 1990, 13.

42 Goering, *Women in Search*, 80, 81, 98.

These international visits made women aware of the desire for leadership training felt by Mennonite-related women around the world. While a program supporting international exchanges had been part of Women in Mission's budget since 1974, a new fund for education and professional training for international women began in 1979, called the Women's World Outreach fund. The fund was designated for international women's travel to future Mennonite World Conference gatherings and for leadership training and seminars in various countries. By the mid-1980s, the fund had been used to enable wives (and sometimes children) of international church leaders to accompany their husbands when they came to study in the United States and to take some classes themselves, as well to aid some attendees of a Hispanic Mennonite women's conference.[43]

I (Marlene) remember after I returned from the 1988 Learning Tour, many North American women were compelled to offer assistance to the Colombian churches, and even to individuals. "What can we do? How shall we respond?" we asked. As I approached the Colombian missionaries and the Commission on Overseas Mission staff, their answer was, "Do not send money; pray for them." But somehow that did not seem adequate. People on both sides were looking for a relationship, or at least a connection. We were interested not just in material aid but also in empowerment. We wanted to help women become leaders, not just send them a diaper (although diapers are important!). Thank God that the women's organization developed other ideas, such as Sister-Link and the International Women's Fund, for scholarships and leadership development.

International support and connection continued to be a concern of future iterations of the women's organizations. In 1997, anticipating the merger of their denominations, the MC and GCMC women's organizations merged and took the name Mennonite Women (eventually becoming Mennonite Women USA and Mennonite Women Canada in 2002). They continued

---

43 Gladys Goering, "Saskatoon Report," 1986, Mennonite Library and Archives (MLA), North Newton, Kansas.

supporting international women who were pursuing theological training, either in the United States or in their own contexts. They also developed Sister-Link projects, which connected women in the United States directly with women in other places, seeking to provide a relationship of blessing and support.

One of the first Sister-Link programs connected women in several Florida churches with women in the Caucasus Mountain region in Russia, where Alice and Phil Shenk were serving with Mennonite Mission Network. The Florida women sent packages for Alice Shenk to distribute to new mothers; the packages included a receiving blanket, an infant outfit, vitamins, socks, and a picture of the giver with a note of congratulations and love.[44] Alice Shenk helped the recipients reciprocate with their own photos and greetings.

Another significant Sister-Link paired North American women with African female theologians, providing scholarships and prayer partners. Several African women who participated in this program, including Rebecca Osiro from Kenya and Sidonie Swana from the Congo, were among the first women ordained in their denominations. Support for women pursuing theological and biblical studies continues to this day through Mennonite Women USA's International Women's Fund.

Women's organizations and the development of their congregations

A 1974 self-study gathered information from 522 GCMC congregational women's groups in Canada and the United States. Given the choices of "strong," "average," or "weak," most respondents (58 percent) rated their congregational group as average, 37 percent said their groups were strong, and 5 percent felt they were weak. Just over half the respondents said their group put a strong emphasis on "handwork," while 20 percent put a strong emphasis on "study and program." Out of several phrases describing the function of groups, the one chosen most frequently was "mate-

---

44 "SisterLink Brings Special Delivery to New Mothers," Mennonite Mission Network 2003–2004 Annual Report, 17.

rial aid contributor" (180 groups), followed by "fellowship" (139 groups). Third and fourth were "financial contributor to the G.C. [denomination]" (105 groups) and "financial contributor to the district/province" (90 groups). This survey shows the strong service and social functions of local women's groups. It also shows that while the denominational organization's leadership was exploring new horizons of leadership, influence, and empowerment, the primary focus for many women continued to be their material and financial contributions.[45]

During the 1970s and 1980s, GCMC women's groups gave time and money to countless projects in their congregations and communities. Most groups near a GCMC higher education institution included it in their giving and supported it with material items. Other activities included cleanup days at homes for the aged, helping with blood drives, serving as hosts for visiting choirs, assisting families during a hospitalization, and volunteering at church-sponsored nursery schools. "Catering meals," Goering notes, "is on the list of numerous [congregational women's] societies as a function performed when it is convenient and often when it is not."[46] Goering points out that the *organization* of church women's societies is especially important.[47] While in many congregations the activities listed above were covered in an ad hoc way, congregations with an established women's group had a source of immediate help.

Women's groups in culturally diverse congregations often both embraced and expanded typical notions of Mennonite women's activities. For example, the women's group at New Holland (Pennsylvania) Spanish Mennonite Church, with participants from ten or more Spanish-speaking countries, started an International Spanish Food Festival in the late 1980s. The festival has become an anticipated community event that draws over

---

45 Self-Study Report, 1974, box 19, folder 246, Women in Mission 1973–77, MLA.
46 Goering, *Women in Search*, 108.
47 Goering, *Women in Search*, 107–108.

five hundred attendees, and the whole congregation participates in preparations.[48] Part of the income from the festival supports congregational projects such as youth group trips and building improvements, and part goes to the women's group (mostly to help people attend Hispanic Mennonite women's conferences). Women in this congregation have also met for Bible study, to support women who have lost their husbands, and to deliver groceries to new families in the area. Wanda Gonzalez Coleman, who was involved in the congregation for many years, said the group even tried to do a bit of quilting, though, she added, "That wasn't our forte!" But the women liked the idea of working on something together and made a quilt that included the names of all the families in the church. They passed the quilt around and committed to pray for the congregation's families when the quilt was in their home. For the New Holland women, a quilt—an item associated with the traditional service commitment of Mennonite women's groups—also fostered a sense of sisterhood as they worked on it together and used it to unite the congregation in prayer.[49]

As Mennonite women's groups found their own niche in congregational life, they also served as a welcoming place for initial connections to a church. In recent years, both Phyllis Tickle and Dorothy Bass have described how "emergent" Christians reverse the traditional religious pattern of "believe, behave, belong" and instead focus first on belonging and then on behaving and believing.[50] Bass uses knitting as an example of this reversal. "In knitting,

---

48 Joan Kern, "New Holland Spanish Mennonite Church to Hold International Food Festival," Lancaster Online, November 4, 2011, lancasteronline.com/features/faith_values/new-holland-spanish-mennonite-church-to-hold-international-food-festival/article_e33f45d4-a754-53e6-b78e-bbc415000efa.html.

49 Wanda Gonzalez Coleman, interview by Anita Hooley Yoder, Jan. 5, 2016.

50 See Phyllis Tickle, *The Great Emergence: How Christianity Is Changing and Why* (Grand Rapids, MI: Baker Books, 2012), 159; Diana Butler Bass, *Christianity after Religion: The End of the Church and the Birth of a New Spiritual Awakening* (New York: HarperCollins, 2012), 201–204.

the process is exactly the reverse of that in church," she writes. "Belonging to a knitting group leads to behaving as a knitter, which leads to believing things about knitting."[51] Maybe Mennonite women's groups, without necessarily realizing it, were poised to continue to thrive as new expressions of Christianity emerged. Women's groups have always stressed belonging (the sisterhood of talking and studying together) and behaving (quilting and doing service projects) as much as, if not more than, believing. They may be able to serve as spaces where the increasing number of "spiritual but not religious" North Americans can come together and work together, even while holding and exploring a variety of beliefs. While most participants in Mennonite women's groups at the beginning of the twenty-first century were older and held somewhat traditional Christian beliefs, the connections fostered by their gatherings could, perhaps, position them to survive and thrive in the atmosphere of emergent Christianity.

When a new woman becomes involved in congregational life, she is usually invited to attend the existing activities. During the time frame for this book, these entry points may have included a women's Bible study, book club, women's retreat, weekly breakfast, sewing circle, or service club. What I (Marlene) have noticed is that multiple entry points into congregational life are highly valued by newcomers. If there is only one option to "join," such as a sewing circle, one particular woman may not be friends with a needle and thread and thereby would never feel comfortable there. However, if there are varied options, held as various times of the day and evening, women are much more likely to find a place that helps them feel like they belong to a supportive community. Belonging first, as opposed to believing or behaving, has become the priority and comfort zone for newcomers. Belonging first makes sense because women are seeking to join a community of faith in which they can engage in the practices of the faith. To serve, sing, study, sew, or eat together in the context of a women's group provides a fine way of learning how the community operates, as well as its boundaries, values, and vision.

---

51 Bass, *Christianity after Religion*, 203.

Women's organizations and the development of their individuals

Besides their outward and even international focus, women's organizations performed a more inward-looking function. The 1970s and beyond saw a shift in mission for the organizations, as they began to focus more on the needs of women in their own congregations. In the pages of their publications, they tackled issues like television exposure, marriage challenges, and sexual abuse. Regional women's organizations pioneered things like groups for business and professional women and weekend women's retreats.

Women's retreats were a contributing factor to an increasing attention to spirituality among Mennonites in the late twentieth century. Women from MC congregations noted that their district retreats sometimes took on the feel of a family reunion, with women spending most of their time in conversations and activities. Beulah Kauffman, executive secretary of the WMSC from 1967 to 1978, felt that Mennonite women generally gave too much time to activities and conversations and not enough time to simply being, and she began promoting the concept of a silent retreat.[52] The WMSC held a silent retreat for its officers, equipping them to travel in pairs to replicate the event in every district. Angie Williams, who served on the WMSC board in the 1970s, attended the first training, where women were encouraged to spend time listening for God's voice. "Being a Mennonite almost all of my life, it was just not what we were used to doing," she remembered. "I mean, God talked to you personally?"[53] But a few women who had experience with the idea made the group feel comfortable, and Williams found herself entering fully into the practice and encountering God in ways she never had before. "To this day I still do some teaching that feeds back into that," she said in a 2015 interview. "I tell people that this has been the single source of the most spiritual growth in my life."[54]

---

52 Jocele Meyer, interview by Anita Hooley Yoder, Apr. 23, 2015.
53 Angie Williams, interview by Anita Hooley Yoder, Oct. 30, 2015.
54 Angie Williams, interview by Anita Hooley Yoder, Oct. 30, 2015.

Promoting retreats was not as great a priority for Women in Mission (the GCMC women's organization) as it was for the WMSC during this time, but some GCMC women did begin having retreats in their areas. Phyllis Baumgartner recalls seeing an article in a Christian magazine in the 1960s about retreats and feeling inspired to organize one for Central District Conference women at their new camp, Camp Friedenswald. Baumgartner, who had five children, worked to organize the retreat with another woman, who had even more children than she did. "It was so good to just have a little free time to read and meditate, to be with other moms who were struggling," Baumgartner said.[55] The Central District Conference women's retreat became an anticipated annual event for women from a variety of backgrounds and locations, including Ivorie Lowe. Lowe served on the denomination's Commission of Home Ministries and remembers having "such turmoil" one year because the commission meeting was the same weekend as the retreat. For Lowe, the retreats were meaningful because they provided an opportunity to "sit down and talk with or listen to women who were organizing something other than what I was involved in." As a school administrator, mother, and active congregation member, Lowe enjoyed hearing how other women balanced their concerns and commitments.[56]

It seems significant that Williams and Lowe, who were both heavily involved in regional or denominational women's retreats, were also some of the earliest women of color who served in denominational leadership roles. Williams was the first African American woman on the WMSC executive committee, beginning her term as WMSC vice president in 1973. Lowe served in many churchwide positions, sometimes as both the first woman and the first African American. Surely connecting with other women gave people like Lowe and Williams much-needed support in navigating the demands of their various settings.

---

55 Phyllis Baumgartner, interview by Anita Hooley Yoder, Oct. 14, 2015.
56 Ivorie Lowe, interview by Anita Hooley Yoder, June 4, 2015.

During this time, Mennonite women of color also started to gather in their own separate retreat spaces. The first Spanish-speaking Mennonite women's conference was held in April 1973 in Moline, Illinois. It was coordinated by Maria Bustos, who joined the WMSC executive committee in 1975 specifically as a representative of Hispanic Mennonite women. Women in Spanish-speaking Mennonite churches had organized into a conference several years earlier, and Bustos facilitated communication between the two organizations. The first Black Mennonite women's retreat, or "fellowship conference," was held in 1977 and coordinated by Frances Jackson. The theme was "Challenges Facing Black Women in the Mennonite Church." Both the Black and the Hispanic retreats served as places for individual women to be supported and to grow in leadership, often having opportunity to preach, teach, and lead music that was not as available in their congregations.[57]

Leadership development was a key function of Mennonite women's groups more generally, even if it was rarely a stated goal. Most participating women took turns leading the group or provided project ideas and offered devotional thoughts and prayer. Often, these women found their voices in these roles, and these experiences led them to additional leadership positions both in and out of congregational life. In a 1992 article on the history of Women in Mission, Gladys Goering wrote that the organization "does not exist to promote women's rights." But, she added, "that happened as leadership skills, otherwise overlooked, were encouraged in women's groups."[58]

In 1988, I (Marlene) was honored to be chosen as the Northern District Conference (GCMC) representative on a Women in Mission learning tour to Colombia in South America. As a young mother with no overseas experience and living in rural South Dakota, I eagerly agreed to participate in this rare opportunity.

---

57 See Yoder, *Circles of Sisterhood*, chapter 5, for a fuller treatment of these gatherings.

58 Gladys Goering, "Still Going after All These Years," *Window to Mission*, Dec. 22, 1992, 3.

The sixteen-day experience was amazing, as we visited many congregations and heard women's stories in Colombian Mennonite churches. We connected with the denomination's missionaries and learned firsthand how the churches in Colombia began. We heard stories of victimization, devastation, and trauma. At the center of each woman's experience was a poignant and enthusiastic expression of Christian faith. Upon return, I was invited to share these stories, relaying the challenges the Colombian women faced daily. As I visited many churches in the Northern District, my public speaking skills developed, and I became a storyteller. I felt a genuine connection to the GCMC and their mission story. This journey impacted my global understanding of Mennonite women, but I was also formed in my own faith, and I grew in confidence in my leadership capabilities. And the next time I was asked to be a leader, I said yes. I was equipped.

In the 1980s, the Mennonite Church was just beginning to permit women to serve in official pastoral leadership positions, and women's groups were often the first place women tested their leadership abilities and callings. Some churches had "WMSC Day," during which a leader from the organization gave the Sunday sermon (or at least a "talk," perhaps while standing to the side of the pulpit). Grace Brunner recalls that five women who were on the WMSC board during her time later went to seminary and became pastors, including herself. "I am sure that if I had never done WMSC, I would never have been ordained," she said in a 2015 interview. "I mean, my whole life changed because of WMSC. And I think it did for some of those women too."[59]

Joyce Shutt started working with the GCMC denominational women's group in her thirties, which included participating in the denomination's Commission on Home Ministries. Her work in this role exposed her to important people and issues in the wider denomination and gave her a chance to exercise her budding leadership skills. Eventually, Shutt decided to enroll in seminary. Her studies spanned a challenging time in her marriage and family life. But after about eight years of intermittent coursework, Shutt

---

59 Grace Brunner, interview by Anita Hooley Yoder, Dec. 11, 2015.

became, in 1980, the seventh female pastor ordained in the US GCMC (see appendix). She served her home congregation, Fairfield (Pennsylvania) Mennonite Church, for twenty years and is now considered a pastor emerita.[60]

Shutt credits the women's group in her congregation and her experience with Women in Mission as instrumental in her awakening as a church leader. Her congregational women's group cheered her on when she wanted to quit. The denominational group, led by Gladys Goering, challenged her to channel her angry energy in a constructive way. Shutt recalled her surprise at the sense of sisterhood and empowerment she experienced through Women in Mission, an organization that she expected to be "a bunch of staid old fuddy-duddies"—which, said Shutt, "they were, in appearance. But they were very empowering." Shutt remembers walking down a hallway en route to a meeting at the denominational headquarters and passing an old woman bent over and using two canes. "You go, girl!" the woman told her.[61]

Conclusions

The end of the twentieth century into the beginning of the twenty-first has been a challenging period in church and society. The decline in church attendance in the United States has been widely documented. Studies have also shown that involvement in social organizations has declined, as Americans have become less connected to social structures in general.[62] These trends have certainly affected women's organizations, as what were vibrant sewing circles or women's sharing groups in some congregations have dwindled to a few members or vanished altogether. Regional or conference-level women's organizations in some places have dis-

---

60 Joyce Shutt, interview by Anita Hooley Yoder, Oct. 16, 2014.

61 Joyce Shutt, interview by Anita Hooley Yoder, Oct. 16, 2014. See also Joyce Shutt, chapter 12, in *Our Struggle to Serve: The Stories of Fifteen Evangelical Women*, ed. Virginia Hearn (Waco, TX: Word, 1979), 142–52.

62 See Robert D. Putnam, *Bowling Alone: The Collapse and Revival of American Community* (New York: Simon & Schuster, 2000).

banded due to shrinking attendance and a lack of women willing to take on leadership roles.

In 1980, Women in Mission estimated it had 10,000 members in 440 groups.[63] In 1991, it reported 7,000 members in 350 units.[64] In 1995, the numbers were 6,500 women in 300 groups.[65] While the 1995 budget had been lowered from previous years, the coordinator still had to announce that it looked as if the organization would not have enough undesignated funds to meet expenses. "This has occurred before in the history of WM but not for several decades," she noted.[66] The numbers for WMSC participation are a bit harder to track since it did not have as much of a focus on dues-paying membership. (WMSC counted 400 local groups in 1995.[67]) But it is not hard to find references to the organization's dwindling finances. Notes from a 1993 executive committee meeting end with: "Finances—are declining." The recorder added, "As I recall, we dismissed rather abruptly and very tired and frustrated."[68] A 1996 treasurer's report in *Voice* noted that receipts were $96,593, while disbursements were $99,809. The report continued, "Because we started this year $1,926 in the red, we are now $5,142 in the red as the year ends. This is very serious."[69]

---

63 Women in Mission brochure, ca. 1980, box 1, folder 3, Women in Mission Promotional items/printed matter 1980s–early 1990s, MLA.

64 Susan Jantzen, "1991 Coordinator's Report to Women in Mission," box 1, folder 29, Women in Mission Minutes, reports, etc. 1960s–1990s, MLA.

65 GCMC Women in Mission and MC Women's Missionary and Service Commission, "Program and Reports," 1995, p. 18, MLA.

66 Susan Jantzen, "1995 Women in Mission Coordinator's Report," p. 14, box 1, folder 33, Women in Mission Minutes, reports, etc. 1960s–1990s, MLA.

67 GCMC Women in Mission and MC Women's Missionary and Service Commission, "Program and Reports," p. 19, Women in Mission 1990s files from Susan Jantzen, MLA.

68 Ruth Lapp Guengerich, WMSC Executive Committee Minutes, July 1993, box 1, folder 3, Women's Missionary and Service Commission Executive Committee Records, Mennonite Church USA Archives, Elkhart, IN.

69 Mary Ellen Kauffman, "Treasurer's Report," *Voice*, April 1997, 5.

Yet, in many places, local women's groups remained strong. Somewhat ironically, given the resistance to women's groups by some male church leaders in earlier eras, by the late twentieth century male leaders often spoke about the value of the women's organizations. In 1981, the moderator of the Conference of Mennonites in Canada called the women's societies the "deacons of our church and conference." He continued, "Your service is the glue that puts stability into our church social functions, and your support of Mission and Service activities at home and abroad is the leaven around which so much of our congregational mission is built."[70] In a 1985 *Gospel Herald* article, Alice W. Lapp wrote that Boyd Nelson, a former MC mission board administrator, "credits WMSC with doing more to promote new ideas, introduce new literature, develop retreats, spread information, and show sensitivity to the feelings of people than any other organization."[71]

One way that the women's organizations dealt with their dwindling numbers and (perhaps) relevance was through collaboration. The MC and GCMC women's organizations were the second agency (after the seminary in Elkhart) to merge as conversations about denominational integration began. They joined to become Mennonite Women in 1997, well before the denominational merging process was complete in 2002. In many areas, regional or conference women's groups had already been collaborating for decades.

As controversy raged in the wider denomination, Mennonite Women USA (the name the organization took in 2003) also faced difficult procedural and theological questions. But as it started new programs to support and connect women in local congregations and around the world, it became what some described as "a bright spot in the denomination."[72] Celebrating one hundred

---

70 Quoted in Gloria Neufeld Redekop, *The Work of Their Hands: Mennonite Women's Societies in Canada* (Waterloo, ON: Wilfrid Laurier University Press, 1996), 100.

71 Alice W. Lapp, "WMSC: Whence and Whither?" *Gospel Herald*, Aug. 6, 1985, 544.

72 Rebekah Basinger, interview by Anita Hooley Yoder, Jan. 22, 2015.

years of ministry in 2017, the organization continues to morph and rethink itself. As it does so, it seeks to honor the productive history of sisterhood and service while at the same time shaping leaders and prophetically proclaiming what being a Mennonite woman is in a new century.

Conclusion
Women said something!
Lois Y. Barrett and Dorothy Nickel Friesen

The years 1972–2006 saw significant expansion of women in leadership in the Mennonite church in North America—as well as challenges to that growth. The contributors to this book have demonstrated this through data from surveys, historical research, and first-person accounts. We hope this retelling of our history will spark even more conversation, and the study guide that follows this conclusion aims to continue this discussion. As editors of the volume, we decided to conclude this volume with our own conversation on women in church leadership over the past decades. Here are the questions we asked each other.

Summing up: What did our voices say forty years ago?

Lois: The first time I went to seminary (1970), I quit after one semester. It was for a variety of reasons, but one of them was that I was not ready to be a "first" in ministry. The seminary (not Mennonite) had only five full-time women students out of a total student body of more than two hundred. The seminary ethos was just so male, and it was hard to go against the stream. Becoming a pioneer sounded so energy-draining! But I ended up being first a lot of times in my career—first woman pastor of my congregation, first woman as executive of the General Conference Commission on Home Ministries, first woman ordained in South Central Conference.

In the introduction to this book, you, Dorothy, talked about that special delegate meeting that South Central Conference called to debate our ministries and our ordinations. The Kansas district ministerial committee had accepted our licensing because of their reciprocal agreement with Western District Conference, but most South Central people did not know about it until you and I went to the regular delegate assembly the next summer and stood on the stage with all the other pastors new to the conference during the past year. Then the discussion exploded!

What changed the discussion in 1985—and at many other points along the way—is that people who had been opposed in theory to women in ministry began seeing us as actual living human beings who had pastoral skills and pastoral hearts and felt called by God. One of the members of my congregation, Mennonite Church of the Servant in Wichita, reported to me after the special delegate meeting that he had been in a small discussion group with a man who went on and on about how women should not be pastors. Finally, the guy from my church had had enough and asked the other man, "Well, then, do you think we should fire Lois?" The man replied, "Oh, no!" When it was women in ministry in the abstract, it was a bad idea. When it was Lois and Dorothy, real embodied people, it was acceptable. I think that, over the past decades, attitudes and biblical interpretations changed in part because people encountered real women in ministry, and it made them go back and read the Bible in a new way.

Context makes a difference in how we read the Bible. Paul M. Miller, the seminary professor who was the keynote speaker at that special session, had much earlier in his career written a booklet promoting the prayer covering for women, which was supposed to symbolize a woman's submission to a man as the head. But when Miller came to the South Central meeting, he began talking about how he had encountered women in ministry on a recent trip to Africa and how that had influenced the way he read the Bible. He said that every time he read the Bible he received new light, and on the issue of women in ministry, he had reread the Bible and had received new light!

Dorothy: I've been musing about the role of women in the Mennonite church after reading hundreds of pages, uncovering old files, and listening to the authors who volunteered their insights for this book. I've also been scanning several recently published books marking decades of denominational ordination of women in the United States.[73] And I have been reminded of the 2015 anti-ordination declaration of Pope Francis: "The Church has spoken and says no. . . . That door is closed."[74] While there are individual stories of the ordination of pioneer women in various denominations (e.g., Antoinette Brown—Congregational, 1835; Helenor Alter Davisson—Methodist, 1866; Anna Bartlett—Free Will Baptist, 1886), it took until the mid–twentieth century for many denominations to begin to regularly ordain women to pastoral leadership. This was also when the two largest North American Mennonite denominations (Mennonite Church in 1973 and General Conference Mennonite Church in 1976) officially began ordaining women. We often think the churches—particularly the Mennonite ones—were late in dealing with the ordination of women, but we Mennonites were right in step with a North American culture that was focusing on women in leadership.

I remember that you, Lois, entered this Mennonite story in the early 1970s with voluntary service before moving into journalism and denominational newswriting. I was a journalist and wife of a seminarian. We "found" each other already in 1972 and—together with Gayle Gerber Koontz, another journalist and my college friend—organized the first "women in the church" ad hoc meeting in Chicago. We three had no idea that during the next decades, we would collaborate repeatedly as each of our vocations in the Mennonite church overlapped. Now, over forty years later and in retirement, our lives are full of stories, memories, some regrets, and some painful events, and yet we tell a remarkable saga of leadership in the Mennonite church body.

---

73 See, for example, Benjamin R. Knoll and Cammie Jo Bolin, *She Preached the Word: Women's Ordination in Modern America* (New York: Oxford University Press, 2018); Fredricka Thompsett, ed., *Looking Forward, Looking Backward: Forty Years of Women's Ordination* (New York: Morehouse, 2014)—Episcopal; Mindy Makant, *Holy Mischief: In Honor and Celebration of Women in Ministry* (Eugene, OR: Cascade Books, 2019)—Evangelical Lutheran Church in America.

74 John L. Allen, "Why Pope Francis Won't Let Women Become Priests," *Time*, March 6, 2015, http://time.com/3729904/francis-women/.

What are some major themes that stood out?

Lois: It is important to remember the back stories of Mennonite women's ordination to ministry. Although the numbers of women in church leadership grew rapidly in the 1970s and 1980s, there were precedents—Anabaptist prophets, deaconesses of one hundred years ago, and missionaries who ministered overseas and in North American city missions in ways that would not have been possible in their home congregations. These foremothers in ministry were part of what gave courage to Mennonite women in the last part of the twentieth century, along with writings and Women in Ministry conferences that put women in conversation with each other and allowed all of us to see the possibilities in the church and in ourselves.

I remember coming to realize during my senior year at seminary that I could do exegesis! It was a skill I had previously thought belonged only to other people (mostly men), and I had always subordinated my own biblical interpretations to those of the people who could *really* interpret scripture. I relied on the commentaries too much. But then I realized that my context, experiences, and skills counted and that I could find new meaning in the text. In this book there are a lot of stories like that—of women breaking out of stereotypical roles and discovering their own callings and gifts. These stories are not only about transformation of the church but also about transformation of ourselves as women.

Dorothy: This book documents the weaving of several threads: the emerging feminist activity of individual Mennonite women in various settings and roles; the collaborating—and often volunteer—work of women in Canada and the United States who felt God's call to leadership; the three Mennonite sociological surveys recording the attitudes of Mennonite church members toward women in leadership; and the merging of nontraditional and institutional efforts from 1972 to 2006 regarding the development of women's roles in the Mennonite church. This tapestry is our experience that continues the weaving of women's stories in the centuries before us. We inherited the patient but persistent work of earlier women. While they often worked with needle and thread, our fingers worked with computers and paper. We organized conferences, wrote articles, developed newsletters, and kept at it! Nevertheless, this resulting story is but a small part of the stories lost, forgotten, suppressed, or hidden. Our story is valuable; it is an invitation for other women to speak up, write down, and bravely share their stories of spiritual calling to proclaim the gospel.

In working on this book, I found anew that the church is affected by its surrounding culture and context. We cannot ignore the 1960s with its civil rights demands and tremendous efforts and forward progress toward social justice. Then, women's liberation was part of every institution and segment of society—including religion and the church. Mennonites could not ignore the historical times, and women could not be sheltered from the reality of protest and new teachings about the role of women in the Bible, theology, the home, and society. We were baby boomers caught up in the enormous cultural change that affected our lives immensely.

What were some surprises?

Dorothy: There were several surprises throughout the process of editing this book. First, the sheer numbers of women who were involved (mostly as volunteers), who organized conferences, wrote for newsletters, hosted women, fed guests who drove all night to attend Women in Ministry gatherings, and published scores of essays, meditations, interviews—well, it is breathtaking. My stack of issues of the MCC *Report* records hundreds and hundreds of women who were "news and verbs" in the church, assuring that women's voices were not stifled.

Second, the emerging revelation of sexual abuse in Mennonite homes, schools, and congregations stunned and stymied women in leadership—especially during the 1970s and 1980s. For example, the very difficult process of years of inquiry, scrutiny, and truth telling concerning John Howard Yoder's sexually abusive behavior—amid his monumental accomplishments in publishing, teaching, research, and global networking—was a journey of pain for the seminary community, the church, and many of us women in leadership. This underbelly of abuse has meant the loss of women in leadership in the Mennonite church. Regret, anger, and then thankfulness for the careful work of institutional repentance and public discussion at Anabaptist Mennonite Biblical Seminary have helped me heal, lead, and understand the responsibilities of leadership. During this book's compilation, we heard from several women who urged us, as editors, to include the fact of sexual abuse of women pastors. We acknowledge that fact but leave the in-depth reporting and theologizing on that issue to others.[75]

Third, the biggest surprise was, and is, that positive attitudes toward women in Mennonite leadership still lag, although often covertly. Women are a distinct minority in prominent roles in the church. And women of color are virtually missing from pastoring, academia, and institutional administrative roles. How can this be? Sexism and racism stain our church. While many things have improved (more women in higher education, higher percentage of women in seminary than forty years ago, occasional congregations that hire two women pastors concurrently, etc.), it is still the fact that "first woman" is attached to too many college presidents, chairs of Mennonite institutional boards, and even pastors of congregations. We learned from this writing project that Mennonite church members share long-standing traditional attitudes toward the role of women in the home, church, and society. Some Mennonite denominations (such as the US Conference of Mennonite

---

[75] See, for example, Elizabeth G. Yoder, ed., *Peace Theology and Violence Against Women*, Occasional Papers 16 (Elkhart, IN: Institute of Mennonite Studies, 1992); Mennonite Central Committee Taskforce on Domestic Violence, *Broken Boundaries: Resources for Pastoring People, Child Sexual Abuse* (Akron, PA: Mennonite Central Committee United States, 1989); Mennonite Central Committee Task Force on Domestic Violence, *The Purple Packet: Domestic Violence Resources for Pastoring Persons*; *Wife Abuse* (Winnipeg: Mennonite Central Committee Canada, 1987); Rachel Waltner Goossen, "'Defanging the Beast': Mennonite Responses to John Howard Yoder's Sexual Abuse," *Mennonite Quarterly Review* 89, no. 1 (Jan. 2015): 7–80.

Brethren) continue to deny ordination for solo or lead women pastors. Some children never hear a woman preach in their congregations. The Bible battle continues from centuries of interpretive affirmations and critiques—often contradictory and with spurious foundations. The use of the Bible is still one pillar of how women are (or are not) leading congregations and Mennonite institutions.

Lois: As I was researching the chapter on women doing theology, I was surprised how many women were taking this seriously and experimenting with new ways of theologizing. As with all experiments, some produced better results than others, but that did not—and should not—stop the experimenting. For example, there was a lot of experimenting around topics of suffering, humility, forgiveness, the cross, and atonement. How could women do theology on these issues without giving in to the stereotypes about women? At the beginning of this era, some women were willing to throw out whole sections of scripture and whole topics of theology—the writings of the apostle Paul or any theory of the atonement that involved suffering, for example. Over time, women pastors have worked their way through these issues and discovered new, authentic ways to preach forgiveness and salvation.

I was also surprised at how much space in the MCC *Report* was devoted to inclusive language for God. I should not have been so surprised because as a writer I know that language matters, especially language about God. This is still an issue in much of the church: Where does one dare use feminine pronouns for God, and where does one use non-gendered language for God?

Why did we stick it out?

Dorothy: I stuck it out because attitudes do change. This change usually happens because brave women step out of traditional roles and claim their call to serve Jesus Christ as pastors, teachers, professors, researchers, and leaders in Mennonite congregations and institutions. We both saw attitudes shift in the major sociological studies from a mere 17 percent support of women's ordination in 1972 to a healthy 67 percent support in 2006. Hallelujah! Yet, two-thirds support signifies a longer, continuing effort for women to occupy significant roles in the church. While overt sexism seems rarer, it is, nevertheless, another pillar of entrenched discrimination against women in religious leadership.

We both can claim our own ordinations from the mid-1980s. We stayed in the Mennonite church even though there were many times of criticism, disappointment, and loneliness. It is important to celebrate the over three hundred women who have been ordained during these early years. We were not alone! We were sustained by the call of God in our lives, the support of many other people, and the gracious call of congregations who loved us into leadership. This is good news.

Lois: I stuck it out because I love the church. I can say that, even though the church at multiple levels has been a source of intense pain for me at several points in my life. Maybe I perceived those experiences as particularly painful because of my love for the church. But all through those experiences there have been people in the church who knew me, listened to me, understood me, and sustained me. And God has kept showing up! One day in 1975, when I was emotionally at my lowest point, I walked through the door of my house, and there in the front hall I physically felt God's unconditional love surrounding me. That experience and subsequent encounters with God have kept me from giving up and have given me a sense that God has a purpose for me: to help the church to proclaim and to be a sign of the reign of God. I resonate with 2 Corinthians 4:1 (NRSV): "Therefore, since it is by God's mercy that we are engaged in this ministry, we do not lose heart."

Final words

Dorothy: Thank you, Lois, for your encouragement, scholarship, and collaboration. This project was fruitful, even though it took its time. Sadly, during our writing we both buried our mothers (yours died in February 2019 and mine in May 2020), marking a loss of strong women of faith. Your mother was a minister's wife and servant of the church. My mother was a church secretary for many years and constant role model of faithful service. Now they rest, and their daughters—and granddaughters—are shouldering their roles of leadership, ministry, and vocation. We are conscious of (and sometimes overwhelmed by) the current racist, classist, and sexist attitudes in the church that still cloud our Christian witness. However, in the end, our writers supplied insights and documentation concerning women's voices. We are grateful. We persist!

Lois: During the time period covered in this book, a guiding scripture for many women in the church was Galatians 3:28 (NRSV): "There is no longer Jew or Greek, there is no longer slave or free, there is no longer male and female; for all of you are one in Christ Jesus." In medieval Europe and during the sixteenth century, the guiding scripture for women's ministry had been Acts 2:17–18:

> In the last days it will be, God declares,
> that I will pour out my Spirit upon all flesh,
>   and your sons and your daughters shall prophesy,
> and your young shall see visions,
>   and your old shall dream dreams.
> Even upon my slaves, both men and women,
>   in those days I will pour out my Spirit,
>   and they shall prophesy.[76]

This passage in Acts, drawn from the Old Testament prophet Joel, gave our foremothers in the faith a biblical justification for women's public ministry of prophecy, proclaiming the Word of God to God's people. But this public ministry had not been routinized; it had been motivated by the Spirit but not embedded in church structures.

---

76 Translation mine. See also Lois Barrett, "Wreath of Glory: Ursula's Prophetic Visions in the Context of Reformation and Revolt in Southwestern Germany, 1524–1530" (PhD dissertation, The Union Institute, 1992), 111–16, 202–206.

What was different, beginning in the 1970s, was that Mennonite women's prophecy connected not only with the Holy Spirit but also with the structures, leadership groups, and official positions of authority. In past centuries, an ad hoc prophetic ministry had been easily pushed aside by patriarchal cultures, traditions, and institutions. This time women would not so easily be pushed aside. Mennonite women were being called as pastors, elected as board members, hired as supervisors, and respected as scholars. These, too, were prophetic roles. These women, too, were proclaiming the good news.

Appendix
Ordained Women in Mennonite Church USA and Mennonite Church Canada (1972–2005)

Compiled by Dorothy Nickel Friesen

Abbreviations

Canadian Conferences before 2002

CMA	Conference of Mennonites in Alberta
CMC	Conference of Mennonites in Canada
CMinBC	Conference of Mennonites in British Columbia
CMM	Conference of Mennonites in Manitoba
CoMoS	Conference of Mennonites in Saskatchewan
MCEC	Mennonite Conference of Eastern Canada (new in 1988 when UM, MCOQ, WOMC, MCEC united)
MCOQ	Mennonite Conference of Ontario and Quebec
UM	Conference of United Mennonite Churches in Ontario
WOMC	Western Ontario Mennonite Conference

Canadian Conferences after 2002

MCA	Mennonite Church Alberta
MCBC	Mennonite Church British Columbia
MCCAN	Mennonite Church Canada
MCEC	Mennonite Church Eastern Canada (name changed from Mennonite Conference of Eastern Canada when MC Canada formed)
MCM	Mennonite Church Manitoba

MCSASK	Mennonite Church Saskatchewan

United States Conferences

ACC	Atlantic Coast Conference
AMC	Allegheny Mennonite Conference
CDC	Central District Conference
CPMC	Central Plains Mennonite Conference (2001 merger of IA-NE and NDC)
EDC	Eastern District Conference
FRC	Franconia Mennonite Conference
FRK	Franklin Mennonite Conference
GCMC	General Conference Mennonite Church
GS	Gulf States Mennonite Conference
IA-NE	Iowa-Nebraska Mennonite Conference
IL	Illinois Mennonite Conference
IN-MI	Indiana-Michigan Mennonite Conference
LAN	Lancaster Mennonite Conference
MC	Mennonite Church
MC USA	Mennonite Church USA
MSMC	Mountain States Mennonite Conference (2006 merger of RMMC and WDC Colorado churches)
NCC	North Central Mennonite Conference
NDC	Northern District Conference
NYMC	New York Mennonite Conference
OMC	Ohio Mennonite Conference
PCC	Pacific Coast Conference
PDC	Pacific District Conference
PNMC	Pacific Northwest Mennonite Conference (formed in 1994 with merger of northern portions of PCC and PDC)
PSMC	Pacific Southwest Mennonite Conference (formed in 1994 with merger of SWC and southern portion of PDC)
RMMC	Rocky Mountain Mennonite Conference
SCMC	South Central Mennonite Conference
SMC	Southeast Mennonite Conference

SWC   Southwest Mennonite Conference
VMC   Virginia Mennonite Conference
WDC   Western District Conference

General

(C)   Church closed
(D)   Death as of completion date

Appendix • 237

Ordination	Last Name	First Name	Conference	Congregation
6/17/1973	Richards (D)	Emma	IL	Lombard Mennonite Church-Lombard, IL
9/19/1976	Miller	Marilyn	WDC	Arvada Mennonite Church-Arvada, CO
11/7/1976	Rupp (D)	Anne Neufeld	CDC	Pleasant Oaks Mennonite Church (C)-Middlebury, IN
12/19/1977	Hochstetler	Betty	CDC	Grace Community Church-Chicago, IL
12/16/1978	Kern (D)	Marilyn	CDC	First Mennonite Church-Bluffton, OH
2/25/1979	Weber	Doris	WOMC	Avon Mennonite Church-Stratford, ON
8/26/1979	Epp	Rosella	WDC	Lorraine Avenue Mennonite Church-Wichita, KS
5/18/1980	Shutt	Joyce	GCMC	Fairfield Mennonite Church-Fairfield, PA
10/19/1980	Neufeld	Doreen	UM	Hamilton Inn-Hamilton, ON
11/30/1980	Epp	Elsie	CoMoS	Wildwood Mennonite Church-Saskatoon, SK
6/28/1981	Janzen	Dorothea	WDC	Trinity Mennonite Church-Hillsboro, KS
4/1982	Good	Martha Smith	MCOQ	Guelph Mennonite Church-Guelph, ON
5/2/1982	Espinoza (D)	Lilia	IL	Iglesia Menonita Hispano-Chicago, IL
5/16/1982	Schwartzentruber	Mary Mae	UM/MCOQ	Stirling Avenue Mennonite Church-Kitchener, ON
7/4/1982	Miller (D)	Elsie	CDC	Oak Grove Mennonite Church-Smithville, OH
7/18/1982	Graber	Rose	CDC	Hively Avenue Mennonite Church-Elkhart, IN
5/1/1983	Dyck	Sheryl	CDC	First Mennonite Church of Champaign-Urbana-Urbana, IL

238 • Appendix

Ordination	Last Name	First Name	Conference	Congregation
9/25/1983	Yoder-Schrock	Marcia	CDC	Hively Avenue Mennonite Church-Elkhart, IN
11/6/1983	Buhr	Linda Neufeld	CMA	Foothills Mennonite Church-Calgary, AB
11/13/1983	Barg	Else	CMM	Charleswood Mennonite Church-Winnipeg, MB
12/20/1983	Childs (D)	Evelyn	IN-MI	Peace Community Mennonite Church-Detroit, MI
1/29/1984	Puricelli	Elizabeth	UM	Toronto United Mennonite Church-Toronto, ON
5/27/1984	Kennel	Pauline	CDC & IL	Christ Community Church-Schaumberg, IL
5/27/1984	Showalter (D)	Ann	CDC & IL	Oak Park Mennonite Church-Oak Park, IL
5/27/1984	Sutton	Norma	CDC & IL	Oak Park Mennonite Church-Oak Park, IL
1/1/1985	Yoder	Ruth	AMC	University Mennonite Church-State College, PA
1/20/1985	Barrett	Lois	WDC & SCMC	Mennonite Church of the Servant-Wichita, KS
2/3/1985	Shelly	Patricia	WDC & RMMC	First Mennonite Church-Denver, CO
2/10/1985	Stucky	Kathee Kime	WDC	Calvary Mennonite Church-Liberal, KS
3/17/1985	Sauder	Renee	WDC	Bethel College Mennonite Church-North Newton, KS
4/28/1985	Friesen	Dorothy Nickel	WDC & SCMC	Manhattan Mennonite Fellowship-Manhattan, KS

Ordination	Last Name	First Name	Conference	Congregation
5/26/1985	Buxman	I Ruth	PDC & SWC	First Mennonite Church of San Francisco-San Francisco, CA
8/1985	Hendricks	Jean	WDC	Lawrence Mennonite Fellowship-Lawrence, KS
9/25/1985	Reusser (D)	Helen	MCOQ	Mannheim Mennonite Church-Petersburg, ON
2/16/1986	Goering	Susan Ortman	WDC	Arvada Mennonite Church-Arvada, CO
3/16/1986	Fisher (D)	Rachel	IN-MI	College Mennonite Church-Goshen, IN
3/16/1986	Kauffmann	Nancy	IN-MI	College Mennonite Church-Goshen, IN
4/20/1986	Smith	Margaret Richer	IN-MI	First Mennonite Church-Indianapolis, IN
5/11/1986	Whitehead	Grace	IN-MI	Parkview Mennonite Church-Kokomo, IN
6/8/1986	Beachy (D)	Eleanor	WDC	Bergthal Mennonite Church (C)-Pawnee Rock, KS
6/22/1986	Kehler (D)	Jessie	CMM	Charleswood Mennonite Church-Winnipeg, MB
6/22/1986	Stueben	Mary	PDC	Shalom Church-Spokane, WA
9/14/1986	Kratz	Clarice	CDC	Maple Avenue Mennonite Church (C)-Pewaukee, WI
1/1/1987	Friesen	Delores	IA-NE	First Mennonite Church of Iowa City-Iowa City, IA
2/15/1987	Naylor	Ruth	CDC	First Mennonite Church-Bluffton, OH
3/29/1987	Brown	Janet	CDC	First Mennonite Church-Nappanee, IN
4/12/1987	Sutter	Janice Yordy	RMMC	First Mennonite Church, Denver, CO

Ordination	Last Name	First Name	Conference	Congregation
5/3/1987	Schiedel	Mary	MCOQ	Elmira Mennonite Church-Elmira, ON
5/10/1987	Landers	Bertha	MCOQ	Bloomingdale Mennonite Church-Bloomingdale, ON
5/24/1987	Rempel-Burkholder	Melita	WOMC & UM & MCOQ	Valleyview Mennonite Church-London, ON
6/7/1987	Steiner (D)	Susan	MCOQ	St Jacobs Mennonite Church-Saint Jacobs, ON
7/19/1987	Lapp (D)	Nancy	CDC & IN-MI	Assembly Mennonite Church-Goshen, IN
10/18/1987	Kraus	Jan	MCOQ	Danforth Morningside Mennonite Church-Toronto, ON
10/25/1987	Hostetler	Donnita	IA-NE	First Mennonite Church-Lincoln, NE
1/1/1988	Shirk	Hazel	SMC	Bayshore Church-Sarasota, FL
3/20/1988	Ruth-Heffelbower	Clare Ann	CDC	Eighth Street Mennonite Church-Goshen, IN
4/24/1988	Hurst	Brenda Martin	WDC	Tabor Mennonite Church-Newton, KS
7/24/1988	Yoder	June Alliman	IN-MI	College Mennonite Church-Goshen, IN
9/11/1988	Schloneger	Florence	OMC	Bethel Mennonite Church-West Liberty, OH
9/19/1988	Glick (D)	Charlotte Holsopple	In-MI	Waterford Mennonite Church-Goshen, IN

Ordination	Last Name	First Name	Conference	Congregation
10/2/1988	Epp-Stobbe	Eleanor	MCEC	Hamilton Mennonite Church-Hamilton, ON
11/12/1988	Williams	Sharon Gehman	FRC	Norristown New Life-Norristown, PA
11/13/1988	Bartholomew	Rebecca	OMC	Powell Community Church-Powell, OH
1/8/1989	Dirks	Doris	CoMoS	Hope Mennonite Fellowship-North Battleford, SK
2/26/1989	Quintela	Helen O'Brien	NDC	St. Paul Mennonite Fellowship, Faith Mennonite Church-Minneapolis, MN
3/5/1989	Mullett	Isabel	OMC	Hillside Chapel-Jackson, OH
6/4/1989	Brunner (D)	Grace	OMC	Beech Mennonite Church-Louisville, OH
9/10/1989	Herr	Mary	IN-MI	Prairie Street Mennonite Church-Elkhart, IN
9/10/1989	Stoltzfus (D)	Ruth Brunk	VMC	Shalom Mennonite Church-Harrisonburg, VA
9/17/1989	Byler	Sharon	CDC & OMC	Oak Grove Mennonite Church-Smithville, OH
11/12/1989	Horner (D)	Thelma	IL	First Mennonite Church-Morton, IL
11/15/1989	Gingrich	Elisabeth	IN-MI	
12/1/1989	Watson	Linda	IN-MI	Paoli Mennonite Church-Paoli, IN
1/1/1990	Kolb-Wyckoff	Martha	FRC	Taftsville Mennonite Church-Woodstock, VT
3/4/1990	Johnson	Norma	WDC	Bethel College Mennonite Church-North Newton, KS
4/22/1990	Schloneger	Enid	OMC	Millersburg Mennonite Church-Millersburg, OH

242 • Appendix

Ordination	Last Name	First Name	Conference	Congregation
5/6/1990	Lehman	Barbara Moyer	OMC	Orrville Mennonite Church-Orrville, OH
6/17/1990	Hurst	Mary	MCEC	Petitcodiac Mennonite Church-Petitcodiac, NB
6/17/1990	Dyck	Mary	CMM	Sargent Avenue Mennonite Church-Winnipeg, MB
6/24/1990	Becker	Ann Weber	MCEC	First Mennonite Church-Kitchener, ON
8/19/1990	Yoder	Brenda	PCC	Eugene Mennonite Church-Eugene, OR
8/26/1990	Ediger	Margaret	WDC	Bethel Mennonite Church-Inman, KS
9/16/1990	Byler	Jayne	OMC	Summit Mennonite Church-Barberton, OH
9/23/1990	Hershey	Jennie	PCC	Ranch Chapel-Crooked River Ranch, OR
9/30/1990	Slough	Rebecca	PDC & SWC	First Mennonite Church of San Francisco-San Francisco, CA
10/14/1990	Bauman	Nancy Brubaker	PDC	First Mennonite Church-Reedley, CA
10/21/1990	Rempel	Kathrine	AMC	University Mennonite Church-State College, PA

Ordination	Last Name	First Name	Conference	Congregation
11/25/1990	Johnson	Janeen Bertsche	WDC	Lorraine Avenue Mennonite Church-Wichita, KS
1/18/1991	Yoder	Elena	RMMC	East Holbrook Mennonite Church-Cheraw, CO
2/16/1991	Longenecker	Catherine	VMC	Broadstreet Mennonite Church-Harrisonburg, VA
2/16/1991	Reid	Kathryn	WDC & SCMC	Austin Mennonite Church-Austin, TX
4/21/1991	Boschman	Kathleen Rempel	CMM	Hope Mennonite Church-Winnipeg, MB
4/28/1991	Juhnke	Christine	WDC	Salina Mennonite Church-Salina, KS
4/28/1991	Smith	Cynthia Neufeld	WDC	Southern Hills Mennonite Church-Topeka, KS
9/22/1991	King (D)	Betty	VMC	Lindale Mennonite Church-Lindale, VA
9/29/1991	Martin	Brenda North	VMC	Raleigh Mennonite Church-Raleigh, NC
10/6/1991	Thi Pham (D)	Xuan	VMC	Vietnamese Christian Fellowship-Falls Church, VA
10/10/1991	Polak (D)	Agnes	WDC	Arvada Mennonite Church-Arvada, CO
10/11/1991	Gascho	Doris	MCEC	Shantz Mennonite Church-Baden, ON
1/1/1992	Shenk	Mary	AMC	Stahl Mennonite Church-Johnstown, PA
1/1/1992	Isaacs	Brenda	PCC	Calvary Christian Fellowship-Inglewood, CA
1/12/1992	Hochstetler	Lois	SCMC	Faith Mennonite Church South Hutchinson, KS

Ordination	Last Name	First Name	Conference	Congregation
6/28/1992	Bechtel	Muriel	MCEC	Warden Woods Mennonite Church (C)-Scarborough, ON-
8/16/1992	Book	Miriam	IN-MI	Belmont Mennonite Church-Elkhart, IN
9/12/1992	Wyse	Joyce	PDC & SWC	First Mennonite Church of San Francisco-San Francisco, CA
9/20/1992	Shenk Kuhns	Edith	VMC	Weavers Mennonite Church-Harrisonburg, VA
9/20/1992	Ediger (D)	Marjorie	WDC	First Mennonite Church-Ransom, KS
11/1/1992	Boehm	Ruth	CMM	Bethel Mennonite Church-Winnipeg, MB
11/22/1992	Kropf	Marlene	IN-MI	Belmont Mennonite Church-Elkhart, IN
1/10/1993	Brenneman	Diane Zaerr	IA-NE	First Mennonite Church of Iowa City-Iowa City, IA
3/27/1993	Yoder	Shirlee	VMC	Park View Mennonite Church-Harrisonburg, VA
5/9/1993	Widmer	Rosemary	IN-MI	College Mennonite Church-Goshen, IN
5/9/1993	Bender	Marilyn	VMC	Raleigh Mennonite Church-Raleigh, NC
6/6/1993	Kurtz	Kathleen	VMC	Daniels Run Peace Church-Fairfax, VA
6/20/1993	Shenk (D)	Evelyn	VMC	Harrisonburg Mennonite Church-Harrisonburg, VA
10/3/1993	Shank	Dorothy	VMC	Ridgeway Mennonite Church-Harrisonburg, VA
10/17/1993	Hopson	Helen	CDC	Evanston Mennonite Church-Evanston, IL
11/14/1993	Friesen	Patty	PCC	Portland Mennonite Church-Portland, OR
11/28/1993	Zimmerly	Karen Martens	CoMoS	Grace Mennonite Church-Regina, SK

Ordination	Last Name	First Name	Conference	Congregation
12/12/1993	Lilliston	Brenda Glanzer	WDC	Hope Mennonite Church-Wichita, KS
12/15/1993	Kreider	Heidi Regier	SMC	Emmanuel Mennonite Church-Gainesville, FL
1/1/1994	Hartman (D)	Lois Ann	OMC	Central Mennonite Church-Archbold, OH
1/11/1994	Youngquist	Sally Schreiner	IL	Reba Place Church-Evanston, IL
2/13/1994	Derry	Ingrid Peters	MCEC	Kingston Mennonite Fellowship (C)-Madoc, ON
4/1/1994	Mellinger	Marianne	FRC	Germantown Mennonite Church-Philadelphia, PA
5/15/1994	Dunn	Kathy Neufeld	CDC	Shalom Community Church-Ann Arbor, MI
6/5/1994	Thiessen	Ingrid Loepp	MCEC	Steinmann Mennonite Church-Baden, ON
6/12/1994	Loewen	Laura	MCEC	Mennonite Fellowship of Montreal-Montreal, QC
6/19/1994	Steckley	Janice	MCEC	Breslau Mennonite Church-Breslau, ON
8/28/1994	Foster	Sandra	VMC	Park View Mennonite Church-Harrisonburg, VA
9/11/1994	deLeon-Hartshorn	Iris	WDC & SCMC	Houston Mennonite Church-Houston, TX
9/12/1994	Claiborne	Maudesta	EDC	Second Mennonite Church-Philadelphia, PA
9/18/1994	Brubaker	Shirley Yoder	VMC	Park View Mennonite Church-Harrisonburg, VA
10/2/1994	Kratz	Dorothy	CDC	North Suburban Mennonite Church-Mundelein, IL
10/30/1994	Laverty	Ruth Anne	MCEC	Elmira Mennonite Church-Elmira, ON

Ordination	Last Name	First Name	Conference	Congregation
11/5/1994	Slater	Jeannette Buller	IN-MI	Communion Fellowship-Goshen, IN
11/27/1994	Moyer	Ann	PSMC	San Diego Mennonite Church-San Diego, CA
1/1/1995	Lance	Ceci	IN-MI	Fairhaven Mennonite Church-Fort Wayne, IN
3/26/1995	Burkholder	Mary	MCEC	Rockway Mennonite Church-Kitchener, ON
4/2/1995	Kruger	Helen	CoMoS	Osler Mennonite Church-Osler, SK
5/7/1995	Caes	Elizabeth	FRC	West Philadelphia Mennonite Fellowship-Philadelphia, PA
7/16/1995	Duerksen	Norma Peters	CDC & OMC	Oak Grove Mennonite Church-Smithville, OH
8/20/1995	Weaver	Dorothy Jean	VMC	Community Mennonite Church-Harrisonburg, VA
8/27/1995	Blatz	Joan	CMM	Thompson United Mennonite (C)-Thompson, MB
10/15/1995	Schultz	Ingrid	CDC	Comunidad de Fe (C)-Schaumburg, IL
11/12/1995	Salo	Anna-Lisa	MCEC	Waters Mennonite Church-Lively, ON
1/21/1996	Yoder	Beth	FRC	Perkasie Mennonite Church-Perkasie, PA
2/11/1996	Dyck	Darlene	CMM	Bergthaler Mennonite Church of Altona-Altona, MB
2/18/1996	Rehan	Anna	CoMoS	CoMoS/Zoar Mennonite Church-Langham, SK
3/3/1996	Yoder	Mary Lehman	IN-MI & CDC	Assembly Mennonite Church-Goshen, IN
4/19/1996	Martin	Jewel	VMC	Park View Mennonite Church-Harrisonburg, VA

Appendix • 247

Ordination	Last Name	First Name	Conference	Congregation
4/28/1996	Wideman	Louise	SCMC	Whitestone Mennonite Church-Hesston, KS
5/19/1996	Peters	Margaret	CoMoS	Hanley Mennonite Church-Hanley, SK
5/26/1996	Walton	Robin	CDC	Columbus Mennonite Church-Columbus, OH
6/29/1996	Shirk	Sylvia	IN-MI	Waterford Mennonite Church-Goshen, IN
8/9/1996	Miller	Wendy	VMC	Immanuel Mennonite Church-Harrisonburg, VA
8/25/1996	Maina	Gladys	CDC	Morning Star Church-Muncie, IN
9/15/1996	Allison-Jones	Susan	MCEC	Wilmot Mennonite Church-New Hamburg, ON
10/27/1996	Yamasaki	April	CMinBC	Emmanuel Mennonite Church-Abbotsford, BC
12/8/1996	Falla	Amanda	SMC	Iglesia Menonita Encuentro de Renovacion-Miami, FL
1/1/1997	Widjija	Magdalena	CoMoS	Grace Mennonite Church-Regina, SK
1/1/1997	Vincent (D)	Lorie	IN-MI	Belmont Mennonite Church-Elkhart, IN
5/11/1997	Swartz	Delores	OMC	Salem Mennonite Church-Waldron, MI
5/17/1997	Simmons	Mary Lou	VMC	Ridgeway Mennonite Church-Harrisonburg, VA
5/18/1997	Paetkau	Brenda Sawatzky	CDC	Eighth Street Mennonite Church-Goshen, IN
6/8/1997	Buller	Jane Stoltzfus	IN-MI	Walnut Hill Mennonite Church-Goshen, IN
6/15/1997	Rudy-Froese	Marilyn	MCEC	Rockway Mennonite Church-Kitchener, ON
6/22/1997	Hershberger	Cheryl	SCMC	Hesston Mennonite Church-Hesston, KS

Ordination	Last Name	First Name	Conference	Congregation
7/13/1997	Ritchie	Amy	CDC	Florence Church of the Brethren-Mennonite-Constantine, MI
7/13/1997	Dick	Jane	RMMC	First Mennonite Church of Denver-Denver, CO
9/21/1997	Schmidt	Debra	WDC	First Mennonite Church-Hutchinson, KS
10/19/1997	Huyard	Rose	VMC	Stephens City Mennonite Church-Stephens City, VA
11/2/1997	Osinkosky	Claire	CDC	Trenton Mennonite Church-Trenton, OH
11/9/1997	Shenk	Donna	ACC	Akron Mennonite Church-Akron, PA
11/16/1997	Nitzsche	Mary	OMC & CDC	Oak Grove Mennonite Church-Smithville, OH
11/30/1997	Stackley (D)	Muriel Thiessen	WDC	Bergthal Mennonite Church (C)-Pawnee Rock, KS
12/28/1997	Dyck	Edna	WDC	Shalom Mennonite Church-Newton, KS
1/1/1998	Martin	Elaine		
1/11/1998	Nofziger	Pauline	CDC	Cincinnati Mennonite Fellowship-Cincinnati, OH
5/3/1998	Penner	Vicki	WDC	Faith Mennonite Church-Newton, KS
5/10/1998	Thomsen	June	CDC	Grace Mennonite Church-Pandora, OH
5/31/1998	Pitts	Katherine	WDC	Salina Mennonite Church-Salina, KS
6/14/1998	Resch (D)	Miriam		
8/6/1998	Maclin	Janace	IL	Bethesda Mennonite Church-Saint Louis, MO

Ordination	Last Name	First Name	Conference	Congregation
10/25/1998	Umble	Jeni Hiett	CDC	Southside Fellowship-Elkhart, IN
11/8/1998	Mears-Driedger	June	IN-MI	College Mennonite Church-Goshen, IN
11/22/1998	Amstutz	Wanda Roth	AMC	Scottdale Mennonite Church-Scottdale, PA
1/1/1999	Shisler	Barbara Esch	FRC	Perkasie Mennonite Church-Perkasie, PA
1/10/1999	Raab	Myra	IN-MI	Parkview Mennonite Church-Kokomo, IN
1/10/1999	Rheinheimer	Jan	WDC	Mountain Community Mennonite Church-Palmer Lake, CO
2/14/1999	Francisco	Karla	VMC	Calvary Community Church-Hampton, VA
2/14/1999	Francisco	Natalie	VMC	Calvary Community Church-Hampton, VA
4/19/1999	Wenger	Kathryn	AMC	Groffdale Mennonite Church-Leola, PA
5/2/1999	Harder	Lois	WDC	Lorraine Avenue Mennonite Church-Wichita, KS
5/23/1999	Rose	Carol	WDC & SCMC	Mennonite Church of the Servant-Wichita, KS
6/27/1999	Maust	Elaine	GS	Jubilee Mennonite Church-Meridian, MS
6/27/1999	Hange	Maren	VMC	Charlottesville Mennonite Church-Charlottesville, VA
7/1/1999	Combs	Joyce	OMC	Southside Mennonite Church-Springfield, OH
7/11/1999	Bean	Heather Ackley	PSMC	Peace Mennonite Church-Claremont, CA
8/1/1999	Mast	Donna	AMC	Scottdale Mennonite Church-Scottdale, PA

Ordination	Last Name	First Name	Conference	Congregation
8/29/1999	Bartholomew	Maxine	OMC	Maple Grove Mennonite Church-New Castle, PA
9/5/1999	Brown	Cora	IN-MI	Church Without Walls-Elkhart, IN
9/19/1999	Harms	Dawn Yoder	ACC	Akron Mennonite Church-Akron, PA
10/17/1999	Fisher	Claire Ewert	CoMoS	Fiske Mennonite Church-Fiske, SK & Ebenfield Mennonite Church-Herschel, SK
11/7/1999	Stoltzfus	Regina Shands	OMC	Lee Heights Community Church-Cleveland, OH
11/14/1999	Ellison White	Julie	MCEC	Tavistock Mennonite Church-Tavistock, ON
11/21/1999	Wightman	Margaret	VMC	Community Mennonite Church-Harrisonburg, VA
12/12/1999	Roth	Charlene	RMMC	Living Waters Fellowship-Greeley, CO
1/9/2000	Bender (D)	Julianna	MCEC	Hamilton Mennonite Church-Hamilton, ON
2/20/2000	Shantz	Kathy	PSMC	Trinity Mennonite Church-Glendale, AZ
2/20/2000	Rempel	Amanda	WDC	First Mennonite Church-Newton, KS
6/4/2000	Sherrill	Teresa	PSMC	Pasadena Mennonite Church-Pasadena, CA
6/11/2000	Bryant (D)	B Elaine	IL	Englewood Mennonite Church (C)-Chicago, IL
6/17/2000	Hartman	Pearl Hoover	CDC & IL	Madison Mennonite Church-Madison, WI
9/10/2000	Yoder	Vickie	OMC	Leetonia Mennonite Church-Leetonia, OH
9/17/2000	Janzen	Anna	VMC	Warwick River Mennonite Church-Newport News, VA

Ordination	Last Name	First Name	Conference	Congregation
10/5/2000	Schrag	LaVerle	WDC	First Mennonite Church-Hutchinson, KS
10/15/2000	Hochstedler	Kathryn	VMC	Harrisonburg Mennonite Church-Harrisonburg, VA
10/22/2000	Schilk	Ruth Preston	CMA	Lethbridge Mennonite Church-Lethbridge, AB
10/22/2000	Morash	Erin	CMM	North Kildonan Mennonite Church-Winnipeg, MB
11/12/2000	Rediger	Anita	CDC	First Mennonite Church-Berne, IN
11/26/2000	Miller	Sharon	IA-NE	Peace Mennonite Church (C)-Burlington, IA
11/26/2000	Klaassen	Renate Dau	MCEC	Bethany Mennonite Church-Niagara-on-the-Lake, ON
12/3/2000	Benner	Mary	FRC	Plains Mennonite Church-Hatfield, PA
12/3/2000	Smucker	Klaudia	IN-MI	College Mennonite Church-Goshen, IN
12/31/2000	Nelson (D)	Dawn	FRC	Methacta Mennonite Church-Norristown, PA
1/21/2001	Greer (D)	Doris	PSMC	Faith and Love Christian Center-Los Angeles, CA
2/11/2001	Miller	Wendy	OMC	Lockport Mennonite Church-Stryker, OH
3/11/2001	Neufeld	Bonnie	IL	Community Mennonite Church-Markham, IL
4/1/2001	Sensenig	Jennifer Davis	CPMC	Cedar Falls Mennonite Church-Cedar Falls, IA
4/22/2001	Dintaman	Pamela	ACC	Community Mennonite Church of Lancaster-Lancaster, PA
4/22/2001	Breeze	Cynthia	CDC	First Mennonite Church of Champaign-Urbana-Urbana, IL

Ordination	Last Name	First Name	Conference	Congregation
4/22/2001	Janzen	Anita	MCEC	Hanover Mennonite Church-Hanover, ON
6/10/2001	Gehring	Barbara Krehbiel	WDC	Manhattan Mennonite Church-Manhattan, KS
7/15/2001	Russell	Juel	PNMC	Salem Mennonite Church-Salem, OR
8/12/2001	Hershey	Phoebe	VMC	Stephens City Mennonite Church-Stephens City, VA
8/19/2001	Kehr	Anita Yoder	IN-MI	Berkey Avenue Mennonite Fellowship-Goshen, IN
9/16/2001	Lanting	Esther	IN-MI	Hudson Lake Mennonite Church-New Carlisle, IN
9/22/2001	Wenger	Tonya Ramer	CDC & IN-MI	Madison Mennonite Church-Madison, WI
9/23/2001	Kauffman	E Elaine	CPMC	First Mennonite Church-Mountain Lake, MN
9/30/2001	Martin	Rebecca	OMC	Pleasant View Mennonite Church-N Lawrence, OH
10/21/2001	Harder	Lois	AMC	Morgantown Church of the Brethren-Morgantown, WV
10/21/2001	Retzlaff	Anita	CoMoS	Nutana Park Mennonite Church-Saskatoon, SK
11/4/2001	Groff	Gwendolyn	FRC	Bethany Mennonite Church-Bridgewater Corners, VT
11/11/2001	Nafziger-Meiser	Linda	PNMC	Hyde Park Mennonite Fellowship-Boise, ID
11/19/2001	Bal	Joan	WDC	Houston Mennonite Church-Houston, TX
1/13/2002	Schrock-Hurst	Carmen	AMC	Pittsburgh Mennonite Church-Pittsburgh, PA
1/18/2002	Tribby	Phyllis	WDC	Arvada Mennonite Church-Arvada, CO

Ordination	Last Name	First Name	Conference	Congregation
3/17/2002	Pipkin (D)	Arlene	ACC	Manhattan Mennonite Fellowship-New York, NY
3/31/2002	Stutzman	Bonita	VMC	Park View Mennonite Church-Harrisonburg, VA
4/21/2002	Penner	Carol	MCEC	The First Mennonite Church-Vineland, ON
5/19/2002	Gustafson-Zook	Gwen	IN-MI	Faith Mennonite Church-Goshen, IN
5/26/2002	Lanctot	Nina	IN-MI	Belmont Mennonite Church-Elkhart, IN
5/26/2002	Kipfer	Anita Schroeder	MCEC	Stirling Avenue Mennonite Church-Kitchener, ON
6/9/2002	Borkholder	CarolSue	CDC	Florence Church of the Brethren-Mennonite-Constantine, MI
6/15/2002	Kennel	Sharon	CPMC	Salem Mennonite Church-Shickley, NE
6/23/2002	Johnston	Ruth	CPMC	Faith Mennonite Church-Minneapolis, MN
7/5/2002	Spires	Tammerie	WDC	Church of Many Peoples (C)-Dallas, TX
7/14/2002	Epp	Charlene	PNMC	Portland Mennonite Church-Portland, OR
8/4/2002	Linsenmeyer	Rebecca	RMMC	Glennon Heights Mennonite Church-Lakewood, CO
10/13/2002	Meyer	Brenda	IN-MI	Benton Mennonite Church-Goshen, IN
10/20/2002	Kirkpatrick	Deborah	MCA	First Mennonite Church-Edmonton, AB
11/17/2002	Zabriskie	Kristin	PSMC	Pasadena Mennonite Church-Pasadena, CA
11/24/2002	Mininger	Mary	IN-MI	Paoli Mennonite Fellowship-Paoli, IN

254 • Appendix

Ordination	Last Name	First Name	Conference	Congregation
12/8/2002	Martin	Ruth	MCEC	Hillcrest Mennonite Church-New Hamburg, ON
12/15/2002	Dutchersmith	Teresa	IN-MI	Faith Mennonite Church-Goshen, IN
1/1/2003	Yoder	Leanne	PSMC	Shalom Mennonite Fellowship-Tucson, AZ
1/12/2003	Kusuma	Rina	PSMC	Upland Peace Church-Upland, CA
2/23/2003	MacMaster	Eve	SMC	Emmanuel Mennonite Church-Gainesville, FL
3/2/2003	Baumgartner	Beverly	WDC	Lorraine Avenue Mennonite Church-Wichita, KS
3/12/2003	Thiessen	Karen	MCBC	West Abbotsford Mennonite Church (C)-Abbotsford, BC
3/23/2003	Smith-Morrison	Barbara	MCEC	St Jacobs Mennonite Church-Saint Jacobs, ON
5/1/2003	Colliver	Kathy	IN-MI	First Mennonite Church (C)-Fort Wayne, IN
6/15/2003	Sawatsky	Margaret	CDC	Hively Avenue Mennonite Church-Elkhart, IN
6/22/2003	Campion	Anne	MCEC	Avon Mennonite Church-Stratford, ON
7/13/2003	Guyton	Cynthia	VMC	Calvary Community Church-Hampton, VA
7/13/2003	Williams	Nan	VMC	Calvary Community Church-Hampton, VA
8/5/2003	Giesbrecht	Kathy	MCM	Springstein Mennonite Church-Springstein, MB
9/28/2003	Leichty	Kristen	IN-MI	College Mennonite Church-Goshen, IN
10/5/2003	Preheim	Lois Janzen	CPMC	Salem Mennonite Church-Freeman, SD
10/5/2003	Evans	Faith	VMC	Washington Community Fellowship-Washington, DC

Ordination	Last Name	First Name	Conference	Congregation
10/26/2003	Hostetler	Sheri	PSMC	First Mennonite Church of San Francisco-San Francisco, CA
12/14/2003	Miller	Beth	CPMC	Kalona Mennonite Church-Kalona, IA
1/25/2004	DeLeon	Seferina	IN-MI	Iglesia Menonita del Buen Pastor-Goshen, IN
3/7/2004	Kaufmann	Lois Johns	IN-MI &CDC	Assembly Mennonite Church-Goshen, IN
3/7/2004	Penner	Ruth	WDC	New Creation Fellowship Church-Newton, KS
3/14/2004	Littman	Elsa	IN-MI	
5/2/2004	Hunsberger	Catherine	MCEC	Rainham Mennonite Church-Selkirk, ON
5/2/2004	Rempel	Jeanne	PNMC	Evergreen Mennonite Church-Kirkland, WA
5/23/2004	Elias	Lillian	IN-MI	Parkview Mennonite Church-Kokomo, IN
5/23/2004	Custar	Deanna	OMC	Salem Mennonite Church-Waldron, MI
6/6/2004	Steinmann	Pauline	MCSASK	Wildwood Mennonite Church-Saskatoon, SK
7/11/2004	Roeschley	Jane	IL & CDC	Mennonite Church of Normal-Normal, IL
8/8/2004	Crockett	Maria	IN-MI	New Foundation United in Christ Mennonite Fellowship-Elkhart, IN
9/12/2004	Yoder	Pamela	IN-MI	First Mennonite Church of Middlebury-Middlebury, IN
9/15/2004	Lumsdaine	Margaret	PSMC	Carlsbad Mennonite Church-Carlsbad, NM
9/16/2004	Klauser	Sylvia	WDC	Houston Mennonite Church-Houston, TX

256 • Appendix

Ordination	Last Name	First Name	Conference	Congregation
9/19/2004	Engle (D)	Naomi	OMC	Aurora Mennonite Church-Aurora, OH
9/26/2004	Bender	Hendrike Isert	MCEC	Nith Valley Mennonite Church-New Hamburg, ON
9/26/2004	Koop	Kathy	MCM	First Mennonite Church-Winnipeg, MB
10/17/2004	Grove	Mary	IN-MI	Benton Mennonite Church-Goshen, IN
10/24/2004	Schlosser	Lynn	WDC	Bergthal Mennonite Church (C)-Pawnee Rock, KS
10/31/2004	Drescher-Lehman	Sandra	FRC	Souderton Mennonite Church-Souderton, PA
1/1/2005	Lapp	Cynthia	AMC	Hyattsville Mennonite Church-Hyattsville, MD
1/16/2005	Carson	Kelly	IL	Chicago Community Mennonite Church-Chicago, IL
1/30/2005	Ranck-Hower	Dawn	FRC	Plains Mennonite Church-Hatfield, PA
4/17/2005	Martin	Lynne	MCM	Arnaud Mennonite Church-Arnaud, MB
5/15/2005	Derstine	Lorene	FRC	Plains Mennonite Church-Hatfield, PA
6/12/2005	Harms	Loanne	IN-MI	Waterford Mennonite Church-Goshen, IN
6/18/2005	Boshart	Shana Peachey	CPMC	West Union Mennonite Church-Parnell, IA
6/19/2005	Lelless	Norma	MCEC	Mississauga Mennonite Fellowship-Mississauga, ON
6/26/2005	Yoder	Helen	CPMC	West Union Mennonite Church-Parnell, IA
7/30/2005	Greenawalt	Kimberlee	VMC	Lindale Mennonite Church-Linville, VA

Ordination	Last Name	First Name	Conference	Congregation
8/14/2005	Mast	Mattie Marie	OMC	Sonnenberg Mennonite Church-Kidron, OH
9/11/2005	Enns	Lisa	MCM	Bethel Mennonite Church-Winnipeg, MB
10/16/2005	Kratzer	Amy	IN-MI	Sunnyside Mennonite Church-Elkhart, IN
11/6/2005	Williams	Angie	VMC	New Beginnings Church-Harrisonburg, VA
11/13/2005	Kramer	Phyllis	MCEC	Windsor Mennonite Fellowship-Windsor, ON

Study Guide

This chapter-by-chapter study guide is offered to help facilitate small group or classroom engagement with the book. Some of the questions recommend additional research beyond the book for further context and understanding. Others encourage more personal engagement with the themes of the book. Readers are encouraged to use this guide however it is helpful to promote discussion, further learning, and application.

Introduction: Women remember

1. What was the cultural situation in the United States and Canada in the 1970s? What were the major political events? (If you were alive during this time, describe your church context.)

2. What roles did women have in your congregation? Did your mother have any leadership positions?

3. This book covers the years 1972–2006. If you were alive during those years, recall what was happening in your life over this span. Share an event that marked your awareness of faith, church, or your giftedness.

1. First gatherings: Women organize

1. Discuss the first meeting of women in Chicago in 1972. What was important?

2. How does change happen? Is it top down or bottom up? In what kinds of situations did women think changes needed to happen?

3. Describe "women's liberation." What are its facets? Do you think Christian feminism is still relevant?

2. If truth be told: Women dare to be activists

1. Author Yoder Nyce describes her experiences in the activist movement regarding the roles of women in the church. How did her mother shape her thinking?

2. Reflect on your family's views of women. What messages did you receive? Did your mother act as role model for you? What role does the Bible play in her thinking? How does the Bible affect your decisions? What does your church teach or practice about the role of women?

3. Notice Yoder Nyce's shift in focus from Christian leadership in the Mennonite denomination to a global interfaith emphasis. Why do you think she made that shift? How do other-than-Christian faiths affect your life?

3. Peace Section advocacy: Women write

1. Research the history of the Mennonite Central Committee (MCC) Peace Section. When did it start? What are today's gender-equity activities? Find materials, publications, and news clippings to share and discuss women's advocacy.

2. The MCC Task Force on Women published the *Report*—a newsletter written by women on diverse topics—which is now archived online at archive.org/details/WomensConcernsReport/ and available in print at the Anabaptist Mennonite Biblical Seminary library. Pick several different copies. What do you notice about the topics? Who are the writers? What perspectives and attitudes are clear? How does Christian faith shape the issues?

3. What Mennonite periodicals do you read? Do they play a role in your church's life? What topics do you wish the church would research, share, write about, teach, and advocate?

4. Blinders and power: Women of color proclaim

1. Retell the early life experiences of both authors. What were critical incidents? Who were role models for them? Who are role models for you?

2. Discuss the double reality of racism and sexism. How does that impact women? Women of color? Men? Men of color?

3. How is power displayed according to these authors? What counsel or advice do these two women share? How will this advice affect you?

5. The great hurdle: Women are ordained

1. What does ordination mean? Review and discuss "Article 15. Ministry and Leadership" of the *Confession of Faith in a Mennonite Perspective* (1995), available at www.mennonite-usa.org/who-are-mennonites/what-we-believe/confession-of-faith/ministry-and-leadership/.

2. Why do you think that ordaining women to be pastors was and, in some places, still is controversial? What biblical texts are used to support or deny ordination for women?

3. If a young girl, college student, middle-aged mother, or senior adult woman sensed a call to be a pastor, what advice would you give her? What resources are available to her? What kinds of education or training would be important?

6. Surveys and conversations: Women pastors speak

1. Review the 1972–1992 survey findings by Sauder. What was interesting, remarkable, surprising, or even historic?

2. Review the 2005 survey findings by Zaerr Brenneman. What were important findings? What changes occurred from the Sauder study?

3. Interview or research a woman pastor. What were factors in her decision to become a pastor? Where did she pastor? What were obstacles to her ministry? What advice (or warnings) would she give to future women pastors?

7. Conferences and publications: Women do theology

1. Discuss the influence of fundamentalism as Barrett describes. How was or is your congregation affected by television and radio preachers, Bible studies, and various educational institutions?

2. Review different topics in theology: biblical and historical models, inclusive language, the role of experience, liberation theology, suffering, forgiveness, atonement, trajectory theology. How do women's perspectives inform these topics?

3. Have you used any of the theological methods discussed in this chapter? What draws you to them?

8. Moving into church structures: Women govern

1. Research the history of women in leadership in your congregation (or where you grew up). Is there a ranking of importance for committees? Who served then and who serves now as chairpersons of committees?

2. Note the figures comparing women and men in denominational leadership positions in 1977 and 2000. What changes do you notice? What about the figures comparing women and men in MCC leadership positions in 1975 and 1985?

3. What does it mean to be the "first" in leadership? Have you experienced being the "first" in church or conference structures? What has been the experience of women who were a "first" in your family, church, or business?

9. Women are "adjunct": Women serve and learn leadership

1. Do you have "women's groups" in your congregation? What is their primary role: projects, celebrations, funding, something else?

2. Name the advantages and disadvantages of having a designated women's organization, or "auxiliary." Share stories of how you, your mother, your grandmother, or someone else you know experienced women's auxiliaries. What is the future of auxiliaries?

3. Should women pastors participate in women's groups? Should clergywomen's spouses be part of a men's group? What do you think are the advantages or disadvantages of such involvement?

Conclusion: Women said something!

1. Pick one chapter. Summarize the chapter's theme. What did you learn? What surprised you? Take turns sharing your summaries.

2. Review the list in the appendix of women who were ordained. How many were ordained in each decade? Where did ordinations occur? Do you know any of the women? Take time to pray for them, write a note of encouragement, or email a greeting. Are there some young girls or women you could encourage for leadership?

3. What are next steps for you, your congregation, and your governance structures regarding women in leadership?

Contributors

Lois Y. Barrett, daughter of a Christian Church (Disciples of Christ) minister, found the Mennonite denomination first as a voluntary service worker in 1969 and then emerged in 1976 as a leader in starting a house church, Mennonite Church of the Servant, Wichita, Kansas, where she was ordained in 1985 and is still an active member. Her professional career in journalism eventually focused on research, teaching, and publishing on theology, history, and service and mission. She has served as executive secretary for the Commission on Home Ministries of the General Conference Mennonite Church, director of the Great Plains Seminary Extension for the Anabaptist Mennonite Biblical Seminary, and professor of theology and Anabaptist studies at Anabaptist Mennonite Biblical Seminary until her retirement in 2018. Lois has degrees from the University of Oklahoma and Mennonite Biblical Seminary and a PhD in historical theology from the Union Institute, Cincinnati, working on the figure of Ursula Jost, a sixteenth-century Anabaptist noted for her ecstatic spirituality. Lois is married to Tom Mierau, and they have three adult children and five grandchildren.

Marlene Harder Bogard served for nearly twenty years as resource librarian and then as minister of Christian formation for the Western District Conference, North Newton, Kansas. She was ordained in 2007 and served as executive director for Mennonite Women USA. She lives in Portland, Oregon, and volunteers with the local international products retail shop.

Diane Zaerr Brenneman was ordained in 1993 and served as co-pastor of First Mennonite Church, Iowa City, Iowa, interim pastor at Washington Mennonite Church, Washington, Iowa, and associate dean at Anabaptist Mennonite Biblical Seminary in Elkhart, Indiana. Diane also served as the denominational minister for Mennonite Church USA's Office of Ministerial Leadership, where she managed the Women and Men in Ministry Survey in 2005. Today she is a farmer and a family leadership training coordinator for the University of Iowa's Child Health Specialty Clinics.

Iris de León-Hartshorn is the associate executive director for operations and director of human resources of Mennonite Church USA. She was ordained in 1994 and has served as a chaplain, co-pastor, mediator, workshop leader, anti-racism trainer, and writer. Living in Portland, Oregon, she is married to Leo Hartshorn, and they are parents to three adult children.

John A. Esau graduated from Goshen College, Mennonite Biblical Seminary, and the United Theological Seminary. He pastored Faith Mennonite Church, Minneapolis, Minnesota, from 1961 to 1971, and the Bethel College Mennonite Church, North Newton, Kansas, from 1971 to 1984. He was the director of ministerial leadership for the General Conference Mennonite Church, Newton, Kansas, from 1985 to 1999. Now retired, he lives in North Newton, Kansas.

Dorothy Nickel Friesen is a graduate of Bethel College (Kansas), the University of Kansas, and St. Paul School of Theology (Missouri). She has been a high school English teacher, editor, pastor, seminary administrator, and Western District Conference minister of Mennonite Church USA. She was ordained in 1985 and, now in retirement, volunteers as a grant-writer, advocates for mental health ministry, and develops online faith formation curriculum. She is married to Richard Friesen, and they have two adult daughters and two grandchildren who live not far from her North Newton, Kansas, home.

Nancy Kauffmann is a retired ordained (1986) minister from Goshen, Indiana. She served for nineteen years on the pastoral team at College Mennonite Church, Goshen, Indiana; nine years as one of the conference ministers for Indiana-Michigan Mennonite Conference; and nine years as a denominational minister for Mennonite Church USA. She received an MDiv from Associated (now Anabaptist) Mennonite Biblical Seminary and a DMin in pastoral counseling and medical ethics from Claremont School of Theology.

Gayle Gerber Koontz graduated from Bethel College, North Newton, Kansas, Lancaster Theological Seminary, and Boston University, where she earned a PhD in philosophy of religion and social ethics. Her roles as writer, editor, college professor, visiting professor in the Philippines, and member of an early Mennonite Central Committee Peace Section task force for women are capped with a nearly forty-year tenure at Anabaptist Mennonite Biblical Seminary, retiring as professor emerita in theology and ethics in 2014. She is married to Ted Koontz, and they have three adult children.

Ted Koontz retired as professor emeritus of ethics and peace studies from Anabaptist Mennonite Biblical Seminary in 2014 after beginning his teaching career there in 1982. Previously he served as associate executive secretary of the Mennonite Central Committee Peace Section, Akron, Pennsylvania, where he served on the Task Force on Women in Church and Society. Ted and Gayle Gerber Koontz live in Goshen, Indiana.

Dorothy Yoder Nyce has been a teacher at secondary, college, and seminary levels. Her Assembly Mennonite Church, Goshen, Indiana, Teaching Elder assignment for several years was primarily with college students. Eight assignments in or trips to India occurred between 1962 and 2017. Interfaith issues focused her DMin degree and more recent writing or speaking opportunities. The mother of two adult daughters, she continues with volunteer tasks and to raise vegetables plus host curry meals with her husband, John.

Regina Shands Stoltzfus is professor of peace, justice, and conflict studies at Goshen College, Goshen, Indiana. Her pastoral ministry in Cleveland, Ohio, and ordination (1999) led to degrees from Cleveland State University, Ashland Theological Seminary, and Chicago Theological Seminary (PhD). Regina is a frequent lecturer and facilitator on racism and sexism intersections.

Anita Hooley Yoder is a freelance writer, campus minister, and theopoet living in Cleveland, Ohio. She is a graduate of Goshen College, Goshen, Indiana, and Bethany Theological Seminary, Richmond, Indiana. Anita is the assistant director of campus ministry at Notre Dame College, South Euclid, Ohio. She and her husband, Benjamin Yoder, are members of Friendship Mennonite Church.

Karen Martens Zimmerly graduated from Anabaptist Mennonite Biblical Seminary, Elkhart, Indiana, and was ordained in 1993. After thirty years in Canada (twenty-one years as co-pastor with her spouse and nine years as denominational minister for Mennonite Church Canada), it was time to fulfill an early marriage promise to do one assignment in the United States. She co-pastors at First Mennonite Church, Iowa City, Iowa. With three sons, their partners, and her first grandchild far away, she is grateful for texts, photos, FaceTime, and visits!

Made in the USA
Middletown, DE
12 June 2023